D1356002

TO BE
DISPOSED
BY
AUTHORITY

SIEGFRIED SASSOON

Now light the candles; one; two; there's a moth;
What silly beggars they are to blunder in
And scorch their wings with glory . . .

'Repression of War Experience' (1917)

Siegfried Sassoon
Scorched Glory

A Critical Study

Paul Moeyes

First published 1997 by
MACMILLAN PRESS LTD
Houndmills, Basingstoke, Hampshire RG21 6XS
and London
Companies and representatives
throughout the world

ISBN 0–333–63285–0

A catalogue record for this book is available
from the British Library.

This book is printed on paper suitable for recycling and
made from fully managed and sustained forest sources.

10   9   8   7   6   5   4   3   2   1
06 05 04 03 02 01 00 99 98 97

Printed in Great Britain by
The Ipswich Book Company Ltd
Ipswich, Suffolk

Published in the United States of America by
ST. MARTIN'S PRESS, INC.,
Scholarly and Reference Division
175 Fifth Avenue, New York, N.Y. 10010

ISBN 0–312–17277–X

Ter herinnering aan mijn ouders

CONTENTS

LIST OF PLATES

1. Weirleigh, near Matfield in Kent, Sassoon's childhood home (*C. D. Wheeler*).

2. Heytesbury House from Keynes, *The Gates of Memory* (*by permission of Oxford University Press*).

3. Alfred Sassoon and his three sons, Siegfried, Michael and Hamo (*The Hulton Getty Picture Collection*).

4. Theresa Sassoon (*by permission of Stanley Jackson and Heinemann, 1989*).

5. Sassoon in 1915 in officer's uniform by Beresford (*The Hulton Getty Picture Collection*).

6. Second Lieutenant Robert Graves (*by kind permission of Richard Perceval Graves*).

7. Robert Nichols from Robert Nichols, *Ardour and Endurance* (*Chatto and Windus*).

8. W. H. R. Rivers (*The Royal Society, London*).

9. Craiglockhart War Hospital (*Napier University, Edinburgh*).

10. G. F. Watts's 'Love and Death' (*The Tate Gallery*).

11. Sassoon and W. B. Yeats, March 1922.

12. Ralph Hodgson (*Associated Press*).

13. Sassoon and his wife Hester from Rosamund Lehmann's album.

14. Sassoon and his son George at Heytesbury from Felicitas Corrigan, *Siegfried Sassoon* (*Gollancz, 1978*).

15. Sassoon in old age (*The Hulton Getty Picture Collection*).

PREFACE

The purpose of this book is to present a general survey and critical examination of the published writings of Siegfried Sassoon (1886-1967). Sassoon's work has elicited little critical attention: Dame Felicitas Corrigan's *Siegfried Sassoon: Poet's Pilgrimage* (1973) is an account of his conversion rather than a critical evaluation of his life and work, which leaves Michael Thorpe's *Siegfried Sassoon* (1966) as the only full-scale critical work entirely devoted to Sassoon's writings. A new critical study of Sassoon's work needs no further justification, then, but it might be useful to explain in which respects this study differs from its predecessor. Thorpe's *Siegfried Sassoon* remains an extremely valuable book and this study makes no claims for superseding it, but Thorpe was forced to decide against following a literary-biographical approach since at the time of writing it Sassoon was still alive, and he was reluctant to supply Thorpe with any information. Neither could the critic draw upon relevant biographical sources, for they were only published after Sassoon's death in 1967: Corrigan's *Siegfried Sassoon: Poet's Pilgrimage* (1973), three volumes of diaries (1981, 1983, 1985), and one volume of letters to Max Beerbohm (1986), all edited by Sassoon's literary executor Sir Rupert Hart-Davis.

In this study I have made liberal use of these autobiographical writings. It might be argued that a largely biographical approach is unsuitable for a work of literary criticism, but I believe that an author who referred to his poetry as his "real biography", and whose seven prose works consist of three autobiographies, three semi-autobiographies, and one biography, at least *invites* a biographical approach, if not making it downright necessary. William Empson once wrote that "in the teasing work of scholarship, a man must all the time be trying to imagine another man's mind; as soon as that stops, he is off the rails".[1] Siegfried Sassoon seems to me to be a prime example of an author whose complete *oeuvre* is best understood in the framework of his own life, and throughout this study I have therefore attempted to "stay on the rails", convinced as I am that both Sassoon's mental development and his authorial aims need to be taken into consideration in order to arrive at a fair critical judgment of his literary work.

A special problem in a critical study of Sassoon's work is where to give which biographical background information. In his works he covers the same ground three times over: the period 1890-1920 is the subject, first of his poetry, then of the Sherston trilogy, and finally of his three autobiographies. It has been my policy to discuss issues and personalities where they seemed most relevant in the context of Sassoon's work. Thus it can happen that Sassoon's relationship with Wilfred Owen is discussed in Chapter 2, whereas his contacts with W.H.R. Rivers feature in Chapter 8, though in reality they took place simultaneously in the summer and autumn of 1917. The reason for this is that the subject of this book is Sassoon's literary work; the biographical details are primarily intended to contribute to a fuller understanding of his work.

A further aim of this study is to determine Sassoon's position as a Georgian writer, and to place the Georgian movement itself in the wider context of early twentieth-century developments in English Literature. Since I believe that Sassoon's views on art were largely those of his mother, I have included a brief discussion of the nineteenth-century art scene in Chapter 3. In this chapter I also trace the ongoing discussion about the artist's position in relation to his audience, which was a major issue among both nineteenth-century painters and twentieth-century Georgians, and which is about the only theoretical matter Sassoon was genuinely interested in.

Sassoon is but one of the Georgian writers to have been neglected by the critics: as yet there are no biographies of Lascelles Abercrombie, John Drinkwater, Gordon Bottomley, W.W. Gibson, Robert Nichols, Ralph Hodgson, John Freeman or Edward Shanks. That there is no biography of Sassoon remains all the more surprising in view of the fact that most other war poets – Brooke, Sorley, Owen, Gurney, Rosenberg, Blunden and Graves – have all been the subject of a biography (and in some cases even more than one). Sassoon remains the elusive character whose war record and poetry are discussed in books on Owen or Graves, and who features in many an index of an (auto-)biographical work of the 1920s and 30s as an 'attendant lord': a member of the entourage, a fellow guest at a dinner-party, or one of the writers mentioned as present at a ceremony. Siegfried Sassoon deserves a better fate, and it is my sincerest wish that this study will make a small contribution to a general reappraisal of a strange but impressive man whose true qualities as a writer have been too often overlooked.

I would like to thank all those who have helped me with this project since it was first begun in March 1987: in particular Mr George Sassoon, who gave me permission to quote extensively from his father's work and answered many of my questions, Professor Dominic Baker-Smith, my supervisor at Amsterdam University, and Dominic Hibberd, who corrected several errors in the manuscript and made many helpful suggestions from which both author and book have benefited considerably.

I am also greatly indebted to all those who, over the past few years, have supplied me with encouragement, advice, practical help and/or relevant material. In particular I would like to mention Charmian Hearne, my editor at Macmillan, Dr C. C. Barfoot, Mady Schuuring-Kohlbrugge, Theo Baart, Su Carlton, Hans Hollander and Mr Roel Leentvaar. Finally, special thanks to my elder brother Fred Moeyes, who helped me out when my o, so limited knowledge of computers and printers had made me cast a nostalgic eye at my other Brother, the typewriter.

P.M.
Amsterdam, April 1996

ABBREVIATIONS

The following abbreviations have been used in the text for references to Sassoon's writings:

D1	– *Diaries 1914–1918*	Edited by Sir Rupert Hart-Davis (London: Faber and Faber, 1983)
D2	– *Diaries 1920–1922*	Edited by Sir Rupert Hart-Davis (London: Faber and Faber, 1981)
D3	– *Diaries 1923–1925*	Edited by Sir Rupert Hart-Davis (London: Faber and Faber, 1985)
LC	– *Letters to a Critic*	Edited by Michael Thorpe (Kent: Kent Editions, 1976)
LMB	– *Letters to Max Beerbohm*	Edited by Sir Rupert Hart-Davis (London: Faber and Faber, 1986)
M	– *Meredith*	(London: Arrow Books, 1959)
MFH	– *Memoirs of a Fox-Hunting Man*	(London: Faber and Faber, 1928)
MIO	– *Memoirs of an Infantry Officer*	(London: Faber and Faber, 1930)
OC	– *The Old Century*	(London: Faber and Faber, 1968)
SJ	– *Siegfried's Journey*	(London: Faber and Faber, 1945)
SP	– *Sherston's Progress*	(London: Faber and Faber, 1936)
WY	– *The Weald of Youth*	(London: Faber and Faber, 1986)

Part I

UNLEARNED ILLUSIONS

*For, having grown world-wise through harshly unlearned
    illusion,*
The traveller into time arrives at this conclusion,–
That life, encountered and unmasked in various shapes,
Dissolves in dust and cloud, and thwartingly escapes.

– Siegfried Sassoon, *Vigils* VII

important role in the literary career of Hamo Thornycroft's nephew Siegfried.

II

After their marriage Alfred and Theresa Sassoon moved to Weirleigh, their country house in a secluded part of the Kentish Weald. The first years they were very happy there, but their shared artistic interests were not enough for a stable relationship:

> She was gentle, but needed more than gentleness to control a volatile and quick-tempered Jew, over-indulged from infancy. He had little need to work and even less inclination. He had considerable gifts and could handle a violin or a lathe with equal skill, but grew bored too quickly. Only a miracle could have made him settle placidly into the Weald of Kent.[6]

They had three sons: the eldest, Michael, was born in 1884, the youngest, Hamo Watts (the painter G. F. Watts was his godfather), in 1887. Their second son, Siegfried Loraine Sassoon, was born at Weirleigh on 8 September 1886. His names were clearly chosen by Theresa: Siegfried reflected her admiration for the music of Richard Wagner and Father Loraine was the name of the canon who had prepared her for confirmation in the Anglican Church in the 1870s.

By 1891 Alfred was apparently tired of waiting for the miracle that would make him put up with family life, and he ran off with a friend of Theresa's. From then on he would only pay occasional visits to his children, when Theresa would lock herself up in her studio. These visits stopped altogether in 1893, when it became clear that Alfred was seriously ill. The children were told by their nurse who, according to Siegfried, "had a relish for the lugubrious", that their father was "in a galloping consumption" (*OC*, 30). They went to see him on his deathbed at Eastbourne, where they also met their Sassoon grandmother and uncle. Theresa was not allowed entrance, though it is unclear whether the orders came from Alfred or his mother. He died in March 1895 (two months after the death of Grandmother Thornycroft, who had died at Weirleigh). There was no message for his estranged wife.

III

When writing about his former self, Sassoon describes someone who progresses from a sensitive and solitary boy to an ignorant and ineffectual young man. Though at times he certainly exaggerates, there seems no reason to doubt the main outline of his life up to the outbreak of the Great War as related in his autobiographies *The Old Century and Seven More Years* (1938) and *The Weald of Youth* (1942).

After their father's departure and early death, the three boys were brought up in a household dominated by women. With Theresa as its central figure, the Sassoon household at Weirleigh in the 1890s consisted of an all-female staff inside the house, and a male staff whose domain was the garden and stables.[7] At first the three boys played together, but Siegfried gradually went his own way, partly because he was a sickly child who could not keep up with his brothers, but also because he did not share his brothers' interest in mechanics. Instead he was drawn to writing, and by the spring of 1896 the then ten-year-old boy began to believe that he was going to be a poet (*OC*, 85). It seems likely, however, that this notion did not emerge spontaneously, but had first been planted there by Theresa:

> My mother had a strong maternal feeling that I was destined to become a great poet. This feeling expressed itself prophetically when she wrote my name in a copy of Coleridge's *Lectures on Shakespeare* on my third birthday (*OC*, 154).

One of the young poet's earliest ventures was a handwritten manuscript with illustrations, entitled "*More Poems* by S.L. Sassoon", which he presented to his mother as a Christmas present in 1897. The eleven-year-old poet had already found some of the themes and genres that were to feature in his later work. One of the poems, 'The Court of Death', was inspired by the G. F. Watts picture of that title which he had seen in London and a prose piece 'Something About Myself' is his first exercise in autobiography (though in this case the narrator is his cat).

One of the causes for the failure of his parents' marriage must have been Theresa Sassoon's dominant and possessive nature. Alfred, used to an unfettered existence, may well have come to see Weirleigh as a prison and Theresa as its warden, but Siegfried never really resented his mother's attention. He always remained very close to her; in *The Old Century* he writes that "My devotion to her was so comprehensive that I had never given any thought to it. I merely took it for granted that we were necessary to one another" (*OC*, 210). As he once told Stephen Tennant, he had always considered himself a mother's boy.[8]

Siegfried must in many ways have reminded Theresa of her husband, and though she had failed to bring out Alfred's latent talents, she was determined to do better with her son and set to work fostering her son's, and probably her own, literary aspirations. Neither the characters of the budding poet and his mentor, nor the rural and isolated setting were conducive to the growth of a poet's mind that could be expected to be either rebellious or innovative. Like his father, the young Siegfried showed no traces of a dogged determination or an unflagging will-power, but whereas his father had had an adventurous spirit, Siegfried was a dreamer who preferred to stand in the garden imagining what the world out there on the other side of the Weald might be like, without ever showing an inclination to actually go and see for himself. His literary interests operated on a similar level: "Poetry was a dream world into which I escaped through an esoteric door in my mind" (*WY*, 28).

Theresa's contributions did little to offset these reclusive tendencies. She kept her son at home until he was twelve, a decision for which she must have had other reasons besides the one Sassoon gives when he says that this was due to her "deep distrust of the feeding arrangements at school" (*OC*, 149). He was then sent to boarding school and Marlborough College (1902-04), after which he went to Clare College, Cambridge, where he read a little law and history, and then followed in his father's footsteps by leaving without taking a degree. Between 1906 and May 1914 he lived mostly at home with his mother, his brothers both being abroad. These were in retrospect the happiest years of his life, when he lived the life of a gentleman-poet. His outdoor activities consisted of fox-hunting, point-to-point racing, and playing golf and cricket, whereas at home he spent his time browsing through booksellers' catalogues, ordering new additions to his book collection,[9] and working on his poetry, though he made few attempts to interest publishers or editors.

In 1906 he had his first volume of verse, simply entitled *Poems*, privately printed in an edition of fifty copies.[10] Sassoon did not retain any of these poems in his *Collected Poems*, which is hardly surprising, though the opening line of the first poem, "Doubt not the light of Heaven upon the soul," would have shown how Sassoon's fifty-year poetic and spiritual pilgrimage was eventually to end where it had started.

In 1962 Sassoon sent Felicitas Corrigan a copy:

> I hope you will have a good laugh at some of the poetizings, their naive moralizing, verbal imprecision, and auto-intoxication with word-sounds. Swinburne was the main influence at the time. I loved Tennyson but was incapable of imitating his distinctness. Dante Rossetti also, and I'd imbibed quite a lot of Browning, *Saul* being my prime favourite. Anyhow, there I was, doing it all on my own steam, with no one to tell me how to do it professionally [...] And I am thankful that I was not a sophisticated youth, and really experienced those aspirations and vague upliftments. Wasn't it better to be like that than to write the stuff most of the young do now – all cleverness and dissatisfaction and uncertainty?[11]

The main impetus in furthering his career came from his uncle Hamo, who had become a trustee on Alfred Sassoon's death. In the final chapter of *The Old Century* Sassoon recalls a visit he paid to his uncle in his studio in Melbury Road, Kensington, in August 1907: "He had been very kind, and had said nothing about my failure at the University" (*OC*, 299). His uncle was then working on a statue of Tennyson and Sassoon never forgot this visit because uncle Hamo asked him to try on Tennyson's wide-brimmed black hat and cloak. His uncle's request may well have had a symbolic importance that Sassoon never appreciated. Tennyson, too, had left Cambridge without taking a degree, and Hamo Thornycroft was determined that his young nephew give up his life of leisure and start to put more energy in the pursuit of his career as a poet. After Sassoon's visit Thornycroft wrote to his friend Edmund Gosse, drawing attention to his literary nephew and asking for his help and advice. Gosse was only too willing to help: he read the poems Thornycroft asked Siegfried to send him, and, recognizing a genuine talent, wrote him an encouraging letter. The young poet, however, was too diffident to push his career, and it was left to his uncle Hamo to keep up a steady stream of letters, in which he informed Gosse about Siegfried's lack of progress, for which Thornycroft blamed "the inferior country intellects" with whom his nephew spent so much of his time.

In the spring of 1913 everything seemed ready for Sassoon to make his appearance on the London literary scene. The preparatory work had been done by his uncle Hamo; invitations to parties at Edmund Gosse's home at 17 Hanover Terrace would have assured him of an ideal introduction to the London literary world and, above all, the times were propitious for the arrival of a new poet. A poetic renaissance had begun around 1911: the established poets, William Watson, Stephen Phillips, W.E. Henley, Alfred Noyes, Henry Newbolt, Maurice Hewlett and Kipling, all staunch supporters of the Empire, were then attacked by a new realistic school of mostly Liberal-minded poets. Two events that heralded the arrival of these new poets were the publication of John Masefield's 'The Everlasting Mercy' in the October 1911 issue of the *English Review*, followed by Rupert Brooke's *Poems* in December. The new school was given a name with the publication of Edward Marsh's first *Georgian Poetry* anthology in December 1912; the book was an immediate success, and a year later it had sold over nine thousand copies. As a result, the anthology market flowered, and publishers were on the look-out for new talent. But Sassoon hesitated too long. He still lingered at Weirleigh, seemingly unaware of the many chances and opportunities he was missing in London. New periodicals were started, with editors who were keen to publish new poets. Edward Marsh's publisher, Harold Monro (1879-1932), started the Poetry Bookshop in December 1912 (officially opened by Henry Newbolt 8 January 1913) and published new poetry in his own quarterly, *Poetry and Drama*. John Middleton Murry's *Rhythm* folded in March 1913, but in May he was back with the *Blue Review*, with Katherine Mansfield as assistant editor. Many young poets made their literary debuts in the pages of A.R. Orage's *New Age*, which counted among its contributors writers as diverse as Arnold Bennett, J.C. Squire, James Elroy Flecker, T.E. Hulme and Ezra Pound. Squire was also literary editor of the *New Statesman*, which first appeared in April 1913 and published poems by W.H. Davies, Hilaire Belloc, Rupert Brooke, Walter de la Mare, W.B. Yeats and Edward Thomas.

It was early in 1913 that Edmund Gosse showed some of Sassoon's poems to Edward Marsh. Marsh commented on these poems in a long letter to Sassoon, which eventually led to a meeting in March 1913. In *The Weald of Youth* Sassoon writes that around this time "I became conscious that there were far too many things in the literary and artistic world that I ought to have heard of and hadn't" (*WY*, 194). He told Marsh about this "state of mental stagnation" (*WY*, 195) and it was Marsh who finally persuaded Sassoon to move to London in the spring of 1914, finding him an apartment at Raymond Buildings, Gray's Inn. The few months in London were not very productive. Sassoon wrote hardly any poetry at all: "I had gradually arrived at my recent realization that I had nothing in me to write about" (*WY*, 262). Nor did he succeed in establishing an acquaintanceship with other writers: an attempt to visit Ralph Hodgson failed when Sassoon found him not at home (they were not to meet for another five years). He did meet two of the Georgian poets, Rupert Brooke and W.H. Davies, at one of Edward Marsh's 'breakfasts' on 9 July, but Davies talked only about the 'business side' of poetry ("this made me feel rather out of it") and when he was left alone with Brooke his attempt to start a conversation had an unpropitious start:

> Hoping that it would go down well, I made a disparaging remark about Kipling's poetry being terribly tub-thumping stuff.
> "But not always, surely," he answered; and then let me off easily by adding, "I used to think rather the same myself until Eddie [Marsh] made me read 'Cities and Thrones and Powers'. There aren't many better modern poems than that, you know." (*WY*, 229)[12]

In any case, a lack of money (partly brought about by his frequent visits to the Opera and the Russian Ballet) forced him to return to Weirleigh later that month. He was still at home when war broke out in August 1914.

CHAPTER 1

YOUNG NIMROD

I

In the early years of this century writing poetry was still an unexceptional activity for a well-educated young man. It was a survival of a romantic age when people were still striving for beauty rather than truth; the poetic young man usually had little or nothing personal to communicate but saw poetry as an exercise in creating beauty with words. And so this poetry was generally derivative, echoing the style and sentiments of the prevailing literary movements. Towards the end of the Victorian period, the English art-scene entered a new phase and became more outward-looking; the Decadent movement of the 1890s cannot be wholly described in terms of a development in the native literary tradition:

> In that it was native the impulsion came directly from the Pre-Raphaelites, and more particularly from the poetry of Dante Gabriel Rossetti and Swinburne. But the chief influences came from France.[1]

It is significant that some of the leading figures in the English 'Art for Art's Sake' movement were foreigners: among the painters James McNeill Whistler, among the writers Oscar Wilde and George Moore. They introduced the work of the French painters and writers in England, thus ending the hegemony of Ruskin and the Royal Academicians, whose doctrines had always emphasized art's moral character and the beneficial influence it had on man's spiritual development. The Aesthetes' claims that art had nothing to do with morality and that there could be beauty in evil shocked the artistic establishment.

But the younger generation, Sassoon's contemporaries, eagerly picked up these foreign ideas: James Elroy Flecker admired Baudelaire and later championed the Parnassians' cause, arguing in the controversial preface to his *The Golden Journey to Samarkand* (1913) that "It is not the poet's business to save man's soul, but to make it worth saving", and Rupert Brooke at seventeen adopted the world-weary tone of the true Decadent. But Sassoon's early work appears to have been conceived in a time warp; there are no foreign influences, and even a languid Decadent tone is absent. In his diaries he refers to his first attempts at writing poetry, around 1906-08, saying that he was then under the "weary influence" of the Pre-Raphaelites (*D1*, 97). These early poems were all about "Eternity and the Tomb", themes of which he was emotionally wholly ignorant; when he attended his uncle's funeral a year or so later, he "experienced a sort of dumb dejection which had nothing to do with the mock-mournfulness of my poems about death and the tomb" (*OC*, 188-9). Most of these early lyrics were imitations of Tennyson's 'In Memoriam' and Rossetti's poems (although in Sassoon there is no deceased Blessed Damozel – women are conspicuously absent), and thus suggest his mother's influence.

She had read to him from the great Victorians and told him about their lives, emphasising the 'great poet – great man' equation (though in the 1890s she thought Swinburne the greatest living poet, Sassoon was not encouraged to read him; he was put off by her stories about Swinburne's undignified behaviour). Apart from introducing him to her own favourite poets, Theresa Sassoon affected her son's poetic career in two fundamental ways: she instilled in him the Victorian values of properness and decency, values that, apart from the war years, he never rebelled against and which caused him to be easily shocked by liberal contemporaries and their work. He dislikes Rupert Brooke's *Poems* for what he called their "modern ugliness", a phrase that might well have been used by his mother. When he first meets Brooke at Edward Marsh's literary breakfast, the sandals Brooke wears remind him of "certain young men – and young women also – of whom my mother was wont to remark she did wish that they wouldn't dress in that sloppily artistic way and talk silly Fabian socialism" (*WY*, 226). The derogatory reference to Fabianism is a clear pointer to Sassoon's intellectual position.

In the early years of the century the universities were centres of the new political ideas. Sassoon's Cambridge contemporaries (Rupert Brooke, James Elroy Flecker, J.C. Squire) became active supporters of socialist ideals and joined the Fabian movement, but Sassoon himself remained oblivious to these developments. Simply echoing his mother's opinions, he adopted both the cultural and his political 'tastes' of an older generation without ever questioning them.

The fact that he was largely out of touch with contemporary developments is also illustrated by the periodical in which four of his poems were published (without him ever getting paid for them). In 1909 and 1910, when the leading poetry publishing periodicals were Ford Madox Hueffer's *English Review* and A.R. Orage's *New Age*, Sassoon sent his poems to the *Academy*, edited by Lord Alfred 'Bosie' Douglas and his infamous assistant T.W.H. Crosland.

More important for Sassoon's writing, however, was Theresa's influence as a painter. She established in her son's mind a link between poetry and the visual arts which helped shape his style. Sassoon's early poetry is an attempt to paint in words the pictures he has conjured up in his mind; it depicts scenes from an, more often than not, imaginary world using evocative, often archaic, words which are not always very precise. The point is that the poet is not trying to convey an experience or opinion that is personal and heartfelt, he is simply trying to write poetry, which for him means the application of the rules of prosody and the use of poetic language.

In *The Weald of Youth* he gave the following description of his ideas about poetry at this time:

> I must explain that abstract ideas are uncongenial to my mind. The sound of words has been more to me than skilful management of their meanings, and verbal exactitude was a late arrival in my literary development. I have always instinctively avoided the use of metaphors, except when they came uncalled-for. Indirect and allusive utterance has never been natural to me. I much prefer the poetry I can visualize and feel to that which needs thinking out afterwards. (*WY*, 112)

II

Before the publication of his first 'official' volume, *The Old Huntsman and Other Poems*, it had been Sassoon's habit to have small editions of his poetry privately printed, which he then distributed among friends and relatives. Between 1906 and 1916 twelve such collections appeared. When *The Old Huntsman* was published by Heinemann in May 1917, it contained, apart from the title poem and the war poems, thirty pieces first published in one or more of these privately printed editions, plus seven other non-war poems of more recent date. Regrouping all these poems for the publication of his *Collected Poems* (1956), Sassoon chose to preserve thirty-three out of a total of thirty-seven in a separate section, *Lyrical Poems: 1908-1916*.

In his critical study of Sassoon, Michael Thorpe is puzzled by the fact that Sassoon retained so many of his early verses in the collected edition. In Thorpe's opinion many of the poems are weak and have "little claim to survival"; as a possible explanation he "prefers to believe that he [Sassoon] wished to offer an honest pattern of his development".[2] This is undoubtedly true, but it is important to recognize the wider implications of this fact. Although at first sight it may seem odd to compare the work of such an introverted, meditative poet as Sassoon with that of the often vigorous and boisterous Walt Whitman, Sassoon's *Collected Poems* should in many ways be regarded as his *Leaves of Grass*. In it he has chronicled the different stages of his life: the dreams and expectations at the outset, the crises, the disillusionment, and the search for inner peace and harmony. Or, as Sassoon himself wrote in a letter to Dame Felicitas Corrigan, "my real biography is in my poetry".[3]

Sassoon's contemporaries did not care much for these early poems. Writing to Robert Nichols in 1917, Robert Graves agrees with him that "S.S. has spoilt his *Huntsman* by one or two quite frigid and meaningless pieces"; in a letter to Edward Marsh he is even more outspoken: "the earlier sort [of poetry] he wrote, though I suppose very perfect technically, means nothing at all to me: a pity, I think, he included it".[4] Thomas Hardy, to whom *The Old Huntsman* is dedicated, was apparently not impressed by them either; in a letter of thanks to Sassoon he praised the war poems but did not once mention the lyrical poems.

Their inclusion is proof of Sassoon's outdated poetic standards and lack of discrimination in assessing the poetic qualities of his own work. In its use of archaic words and such old-fashioned subjects as nymphs and dryads it has a distinctly nineteenth-century atmosphere. In true Arthur O' Shaugnessy-vein, the young poet is a music-maker and dreamer of dreams rather than a modern poet in tune with the society around him. At the same time, the presence of these poems casts doubt on the modernity of Edward Marsh's taste, for in making his selection Sassoon followed his advice: in *The Weald of Youth*, Sassoon quotes from a letter in which Marsh reviews some of the early poems Sassoon sent him (*WY*, 138-39). In all, six poems are mentioned; Marsh approves of four and rejects two. Only the four poems that met with Marsh's approval are included in *The Old Huntsman* (and were preserved in the *Lyrical Poems* section). Also, Marsh would seem to have not always been consistent in his criticism: Robert Graves reports that when he first showed Marsh some of his poems in 1912, he was told that he was "using 'an outworn vocabulary' and must reform it"; according to him this made him dispense with the use of 'thou', 'thee' or 'where'er'.[5] So why didn't Marsh object to Sassoon's archaisms? The most likely answer is that Marsh wanted to draw Sassoon's attention to the fact that some of his poems lacked meaning altogether ("It seems a necessity now to write either with one's eye on an object or with one's mind at grips with a more or less definite idea. Quite a slight one will suffice") and refrained from further critical remarks so as not to discourage the young poet.

That Sassoon decided to retain these poems in *The Old Huntsman* and even in his collected edition of 1956 cannot simply be taken as evidence of the poet's critical shortcomings. The intensely private nature of the man who after the war continued to publish his poetry in private editions before bringing out a trade edition seems to have manifested itself at the outset of his career. Sassoon's characteristic attitude towards all his literary work throughout his career was never to judge it by literary standards only: at least as important was the emotional value it had for him personally. *The Old Huntsman* was published in the middle of the Great War, when his strained nerves had already made him seek solace. In *Siegfried's Journey* he writes about the period of poetic inspiration he experienced in the early months of 1915, when he was at home convalescing from a badly broken arm. It was then that he wrote 'The Old Huntsman' and several other lyrics: "I had been happiest in a dozen war-oblivious lyrical pieces which had arrived spontaneous and unexpected" (*SJ*, 17). These poems appeared in two privately published volumes, *Discoveries* (April, 1915) and *Morning-Glory* (1916); of the thirty lyrical poems in *The Old Huntsman*, twenty first appeared in these two volumes. So above all, their inclusion in *The Old Huntsman* reflects this emotional importance.

III

This is not to say that personal fondness for a poem was the sole criterion for publication. In *The Weald of Youth* (123-26) Sassoon describes with some pride how he came to write 'The Daffodil Murderer', a long dramatic monologue which was intended to parody John Masefield's 'The Everlasting Mercy' (1911). On 14 March 1922, in the middle of one of his staler periods, Sassoon referred to the poem in his diary: "I still think it one of my finest achievements. I wish I could write something as good, in the style of Sassoon instead of in imitation of Masefield." This may seem high praise for a poem of little merit, but it should be remembered that it was written at a time Sassoon had dried up completely, and was desperately looking for a 'poetic voice'. 'The Daffodil Murderer' remained dear to him because it marked an important development in his writing: "I was really feeling what I wrote - and doing it not only with abundant delight but a sense of descriptive energy quite unlike anything I had experienced before" (*WY*, 124). Again there is the emotional importance: in his mind the poem is associated with a period of poetic inspiration.

Still he had enough sense to see that the poem did not merit inclusion in one of his official publications. Sassoon himself financed the edition of 1000 copies which was published by John Richmond (a small publishing company run by T.W.H. Crosland) in February 1913 with a preface by Crosland, but did not include it in either *The Old Huntsman* or his *Collected Poems*. He did, however, give permission to Michael Thorpe to reprint it as an appendix to his critical study, which seems to suggest that as late as 1966 he still liked the poem.

'The Daffodil Murderer' starts off as a parody and ends a pastiche. The title was added as a reference to 'The Daffodil Fields', the fourth of Masefield's long narrative poems which had just been published when Sassoon finished his poem. It can hardly be called an inspired choice, for Sassoon's poem has nothing to do with daffodils. As a parody its main problem is that it is not funny. Masefield's poems left enough scope for successful satire, as J.C. Squire amply illustrated in some of his efforts,[6] but Sassoon's effort fails to amuse, as was pointed out in the only review of the poem in *The Athenaeum* of 22 February 1913, where it was given short shrift: "This is a pointless and weak-kneed imitation of 'The Everlasting Mercy'. The only conclusion we obtain from its perusal is that it is easy to write worse than Mr. Masefield."

Masefield's narratives were often condemned for their violence and abusive language; in 1918 a critic said that in these poems Masefield confused "crudity and brutality with strength"[7] - his use of the word 'bloody' in particular was greatly resented. In the opening lines of 'The Everlasting Mercy', two poachers quarrel over who can poach a particular field. One of the poachers accuses the other of not sticking to the division they agreed on:

> "Out now", he says, "and leave your wire;
> It's mine."
>   "It ain't."
>   "You put".
>   "You liar."
> "You closhy put."
>   "You bloody liar."

In Sassoon's poem there is also a quarrel, this time between two farm-hands who dispute the ownership of a mug in a Sussex pub:

> "It's mine, I say, you lump o' dirt."
> "I say it ain't."
>   "It's mine, I tell 'ee."
> "Then, Bert, your beer's gone down my belly."

"Gimme that jug, you blasted skug,
"Or else I'll bash your ugly mug."
"I won't."
   "You will."
      "Leggo my ear."

Sassoon says that after some fifty lines he gave up the idea of a parody and started to really 'feel' what he wrote; this scene takes place after more than 250 lines, so presumably the fight is as the poet saw it with his mind's eye. It thus shows the limitations of his Marlborough/ Cambridge experience (and perhaps his mother's dislike of coarse language), for the ear-pulling is reminiscent of *Tom Brown's Schooldays* rather than two rural ruffians. This is not the only instance in which the speaker's background is that of a Kent gentleman rather than that of a Sussex yokel: thinking of his victim, he is reminded of the cricket matches they played together, and he associates the "golden autumn weather" with the huntsman blowing his horn.[8]

Though the poem is certainly not all bad Sassoon was right not to include it in his *oeuvre*: in subject, form and tone it is wholly derivative and he lacked the empathy to impersonate successfully a simple farm-hand. The importance of the poem lies in the fact that it is Sassoon's first attempt to write 'physically', and the poem can thus be linked with the war-poetry that was to establish him as a poet.

IV

The poems in the *Lyrical Poems* section of the *Collected Poems* are of the sort of juvenilia that only get reprinted when their author goes on to make a name for himself as a writer with different, and better, poetry. At best they can be called pleasant or competent, but in some cases even these epithets seem too extravagant. Most of them were written in the years 1915-1916, but there are some of the author's old favourites, as their printing history reveals: 'Villon', a short monologue by the French poet with strong religious overtones, was printed in three private editions and Alfred Lord Douglas' *The Academy* (this is the poem Sassoon refers to on the opening page of *The Weald of Youth*) before its inclusion in *The Old Huntsman*. They are mainly interesting for biographical reasons, in that they give an idea of Sassoon's poetic beginnings. Undoubtedly this is at least partly why they were preserved in the *Collected Poems*.[9] What they illustrate above all, however, are the young poet's main problems: he had little to say and no poetical voice to say it with.

The section opens with a piece that is only remarkable for its exuberant mood. In a short poem of only eight lines young Nimrod comes galloping by "With jollity of horn and lusty cheer". 'Nimrod in September' celebrates the young sportsman, and it is notable that it is only in this hunting poem that the tone is buoyant. The poetic qualities of the piece are negligible, so it must have been Sassoon's intention to give the reader a glimpse of himself as the naive, carefree sportsman he was at the outset of his poetic journey in the very first poem of this *Lyrical Poems* section. The poem was deliberately used as the opening poem: it was first published in *Discoveries* (1915), the last but one of Sassoon's privately published editions to appear before *The Old Huntsman*. Several of the poems that follow are from a much earlier date.

The second poem, 'Morning Express', is a much better piece, praised by Virginia Woolf as "a solid and in its way beautiful catalogue of facts" and a source of despair for Wilfred Owen ("everyone says 'I could have done that myself!'").[10] It describes the arrival and departure of a morning train:

> Under the arch, then forth into blue day,
> Glide the processional windows on their way,
> And glimpse the stately folk who sit at ease
> To view the world like kings taking the seas
> In prosperous weather: drifting banners tell
> Their progress to the counties
>
> > (ll. 19-24)

When reading the autobiographies it becomes clear that for the young Sassoon trains had a particular meaning; he associated them with discovering 'the world'.

> Ten miles was a long way when I was a child. Over the hills and far away, I used to think to myself, as I stared across the orchards and meadows of the weald, along which ran the proverbially slow railway line to London. (*MFH*, 27)

These ideas are also expressed in the poem; not only does the simile in ll. 21-23 suggest that the poet considers travelling a privilege, but on their journey the passengers do not look at the counties or the countryside, but they "view the world". What the two opening poems have in common is that the poet does not take part in the activities; he is the passive observer who watches young Nimrod gallop towards his adventures and sees the train leave on its journey to the world outside.

'Ancestors' reflects Sassoon's interest in his paternal family history. In his autobiographies he is somewhat reticent about the Sassoon connection, simply saying what his mother told him about his illustrious great-grandfather David Sassoon, "whom [she] had encouraged me to venerate vaguely as a man of noble character and wonderful ability, though I had found it difficult to connect myself with an ancestor who couldn't speak English and dressed like a biblical patriarch" (*WY*, 250-51). But it seems that Sassoon is consciously underplaying this curiosity about the Persian Sassoons. Both Fitzgerald's *Rubaiyat* and C.M. Doughty's *Travels In Arabia Deserta* were among his favourite reading, and when he briefly corresponded with Doughty in 1907 he was much intrigued to hear that Doughty had actually met some of his relatives in Poona (*WY*, 20). As in all these early poems, however, Sassoon never takes the personal angle; even here, where the subject offers him an ideal opportunity for a more personal approach, he produces a competent but essentially mannered poem, an exercise in Swinburnian word-music:

> And oft in pauses of their conference,
> They listen to the measured breath of night's
> Hushed sweep of wind aloft the swaying trees
> In dimly gesturing gardens; then a voice
> Climbs with clear mortal song half-sad for heaven
>
> (ll. 7-11)

The poem evokes a purely sensuous picture, but does not seem to have any particular meaning and clearly shows the truth of Sassoon's earlier quoted comment that "The sound of words has been more to me than skilful management of their meanings, and verbal exactitude was a late arrival in my literary development".

The other poems in this section hardly merit individual discussion. Keatsian fauns and dryads pipe drowsy notes ('Night Piece') or "Move in the gloom of the glade" ('Dryads'), and archaic words (a result of Sassoon's admiration for the works of C. M. Doughty) are either somewhat embarrassing, if not to say ridiculous, as in "Raise your bowed heads, and let/Your horns adore the sky, ye patient kine!" ('Storm and Sunlight', ll. 17-8), or completely superfluous as in 'October', where the leaves of "drooping cherry orchards" are described as hanging "silent and whist" (l. 3), the only merit of "whist" being that it rhymes with "mist" in line 1. The range of vocabulary is limited, the poetry bloodless, and the poet's fondness of certain words like "blundering", "blustering" and "glade" leads to their over frequent use.

One of the more powerful poems is 'Haunted', a nightmarish vision of a man pursued by evil creatures in a dark forest. No explanation of how the man came to be there is given, the reader is dropped right in the middle of the action. As such it is reminiscent of Walter de la Mare's 'The Listeners',[11] a poem that must have greatly impressed Sassoon, for the first stanza of 'Special-Constable' (written around the same time but deleted from the *Collected Poems*) seems a direct echo of de la Mare's 'haunting' poem:

> "Put out that light!" he cried.
> But no one put it out.
> No one replied,
> And silence gulped his husky shout.

Sassoon's poem reads as a parody of 'The Listeners', for the special-constable, slightly the worse for drink, becomes over-zealous and orders the night sky to black out, hurling his truncheon "Up at the lit and lawless sky". The poem is not unfunny, but perhaps Sassoon, who later became a close friend of de la Mare's, decided to leave it out of his collected edition because he felt it a too irreverent treatment of one of his admired friend's best poems.

Looking back over the limited subject-range of his early poetry, Sassoon came to the conclusion that "the two things about which I wrote with most fullness of feeling were music and the early morning" (*WY*, 35-6). Music would always remain important to Sassoon: though his own qualities as a pianist could not be compared to those of his father as a violinist, it would always remain an important feature of both his poetry and his life. But the favourite theme of his early poetry is without question the early morning, as is clear from such titles as 'Morning-Land', 'At Daybreak', 'Morning Glory', 'Today', 'Daybreak in a Garden' and 'Before Day'. Again I think Sassoon intentionally chose to preserve so many of these poems in this section. Quite apart from their individual qualities, which are debatable, he wanted to establish himself as a 'morning-poet'. Especially in his later work, spring, dawn and the early morning were to become symbols of youth, high-spirited optimism, innocence and expectancy. The idea of associating the early morning with optimism and vigour was suggested to him by the work of George Meredith. Sassoon first read him in 1908 and was thrilled by the "exultant energy and descriptive loveliness" (*WY*, 30) of the lyrical poems. In his biography of Meredith, written forty years later, he associated Meredith's optimism with the early morning. Discussing 'The Thrush in February' he writes: "Its twilight mood and setting are unusual for him, who was morning-minded and loved to meet the sun upon the upland lawn" (*M*, 239). The young Sassoon was equally morning-minded, and though the early poems themselves may be too self-consciously literary, they do serve to convey the image of a young poet, eagerly awaiting what 'the world' is going to offer him.

Whether the classification 'Lyrical Poems' is well chosen is doubtful. Many of the poems are purely descriptive and lack a personal, emotional tone. Again this may indicate the fact that Sassoon had nothing personal to say, though it is rather surprising that the theme of human love is completely absent. It is fruitless to speculate whether this was because Sassoon as yet had had no experience of love, but it seems reasonable to assume that his reticence on the subject was at least partly due to his homosexuality.

In July 1911 Sassoon had sent a few of his sonnets to Edward Carpenter, explaining in an accompanying letter that they were meant to express the gratitude he felt towards Carpenter after a chance reading of his *The Intermediate Sex* in October 1910 had "opened up a new life" for him. Edward Carpenter (1844-1929) was, with Havelock Ellis, among the leading English experts on 'sexual inversion'. Himself a homosexual, Carpenter introduced in his writings the new ideas on homosexuality of German and Austrian theorists such as Magnus Hirschfeld and Karl Ulrichs, proclaiming that to follow one's own natural impulses was in fact to follow nature itself, but that such a life-style required courage and discipline. *The Intermediate Sex*, first published in 1908, was a collection of essays and articles Carpenter had written on the subject of homosexuality. The volume also reprinted his controversial pamphlet 'Homogenic Love, and its Place in a Free Society' (first published in 1895, a few months before the Oscar Wilde trials) in which Carpenter defended homosexuals as normal and healthy people and claimed that homosexuality was no more and no less than "*a distinct variety of the sexual passion*". The main difference was that homosexuality could not be expressed as freely and perfectly as heterosexual love, and homosexual love therefore tended "to run rather more along emotional lines". Carpenter then went on to claim that heterosexual love had a purely natural function, i.e. the propagation of the race, whereas homosexual love was necessary for a society to generate "those children of the mind, the philosophical conceptions and ideals which transform our lives and those of society".[12] For Sassoon, this view of homosexuality as a superior kind of human love denoting a philosophical or artistic nature must have tied in well with his own belief that he was going to be a poet and with what his mother had told him about a great poet being a superior human being.

As he explained in his letter, it was through Carpenter's writings that Sassoon had first come to terms with his own homosexuality:

> your words have shown me all that I was blind to before, & have opened up a new life to me, after a time of great perplexity & unhappiness. Until I read the 'Intermediate Sex', I knew absolutely nothing of that subject, (& was entirely *unspotted*, as I *am now*), but life was an empty thing, & what ideas I had about homosexuality were absolutely prejudiced, & I was in such a groove that I couldn't allow myself to be what I wished to be, & the intense attraction I felt for my own sex was almost a subconscious thing, & my antipathy for women a mystery to me [...] I write to you as a leader and a prophet.[13]

Carpenter immediately replied, inviting Sassoon to visit him at his home in Millthorpe, where in 1883 he had set up as a market gardener, only then to gradually convert his farm into a socialist cooperative which aimed to realize the ideals of Walt Whitman's *Democratic Vistas* and Henry David Thoreau's *Walden*. Though in his letter Sassoon had called Carpenter a "leader and prophet", his visit to Millthorpe did not induce him to become a faithful disciple, mainly because Carpenter's socialist ideals did not appeal to him. But he did share Carpenter's enthusiasm for Walt Whitman's *Leaves of Grass*, which was to be a profound influence on the contents of his *Collected Poems*. He kept in touch with Carpenter, sending him a copy of his 'Statement against the War' in 1917 (a protest action Carpenter warmly applauded), but the initial admiration for Carpenter as expressed in his 1911 letter never matured into an intimate friendship.

Sassoon's letter reveals that though in 1911 (when he was 25) he was still sexually inexperienced, he did feel a definite sexual attraction towards his own sex, so that the absence of love as a subject in the *Lyrical Poems* section remains puzzling. It must be remembered, however, that when *The Old Huntsman* was published in May 1917, Sassoon, through his friendship with Robert Ross, was already well aware of the need for discretion on the subject of homosexuality. But whatever the reason, the absence of love poetry is yet another example of the curious paradox in this *Lyrical Poems* section, where the reader is left with the impression that all personal involvement has been carefully avoided.

V

The title piece of his first volume is one of the longest poems Sassoon ever wrote. Although 'The Old Huntsman' does not have all the characteristics of the dramatic monologue (except for the last 3 lines there is no other person present), he undoubtedly considered it to be one: "I have always preferred brevity to amplitude in poetry. If a poem must be long, I want it to be in the form of a dramatic monologue – subjective utterance rather than impersonal narrative" (*M*, 209). It was written early in 1915, shortly before Sassoon first went to France, and is his most successful piece of non-war poetry up to that time. What must have contributed to this success is the fact that here, for the very first time, Sassoon makes use of his own expert knowledge. Relying on his experiences as a sportsman, he creates the persona of an old huntsman who, at the end of his career, has used the

Squire's three hundred pound testimonial to sign "A seven years' bargain for the Golden Fleece" (a pub), a venture which has not proved to be altogether successful:

> 'T was a bad deal all round; and dear enough
> It cost me, what with my daft management,
> And the mean folk as owed and never paid me,
> And backing losers;and the local bucks
> Egging me on with whiskys while I bragged
> The man I was when huntsman to the Squire
>
> (ll.3-8)

The colloquial tone of voice is quite convincing (Sassoon must have heard it often enough when out hunting), and it is a pity that at times the too-lavish style of the early poetry intrudes:

> wind the clock
> That keeps the time of life with feeble tick
> Behind my bleared old face that stares and wonders
>
> (ll.25-7)

The old huntsman has the same meditative inclinations as the young poet, and begins to ruminate about his active days as a huntsman. The most interesting feature of this part of the poem is, for the non-aficionado, the gruesomely detailed description:

> We've been digging
> In a steep sandy warren, riddled with holes,
> And I've just pulled the terrier out and left
> A sharp-nosed cub-face blinking there and snapping,
> Then in a moment seen him mobbed and torn
> To strips in the baying hurly of the pack
>
> (ll. 29-34)

By the time Sassoon came to write *Memoirs of a Fox-Hunting Man* (1928) this side of hunting remained unmentioned: such bloody scenes would not have served his purpose of creating an idyllic and pastoral Edwardian world as a contrast to the senseless slaughter of the Great War.

The hunting-memories and his conversations with the parson on religion (ll.48-72) blend with the dream of Hell the old man used to have in his early days as a huntsman:

> Hell was the coldest scenting land I've known,
> And both my whips were always lost, and hounds
> Would never get their heads down
>
> (ll. 85-7)

The poem offers an affectionate description of a man who has only lived for hunting, and who has never consciously realized how happy he has been:

> So I've loved
> My life; and when the good years are gone down,
> Discover what I've lost. I never broke
> Out of my blundering self into the world,
> But let it all go past me, like a man
> Half asleep in a land that's full of wars
>
> (ll.177-182)

The regrets of the huntsman are the fears of the poet. The old man never realized how happy he was because his cocooned existence he led as a huntsman had not allowed him to go out in the world and gather the outside experience he might then have used as a means of comparison.

But the man who observes that as yet he has never broken out of his "blundering self" is not the huntsman; it is the voice of the poet who now speaks out openly, knowing that the time has come for him to wake up and go out into a world "full of wars".

CHAPTER 2

AN OFFICER AND TEMPORARY REBEL

I

The story of the soldier-poet Sassoon is that of a latter-day Doctor Faustus. The young man who was so eager to become a famous poet saw his dream fulfilled, only then to start wondering if the price had been worth paying: the war that made the poet destroyed the man, and Sassoon's post-war life is mainly one long attempt (he called it his spiritual journey) to find a new equilibrium after a profound experience that left him spiritually and emotionally unsettled. In later life Sassoon complained that his reputation as a war poet had become a burden to him, at the same time expressing amazement at the fact that the naive young man who went to war had succeeded as a war poet at all: "I was immature, impulsive, irrational, and bewildered by the whole affair, hastily improvising my responses, and only saved by being true to the experiences which I drew upon" (LC, 14).

At the outbreak of the war, Sassoon enlisted as a trooper in the Sussex Yeomanry. In May 1915 he was commissioned in the Royal Welch Fusiliers, and between November 1915 and April 1917 Sassoon served in the First and Second Battalions RWF, both of which were to distinguish themselves as elite fighting units, known for there active and aggressive trench tours.[1] Sassoon first arrived in France on 17 November 1915, and a week later he joined the First Battalion RWF near Béthune in the Artois sector, where the Battle of Loos had been fought on 15 September.

The first month he was put in charge of several working parties that were sent up to the front-line on repair duties. In January 1916, before his Battalion was sent up the line to serve in the trenches, he was appointed Transport Officer, a job he accepted with reluctance since it meant that he would spend most of his time in relative safety behind the lines. He thus did not arrive in the front-line trenches for a longer period until 26 March 1916.

By then he had suffered his first personal loss: on 1 November 1915 his younger brother Hamo was buried at sea after being mortally wounded at Gallipoli. Then, on 18 March 1916, 2nd lieutenant D.C. 'Tommy' Thomas, a friend of both Robert Graves and Sassoon, was killed by a stray bullet. The following evening Sassoon, who as a boy had hardly ever attended funerals because of his nervous disposition, noted in his diary how he saw Thomas' "shrouded form laid in the earth", Robert Graves, "with his white whimsical face twisted and grieving", standing beside him. Sassoon had been secretly in love with Thomas, and it is moving to read his record of their last meeting:

> When last I saw him, two nights ago, he had his notebook in his hand, reading my last poem. And I said good night to him, in the moonlit trenches. Had I but known! – the old, human-weak cry. Now he comes back to me in memories, like an angel, with the light in his yellow hair, and I think of him at Cambridge last August [1915, when they were on a training course] when we lived together four weeks in Pembroke College in rooms where the previous occupant's name, Paradise, was written above the door. (*D1*, 44-5)

Though these losses did upset Sassoon personally, they at first did not affect his poetry: there is as yet no trace in his poems that would suggest the bitter war-satires he was to write later on. At this stage Sassoon and his early war poems do not differ greatly from the poets and poems that are usually quoted to illustrate an initial war enthusiasm, Rupert Brooke's *1914* sonnets and Julian Grenfell's 'Into Battle'. Brooke, especially, caught the mood of many a soldier who had not yet had any front-line experience, and many of the war poets that are usually juxtaposed with Brooke shared his enthusiasm when still inexperienced. Though he later wrote some sonnets that were meant as an antithesis to Brooke's blind enthusiasm, Ivor Gurney, when still in England, wrote to a friend in April 1915 that Brooke had written "two sonnets which outshine by far any thing yet written on this upheaval".[2] And when Herbert Read tried to explain his happiness at the prospect of being sent up the line, he wrote that his gladness was akin to that expressed in Brooke's 'Peace', of which he then quoted the opening lines.[3]

Sassoon's early war poems are in a similar celebratory mood. Characteristic of these poems is the indiscriminate use the poet makes of the personal pronouns 'I' and 'we', as if as yet it had not occurred to him that not everybody may share his enthusiasm for the war. It is, however, also possible that this too is in unconscious imitation of Brooke's *1914* sonnets, which are their major influence, especially in 'Absolution':

> War is our scourge; yet war has made us wise,
> And, fighting for freedom, we are free

The paradoxical nature of these lines echoes Brooke's sonnet 'Safety': "Safe though all safety's lost; safe where men fall", and when in the final lines Sassoon writes:

> Now, having claimed this heritage of heart,
> What need we more, my comrades and my brothers?

it is clear that "this heritage" consists of the Holiness, Love, Pain, Honour and Nobleness that Brooke welcomes as "our heritage" in the sestet of his third sonnet, 'The Dead'. These heroic qualities, with death as the hero's ultimate achievement, are also referred to in 'To My Brother', in which Sassoon commemorates his brother Hamo's death in heroic mood: "in the gloom I see your laurell'd head / And through your victory I shall win the light".

This first stage of Sassoon's career as a war poet is perhaps best illustrated by a quotation from his war diary. On 2 December 1915, still safely behind the lines, Sassoon continued his pre-war life and went out riding with a fellow officer:

> Saw a heron, which sailed slowly away across the misty flats of ploughed land; grey, still evening, gleaming dykes, willows and poplars; a few lights here and there as we rode home, and flicker of star-shells in the sky beyond Bethune. Robert Graves lent me his manuscript poems to read: some very bad, violent and repulsive. A few full of promise and real beauty. He oughtn't to publish yet. (*D1*, 21)

What this passage so clearly shows is that Sassoon had as yet not changed his ideas about the nature of poetry: he still believed that it was the poet's task to create beauty, and in this description of the French countryside that is exactly what he is trying to do, even going so far as to incorporate the "flicker of star-shells" of the distant front into his idyllic picture. No wonder he did not approve of Robert Graves' harshly realistic war poems. Graves was first in the trenches in May 1915, and therefore, though Sassoon's junior by nine years, vastly superior in front-line experience. In *Goodbye to All That* (1929) Graves recounts a meeting with Sassoon when he showed him some of his poems:

> He [Sassoon] frowned and said that war should not be written about in such a realistic way. In return, he showed me some of his own poems. One of them began:
>> Return to greet me, colours that were my joy,
>> Not in the woeful crimson of men slain ...
> Siegfried had not yet been in the trenches. I told him, in my old-soldier manner, that he would soon change his style.[4]

The lines Graves quotes are from 'To Victory', a poem that is interesting for two reasons, one personal and one poetical. Sassoon dedicated it to Edmund Gosse and sent it to him immediately after its completion on 4 January 1916. Gosse published it anonymously in *The Times* on 15 January, when it was read by Lady Ottoline Morrell.[5] She thought the poem had "real beauty", became interested in its author and made enquiries, which eventually led to a correspondence between Sassoon and Lady Ottoline, and still later to regular invitations to Garsington Manor, Lady Ottoline's country house near Oxford. Sassoon thus gained what was to be an important social contact before he became known as an angry war poet. But the poem also heralds the major change in Sassoon's war poetry: the "woeful crimson of men slain" suggests the emergence of a growing concern for his men, a concern that was to be the main reason for Sassoon's eventual revolt.

II

From the moment he arrived for his first spell in the trenches there is a gradual development of two different strains in his poetry, which usually co-exist without any problems, but which sometimes oddly clash. On the one hand there is Sassoon's personal voice, the voice of the privileged young man who struggles to come to terms with the realities of war. But on the other hand there is the voice of the subaltern, the young officer who develops a sense of responsibility for the men under his command.

Sassoon was a second lieutenant, the lowest officer-rank, and in command of a platoon which at the outbreak of the war would have consisted of four sections of fourteen men. But as the war progressed this standard size was hardly ever maintained, and a platoon might come to consist of a curious hotchpotch. When Sassoon joined the 2nd Battalion of the Royal Welch Fusiliers in March 1917, he was posted to B Company:

> I found myself in command of No. 8 Platoon, which contained 8 Private Joneses. Its total strength numbered 34, including two sergeants, 1 corporal and 6 lance-corporals. Eight of the 34 were Lewis gunners. These being deducted my compact little unit was unimpressive on parade and seldom mustered 20 strong.[6]

A second lieutenant would be in the trenches with his men, know about their living conditions, and one of his duties would be to act as censor. Company officers had to read and sign each of their men's correspondence and they were held responsible for any breaches of security in these letters that were discovered by security officers at the base. Many company officers found this yet another chore; Raymond Asquith, in billets in October 1915, wrote to his wife that "The most laborious thing one does is reading through and censoring the soldiers' letters. They are usually very long and very dull and full of formulae which hardly amount to idiom".[7] But some felt that censoring did have a positive effect:

> As we sat round the dugout table, reading piles of letters by the
> light of one candle-end, we got to know our men with a new
> intimacy, not because they opened their hearts in letters which
> would be so public, but because they revealed their characters.
> Whatever else, this sharing of privacy tightened the bond
> between officers and men.[8]

For Sassoon the reading of his men's letters was a real eye-opener.
Not only did it make him realize that not everybody shared his
reckless fighting spirit, but it also gave him an insight into their
backgrounds, their private lives, jobs, living conditions, families,
thoughts and cares. It brought home to him the simple but all too
easily overlooked truth of the remark made by one of the characters in
Henry Barbusse's famous war-novel *Under Fire* (1916): "We are not
soldiers ... we're men".[9]

On 10 February 1916 Sassoon wrote what he later called the "first
of my 'outspoken' war poems".[10] Undoubtedly inspired by the insights
he had gained as a censor, he for the first time attempted to use the
voice of the average Royal Welch Fusilier. 'In the Pink' begins with a
soldier writing a letter home to his girl, the day before he has to go
back in the trenches: 'So Davies wrote: "This leaves me in the pink" /
Then scrawled his name: "Your loving sweetheart, Willie".' In the
second stanza of the poem the personalization of the soldier continues
with the poet giving an insight into the young man's mind:

> He groaned and thought of Sundays at the farm,
> And how he'd go cheerful as a lark
> In his best suit, to wander arm in arm
> With brown-eyed Gwen, and whisper in her ear
> The simple, silly things she liked to hear

This picture is too idyllic and simple to really work well. In
comparison with 'The Old Huntsman' the poet's grasp is not as sure;
he is not well enough acquainted with this life to give as original a
picture as he could do in 'The Old Huntsman'. Rather he has to rely on
bloodless cliches that are too trite to make the soldier come to life for
the reader. In the concluding lines an authorial voice intrudes: "Tonight's he's in the pink; but soon he'll die / And still the war goes on -
he don't know why".

It is this concern for the common soldier, for the little lives of the men who arrive at the front, are sent into battle and go under anonymously, that was to become the underlying theme in Sassoon's war poetry. The responsibility and deep sympathy he felt for these simple men developed into a feeling of love for the common soldier and anger towards those at home and in authority who were blind to the soldiers' sufferings.

III

Besides this growing concern for his men Sassoon was also driven on by purely personal motives. At the front the Poet Sassoon and the Sportsman Sassoon, two facets of his personality which before the war had led separate existences, blended into the Soldier Sassoon. Entries in his 1916 war diary give an astonishing picture of a man who combines the thrills of outdoor sports with the fanaticism and idealism of a personal crusade:

> Last night [...] found me creeping about in front of our wire [...] Got quite near the German wire [.....] I found it most exhilarating – just like starting for a race. Great thing is to get as many sensations as possible. No good being out here unless one takes the full amount of risks, and I want to get a good name in the Battalion, for the sake of poetry and poets, whom I represent. (*D1*, 50-1)

Not only does this passage show the highly romantic image Sassoon had of the Poet, it also confirms his own unshakeable belief that he himself was a poet. Shy and diffident, as a poet virtually unknown and at that time with no official publication to his name, he did regard himself as the unofficial representative of "poetry and poets". His soldiering gave him the physical exhilaration that he had known as a sportsman, but it also provided him with experiences of life, and that, according to Sassoon, was the stuff poetry was made of:

> I used to say I couldn't kill anybody in this war; but since they shot Tommy [Ltn. Thomas] I would gladly stick a bayonet into a German by daylight. Someone told me a year ago that love,

sorrow, and hate were things I had never known (things which every poet *should* know!). Now I have known love for Bobbie [Hanmer] and Tommy, and grief for Hamo and Tommy, and hate has come also, and the lust to kill. (*D1*, 52)

Sassoon got every opportunity to vent his desire for action, for both the First and Second Battalions RWF were renowned fighting units. Whereas many other battalions happily conformed to the 'live and let live' system that gradually developed at the front and kept quiet as long as the enemy did the same, the First and Second Battalions RWF maintained a policy of aggressive patrolling in no man's land, which was mainly intended to keep up a fighting spirit among the troops. But even in these active battalions Sassoon's keenness was exceptional. During his first months at the front, his fellow officers suspected him of trying to get killed, which is quite likely, though he himself only talks about something that drove him on "to look for trouble" (*D1*, 51). The deaths of his brother and his friend upset his nerves and he found it impossible to sit still; he needed to work it off:

I am bound to get it in the neck sometime, so why not make a creditable show [....] And death is the best adventure of all – better than living idleness and sinking into the groove again and trying to be happy. Life is precious to us all now; too precious to keep long. (*D1*, 53)

There is an over-excited determination in these words: not only does he want to get his own back for the deaths of his brother and his friend, but also he wants to prove to himself that he has cut himself loose from his former existence. It is the 'death or glory' maxim reduced to 'death *is* glory'. Death is just the splendid culmination of a heroic life lived to the full. Julian Grenfell had expressed a similar attitude in his 'Into Battle', but he never had the chance to find out if it was just a passing mood: he died of wounds in May 1915. Sassoon survived all his reckless exploits and had time to discover that he was no Robert Graves, who could say 'goodbye to all that'. No matter how much he wanted to, or thought he wanted to, Sassoon could never cut himself loose from his former life. The young poet who celebrated the beauty of nature was in him still, and could not be suppressed. Only ten days later, after a night in which he has been dreaming of English landscapes, he notes in his diary:

> The existence one leads here is so much a thing of naked outlines and bare expanses, so empty of colour and fragrance, that one loves these things more than ever, and more than ever one hungers for them – the music and the graciousness of life. (*DI*, 55)

In December 1916 he wrote two poems that illustrate this dichotomy of the nature-poet looking for beauty and the soldier-poet who finds satisfaction in fighting. In 'The Poet as Hero' Sassoon discusses the change that has occurred in his poetry. Throughout the poem he makes use of a chivalrous metaphor that gives the poem a distinctly Pre-Raphaelite flavour. The opening stanza asks why the poet gave up his "silly sweetness" and changed his ecstasies to "an ugly cry". The answer is that formerly he was a knight in search of the Grail, i.e. a poet in search of Beauty, whereas "now I've said goodbye to Galahad"

> And am no more the knight of dreams and show:
> For lust and senseless hatred make me glad,
> And my killed friends are with me where I go.

This bloodthirsty attitude ties in with the over-excited diary entries recording Sassoon's reckless exploits in no man's land. That same diary shows, however, that once his nerves had calmed down, he often sought solitude to contemplate and enjoy what natural beauty could be found behind the lines. This is the theme of the second poem, 'Secret Music', which is a celebration of the creative imagination that allows him to cope with the horrors of war and restores his mental sanity:

> I keep such music in my brain
> No din this side of death can quell;
> Glory exulting over pain,
> And beauty, garlanded in hell.

The fact that these contrasting poems were written in the same month is indicative of Sassoon's volatile state of mind.

IV

One of the features of his early poetry that Sassoon could now put to
better use was the visual aspect of his writing. Many of his best war
poems contain descriptive passages that give the reader a vivid
impression of life (and death) in the trenches. One of the first poems
to show this quality is 'A Working Party', written in March 1916. The
first part of the poem gives a detailed description of a soldier in a
working party stumblingly finding his way through the trench-
system:

> Three hours ago he blundered up the trench,
> Sliding and poising, groping with his boots;
>   ...
> He couldn't see the man who walked in front;
> Only he heard the drum and rattle of feet
> Stepping along barred trench-boards, often splashing
> Wretchedly where the sludge was ankle-deep

The careful observation is reminiscent of the young poet describing
the train's stop at the station in 'Morning Express', as is also the use of
some of his favourite words, "blundered" and "groping". But this time
the overall effect is far more successful. This is partly due to the
subject; a detailed description of a working party in the trenches is
more interesting than that of the arrival of a train for the simple
reason that the reader is not familiar with this experience. But not
only is the poet more knowledgeable on his subject, his poetic
craftsmanship shows signs of improvement as well: "sludge" (l.8) is
well-chosen and has onomatopoeic qualities, and when the poet
writes that "rifle-shots/would split and crack and sing along the night"
(ll. 22-3) he is not only again careful in his choice of short, sharp
words, but also casually suggesting the presence of snipers. In line 26,
there is a sudden change in the poem. First the poet bluntly announces
that the soldier is dead (the final stanza of the poem makes clear that
he was killed by a sniper), then he goes on to personalize the soldier:
"He was a young man with a meagre wife / And two small children in
a Midland town" (ll. 30-1). This is the same technique he used in 'In
the Pink': the first person pronouns that marked the first phase of his

war poetry are now replaced by "he", and the main subject of the poems is no longer a war-happy, anonymous warrior, but a private soldier, trying to make the best of the miserable conditions he is living in.

In the first draft of 'The Working Party' there is a final stanza Sassoon chose to delete when he included the poem in *The Old Huntsman*.[11] The first two lines of this stanza, "That's how a lad goes west when at the front / Snapped in a moment's merciful escape", show a change in the role of the poet. Apart from the fact that death is no longer a heroic climax but a "moment's merciful escape", the poet is here not the narrator, but is actually addressing the reader. This new role, one that Sassoon was to adopt more often in his later war poems, and which occurs in most of his angry war satires, is indicative of a new feature in his poetic personality coming to the fore: that of the Prophet.

What it was that made him feel a Prophet is difficult to say. Partly, it is a logical extension of his romantic concept of 'the Poet', and partly it may have been caused by his growing fascination for his Jewish ancestry. It may even have been due to the fact that mentally he could not cope with his gruesome experiences in the trenches. Just as he had had to work off the emotional upset caused by the loss of his brother and friend, so now he felt the need to do something with his emotional experiences of trench life. The most important reason, however, was undoubtedly the concern he felt for his men. His sense of responsibility gradually became a sense of guilt, in that he felt an accomplice in the continuation of a war that was organised and kept going by one part of the population (politicians, senior officers, the Home Front), but in which another part, the common man, fought and suffered.

Jon Silkin writes that the violence in Sassoon's later war poetry, and his hostility towards the people he held responsible for the continuation of the war "testify to the impact of it [the war] on him as well as to the suddenness of his development".[12] It was the adoption of the prophet-role that more than anything else accounts for Sassoon's sudden development. Sharing his experiences with the reader and describing the horrors of the war were a necessary outlet for him. Sassoon himself wrote in a letter:

As a poetic spirit I have always felt myself – or wanted to be – a kind of minor prophet. I suppose most poets aim at being prophetic communicators. But the idea has always been very strong in my mind. And found utterance in the war poems of course.[13]

The prophet-role Sassoon adopted did not just come out of the blue; from the start a religious theme is a constant presence in his war poetry. Titles such as 'The Redeemer', 'The Prince of Wounds', 'Golgotha' and 'Christ and the Soldier' tell their own story, but Sassoon's Christianity is highly personal. In a footnote added later to 'Christ and the Soldier' he writes that at the time he

was a very incomplete and quite unpractising Christian, and understood little more than he [an "ignorant private", the Soldier in the poem] of the meaning of the Lord's teaching. Like Wilfred Owen, I was anti-clerical, and the Churches seemed to offer no solution to the demented doings on the Western Front.[14]

Characteristically, he underplays his own religious feelings in this passage. A religious vocabulary is not an unusual feature in war-poetry descriptions of the frontline. That Sassoon refers to the battle and the front as hell or Armageddon is therefore in itself not remarkable. While behind the lines at the Somme on 21 July 1916 he continued this metaphor, describing soldiers returning from the frontline as ghosts: "Then, like flitting ghosts, last began to come the foot-weary infantry – stumbling – limping – straggling back after eight days in hell" (*D1*, 97). Much later, in April 1918, he developed this theme into a Dantesque vision in 'Concert Party'. The poem describes a concert party in Egypt (where Sassoon was then stationed). The men turn out to watch and listen to the dancers and musicians who sing the familiar songs that remind them of home. But whereas the entertainers will soon return home, the soldiers are simply reminded of things they once knew but which are now beyond their reach. The poem describes this concert as a scene from Dante's Inferno, with the musicians in the roles of Dante and Virgil and the soldiers as the ghosts who cannot follow them back to a civilian world of relative normality:

We hear them, drink them, till the concert's done.
Silent, I watch the shadowy mass of soldiers stand.
Silent, they drift away, over the glimmering sand.

Perhaps the most striking example of Sassoon's religious desire is to be found in 'The Dream', a poem written in Limerick in January 1918, for in the third section of this poem Sassoon explicitly states his guilt-complex. The poem recounts a dream in which the poet/officer inspects the feet of his men after a long day's march. There is a feeling of comradeship between soldiers and officer, "for each of 'em knows / That I am as tired as they are", but the officer feels more than just physical exhaustion:

> Can they guess
> The secret burden that is always mine?–
> Pride in their courage, pity for their distress;
> And burning bitterness
> That I must take them to the accursed Line.
> ...
> And I must lead them nearer, day by day,
> To the foul beast of war that bludgeons life.

This third section of the poem was first conceived as a separate poem, written in April 1917, and entitled 'Foot Inspection'. There are two major differences with the later version, both suggesting that in revising the poem Sassoon felt the need to make it less direct. Not only does 'Foot Inspection' not use a dream-setting, even more remarkable are the lines where the poet introduces a religious metaphor, inspired by the foot inspection/foot washing association. Asking one of the soldiers about the condition of his boots, the officer considers how the soldier will never know "How glad I'd be to die, if dying could set him free / From battles". This identification with Jesus the Redeemer and the explicitly stated desire to sacrifice himself for his men, reveal an intensity of feeling for his men that is not found in the work of any other officer-poet.

V

The sense of responsibility they felt for their men rarely occurs as a subject in the work of other officer-poets. When writing about their platoon they usually focus on the camaraderie between officer and men, as in Edmund Blunden's 'Their Very Memory'. Blunden, a young subaltern in the Royal Sussex Regiment, celebrates the cheerful spirit of his men that brought life to the otherwise desolate landscape, emphasizing the pride he felt in being with them and his gratitude for the way they could uplift his own spirit.

One of the few poems that goes further in describing the feelings of the officer for his men is Herbert Read's 'My Company'.[15] Here too there is pride and gratitude:

> we've fought together
> compact, unanimous
> and I have felt the pride of leadership.

But in the following lines the emotion deepens, culminating in a surprising and somewhat sentimental outburst: the bonds that have grown between officer and men are like family ties, to be severed when the war ends. The outburst that follows is like a father who cannot cope with his children leaving home:

> I know that I'll wonder with a cry:
> "O beautiful men, O men I loved
> O whither are you gone, my company?"

Peace is the major threat to the company as a unit, for it will mean its complete annihilation, and it thus becomes, paradoxically enough, the biggest enemy. The individual human losses within the company that are suffered in the course of the war are in comparison apparently less important, for, as the poet suggests in the last section of the poem, he can still distance himself from the realities of the war and the suffering of his men. It is in this respect that he differs completely from Sassoon:

I can assume
a giant attitude and godlike mood
and then detachedly regard
all riots, conflicts and collisions.

The men I've lived with
lurch suddenly into a far perspective:
They distantly gather like a dark cloud of birds
in the autumn sky.

Sassoon was incapable of taking a similarly detached view; he could not help 'mothering' his men and he was unable to shrug off the responsibility he felt towards them.

On 16 April 1917 Sassoon was hit in the shoulder by a sniper's bullet while leading his company in an attack on Fontaine-les-Croisilles on the Somme front. Four days later he was back in England, recovering in the Fourth London Hospital at Denmark Hill. On 12 May he was moved to Chapelwood Manor in Sussex, the home of Lord and Lady Brassey (the Lord and Lady Asterisk of *Memoirs of an Infantry Officer*), who contributed to the war effort by making their country house a convalescent home for officers.

It was during the following weeks that Sassoon began to feel compelled to make a more outspoken protest against the war. This was partly brought on by his peaceful, comfortable existence at Chapelwood Manor which was in such sharp contrast with the horrors of the front he had only recently left behind and which his men were still experiencing. On 20 May he noted in his diary

tonight the rain is hushing the darkness, steady, whispering rain
– the voice of peace among the foliage. And men are cursing
the downpour that drenches and chills them, while the guns
roar out their challenge (*D1*, 171).

A few days after leaving Chapelwood Manor on 4 June he visited Ottoline Morrell at Garsington. Robert Graves had been a regular guest there while a convalescent in February 1917. When he had realized that the state of his nerves made him unfit for active service, he had asked his Commanding Officer if he could be appointed an instructor in the Officer Cadet Battalion stationed at Wadham College, Oxford.[16] Some of Sassoon's friends now urged him to apply for a similar position as instructor with the Officers' Training Corps at Cambridge, but Sassoon told Lady Ottoline that he was reluctant to do so: "How could he possibly train others to go out there knowing what they would have to go through. 'They will all be killed or maimed'".[17] He then told her about his desire to make a forceful protest against the war.

Lady Ottoline was keen to help him with his protest. She had been involved with anti-war movements since the outbreak of hostilities in August 1914, when her house in Bedford Square had become the meeting place for a group of Socialist and Liberal campaigners who went on to found the Union of Democratic Control (U.D.C.) in December 1914. One of these campaigners was Bertrand Russell, and according to Lady Ottoline's account she arranged for Sassoon to meet Russell and John Middleton Murry for lunch at a London restaurant on 12 June. Russell advised him to draw up a short statement against the continuation of the war, for which he would then try to get as much publicity as possible. Sassoon went home to Weirleigh and made a first draft which was far too long, and on 15 June he returned to London to see John Middleton Murry, who helped him in clarifying the text and reducing it to its right length. Katherine Mansfield met Sassoon for the first time that evening, and she wrote to Lady Ottoline the next day that Sassoon seemed to her "at present, in the *Dostoievsky* sense, 'delirious'".[18]

The final draft of Sassoon's 'Soldier's Declaration' is dated 15 June[19] and runs as follows:

> I am making this statement as an act of wilful defiance of military authority, because I believe that the War is being deliberately prolonged by those who have the power to end it. I am a soldier, convinced that I am acting on behalf of soldiers. I believe that this War, upon which I entered as a war of defence and liberation, has now become a war of aggression and conquest. I believe that the purposes for which I and my fellow-soldiers entered upon this War should have been so clearly stated as to have made it impossible for them to be changed without our knowledge, and that, had this been done, the

objects which actuated us would now be attainable by negotiation.

I have seen and endured the sufferings of the troops, and I can no longer be a party to prolonging those sufferings for ends which I believe to be evil and unjust.

I am not protesting against the military conduct of the War, but against the political errors and insincerities for which the fighting men are being sacrificed.

On behalf of those who are suffering now, I make this protest against the deception which is being practised on them. Also I believe that it may help to destroy the callous complacence with which the majority of those at home regard the continuance of agonies which they do not share, and which they have not sufficient imagination to realise.[20]

The second and fourth paragraphs of this statement, which refer to the suffering of the men and the ignorance of the home-front, clearly represent Sassoon's own views. But it is hard to believe that the third paragraph, which explicitly states that this is not a protest against the military conduct of the war, had been included in his original first draft. Only two months earlier, while recovering from his wound in hospital at Denmark Hill, Sassoon had written his poem 'The General', arguably his fiercest attack on the incompetence of the military leadership.

In the opening paragraph of his Declaration Sassoon claims to have entered the war thinking that it was a war of defence and liberation; but this claim suggests a degree of political awareness and idealism that was in fact totally absent in the innocent and ignorant young man he had been in August 1914. Sassoon never mentions political arguments in his war diaries, and yet his protest is solely based on political motives: the political leaders are accused of having altered the original war aims which had never been clearly defined in the first place (this would seem to beg the question how he can be so sure that the war aims had been altered) and they are also held responsible for prolonging the war unnecessarily. It is especially in this opening paragraph that the influence of Bertrand Russell, and, through him, the Cambridge philosopher G.E. Moore, is clearly detectable. For it was Moore, also a member of the Union of Democratic Control, who had devised a defence of conscientious objection not on absolute grounds, but on political and moral grounds pertaining only to the war then in progress.[21]

Sassoon's statement was read out in the House of Commons by the Liberal MP for Northampton H.B. Lees-Smith on 30 July 1917. In his reply the Under-Secretary for War called upon the Honourable Members not to exploit this action by a gallant officer who was at present in a disturbed state of mind, thus managing to avoid any further discussion on the subject. The following day the statement was published in *The Times* and *The Daily Mail*, but though other papers did take up the story, Sassoon's action never generated enough interest to become a major news story.

Though the bold claim "I am a soldier, convinced that I am acting on behalf of soldiers" suggests otherwise, Sassoon embarked on his Quixotic action without either his fellow officers or his men knowing anything about his plans. In *Siegfried's Journey* Sassoon recalled the hesitations he felt shortly before he decided to go through with its publication:

> Possibly what I disliked most was the prospect of being misunderstood and disapproved of by my fellow officers. Some of them would regard my behaviour as a disgrace to the Regiment. Others would assume that I had gone a bit crazy. How many of them, I wondered, would give me credit for having done it for the sake of the troops who were at the Front? (*SJ*, 52).

As it turned out there were precious few who admired his independent action. The only enthusiastic reaction was a short note from Edward Carpenter ("Well done, good and faithful!"). His literary friends Edward Marsh, Robert Ross, Edmund Gosse and H.G. Wells thoroughly disapproved of his protest. Arnold Bennett, who was also sent a copy of the 'Soldier's Declaration', pointed out the errors of Sassoon's ways in what he "thought to be a judicious letter", which unfortunately never seems to have reached him.[22]

His worst fears were also realized in that his fellow officers did not approve of his action either: his pre-war friend and fellow officer in the Royal Welch Fusiliers Robert Hanmer wrote from the Reading hospital where he was convalescing that he thought it all a "damned nonsense" and Robert Graves gave his initial reaction in a letter to

Edward Marsh, dated 12 July 1917: "It's an awful thing – completely mad – that he's done. Such rotten luck on you and me and his friends, especially in the Regiment. They all think he's mad...".[23] Sassoon's claim that he was speaking for the troops was also denied by a fellow officer in the Second Battalion RWF, who gave this verdict on Sassoon's action in August 1917:

> Sassoon gave a moral flavour to a gibe everywhere current at the front for a couple of years, that a lot of individuals in cushy jobs don't care how long the War lasts. It used to be said laughingly, now it is said bitterly. But for one in the Army with an interest in the prolongation of the War there are now hundreds of 'indispensables' at home in well paid war-jobs. The affluence and the squeals of the indispensables have made it hard for the serving-men's families, and exasperated the serving men, many of whom have been taken from increasing affluence for service. But I have not heard any stop-the-war talk among front-line troops, whatever may be spoken among the Base tribe: Base canteen workers have told me that the talk there is pretty alarming. On that point Sassoon did not speak the feeling of those with most to lose by the War.[24]

VI

It was his concern and compassion for his men that led Sassoon to his public opposition to the war. When at this stage he speaks out against the war, his condemnation no longer stems from any personal grievances but from his sympathies for, and gradual identification with, the grudges of the private soldiers. These grudges were, of course, partly based on class distinction: at the beginning of the war, before severe losses made it easier for soldiers to rise through the ranks, officers were picked from the privileged classes. Regardless of the fact that he himself owed his commission to this system, Sassoon's solidarity with his men made him share their dislike for officers. When on 9 June 1916 he was sent on leave, Sassoon shared his train carriage with "three Manchester officers[25] and one Suffolk":

all of them the last word in nonentitude and flatness and commonness. How rotten these people seem compared with the men who get orders from them, and go on leave once in twelve months if they are lucky. I can't see that the officers' class (second-rate) have any more intelligence than the private soldier. (*D1*, 77)

But these budding socialist tendencies are as yet not well thought-out. The curious consequences of this are best shown in the poems that criticize high-ranking officers. In 'The March-Past' (written in December 1916), the soldiers, on their way to the front line, pass the Corps-Commander:

> He was their leader, and a judge of Port-
> Rode well to hounds, and was a damned good sort.

The Corps-Commander remains at the Base and watches the soldiers march off to the front. One of the suggestions of the poem seems to be that one's position in the army is determined by the social class one belongs to. The lines here quoted are supposed to point out the class-division: the Corps-Commander is a keen fox-hunter, and a "damned good sort" is an example of his speech (as opposed to the "he don't know why" of private Davies in 'In the Pink'). Where the sympathies of the poet lie is unequivocally clear: he refers to the officer as "our" leader (thus siding with the men) and calls him "The corpse-commander".

But while giving voice to the thoughts and complaints of the soldiers, Sassoon seemingly forgets his own position and background. Much as he wanted to identify with the plight of the soldiers, according to the classification he applied it remained a fact that he himself, the enthusiastic sportsman who would describe himself as an "ordinary sort of chap",[26] belonged very much to the officer class. As soon the men were in billets behind the lines, the sharp divisions between officers and men immediately established themselves:

> Out of the line, the officer was a man apart. He never visited the estaminet of the men and they had to stand to attention when addressing him, and could get an interview only by written note to the orderly room [...] In the line all was

changed. Trappings like insignia, saluting, social distance gave way to survival and were largely omitted. Instead the officer was seen constantly by his men.[27]

The situation described in 'The March-Past' marks the transition between life at the Base and trench-life. It is not hard to imagine that whenever this happened it must have led to frequent grumbling remarks about the 'cushy' jobs at the Base among the men. Such remarks will not have escaped a 2nd lieutenant marching with them.

Sassoon's sympathy for his men led him to see the war through their eyes, but by focusing on the officers at the Base (he returned to this theme is such poems as 'The General' and 'Base Details') he never came to understand his own hybrid position. That he was completely unaware of these inconsistencies can be seen in one of his otherwise most successful war satires, 'Does It Matter?'.

The mood in 'Does It Matter?' is one of carefully controlled anger. It was written while Sassoon was being treated for his so-called nervous breakdown at Craiglockhart War Hospital in the autumn of 1917, and is of importance in this context for two reasons. The three stanzas each deal with a particular war-injury: the loss of legs, the loss of sight and "those dreams from the pit". The main point the poem makes is that whereas physical injuries are at least recognized by the people at home (who then consider it their patriotic duty to kill the soldier with kindness), the horrific thing about mental wounds is that nobody recognizes they exist, with the result that the best you can hope for is that "people won't say that you're mad". That Sassoon is here speaking for himself and not trying to be one with his men is nicely illustrated by the first stanza, which sarcastically claims that the loss of one's legs is amply compensated for by the kindness of other people:

> And you need not show that you mind
> When the others come in after hunting
> To gobble their muffins and eggs.

This is a far cry from the poet of 'The March Past' who used fox--hunting in a negative connotation, to mark the class distinction between the men marching to the front and the Corps-Commander;

rather this is Sassoon the Sportsman, who can imagine only too well what it would be like never to be able to hunt again.

VII

The way the military authorities handled the Sassoon affair may well have been induced by their desire to avoid any unwanted publicity, but they had every reason to be pleased with the outcome. Not only did their humane response eventually lead to the return to the front of a brave and useful officer, but by sending him to the Craiglockhart War Hospital for shell-shocked officers near Edinburgh they were directly responsible for a historic meeting between two major British war poets.

Wilfred Owen, a second lieutenant in the 2nd Battalion, Manchester Regiment, had been at Craiglockhart since 29 June; Sassoon arrived on 23 July, followed four hours later by his military escort consisting of Robert Graves and another officer, who had both managed to miss the train. In a letter to his mother, dated 15 August 1917, Owen writes:

> I have just been reading Siegfried Sassoon, and am feeling at a very high pitch of emotion. Nothing like his trench life sketches has ever been written or ever will be written. Shakespere [sic] reads vapid after these. Not of course because Sassoon is a greater artist, but because of the subjects, I mean. I think if I had the choice of making friends with Tennyson or with Sassoon I should go to Sassoon.[28]

These lines occur in the second part of a letter which is interrupted after the first two paragraphs by the single word "Friday" in brackets. This suggests that Owen started this letter on the 15th, and continued it on Friday the 20th.

On Sunday 22 August he wrote to his cousin Leslie Gunston: "At last I have an event worth a letter. I have beknown myself to Siegfried Sassoon. Went in to him last night (my second call). The first visit was one morning last week."[29] Since he does not mention this first visit to Sassoon in the letter to his mother, it would be tempting to think that he went to see him on the spur of the moment on Friday 20

August, immediately after completing the letter to his mother. Against this interpretation pleads a postscript Owen added at the bottom of the letter: "*Friday aft*. Just had yours. Haven't given it close attention yet," but it could be argued that Owen added that line in haste, shortly before sealing the envelope and posting it, just to let his mother know that he had received her letter, for at the same time the postscript does confirm that the second part of the letter was written on the Friday *morning*.[30]

That the brief period they spent together (Owen left Craiglockhart in the first week of November) was of major importance in the development of Owen's poetry is generally recognized. Dominic Hibberd concludes that if Owen had not been sent to Craiglockhart "some of the finest war poems in the English language might never have been written".[31] Sassoon's presence had a major effect on Owen's life: in the letters there are several small instances that show how susceptible Owen was to the older man's influence. In his letter of 22 August to his cousin Leslie Gunston Owen wrote that Sassoon had warned him not to publish too soon; in the same letter he said that he was looking forward to the volume of poetry that Gunston was having published at his own expense. Three weeks later he wrote to his mother to say that "Sassoon considers E.L. Gunston['s poetry] not only flatulent, but hopeless. I do think it a pity Leslie is in such a hurry".[32] The last remark is totally irrelevant, since Gunston's poems were, according to Sassoon, beyond hope, but Owen was simply echoing Sassoon's advice.

Another example of Sassoon's influence is Owen's appreciation of Thomas Hardy. In August 1917 he writes that he does not share Sassoon's enthusiasm for Hardy's work; but in April 1918 he recommends *Under the Greenwood Tree* to his mother.[33] And whereas up to Sassoon's arrival Owen had been happy to busy himself with the editorship of *The Hydra*, the Craiglockhart magazine, he writes to his mother in September that "Sassoon is too much the great man to be bothered with it, and I wish I had back again the time I have wasted on it".[34] That he considered his editorship a waste of time is probably because, stimulated by Sassoon's presence, he by then felt that he would have been better occupied writing poetry.

Sassoon's influence on the development of Owen as a war poet is considerable; not only did he comment on the poems Owen wrote,[35] but Owen also copied Sassoon's criticism of staff officers and the

Home Front, and used Sassoon's colloquial style in such poems as 'Conscious' and 'The Letter'. The latter poem is an interesting case in that it shows Owen using a Sassoon poem as a starting point, only then to diverge into a different direction. The voice in both Sassoon's 'In the Pink' and Owen's 'The Letter' is supposed to be that of a private soldier writing a letter home. But whereas Owen uses a dramatic setting, interspersing the soldier's letter with his asides to his mate in the trenches (thus making the poem into a dramatic monologue) and ending the poem with the soldier's dying words after he has been hit by a shell, Sassoon in his poem steps in as the omniscient author driving his message home by directly addressing the reader:

> (Eh? What the 'ell! Stand to? Stand to!
> Jim, give's a hand with pack on, lad.
> Guh! Christ! I'm hit. Take 'old. Aye, bad.
> No, damn your iodine. Jim? 'Ere!
> Write my old girl, Jim, there's a dear.)
> ('The Letter', ll. 18-22)

> And then he thought: to-morrow night we trudge
> Up to the trenches, and my boots are rotten.
> Five miles of stodgy clay and freezing sludge,
> And everything but wretchedness forgotten.
> To-night he's in the pink; but soon he'll die.
> And still the war goed on – *he* don't know why.
> ('In the Pink', ll. 13-8)

The setting and subject of several other Owen poems seem to have been derived from Sassoon: a further example is the meeting with a dead German and the "profound dull tunnel" through which the speaker escapes out of battle in Owen's 'Strange Meeting', which seem to have been suggested by Sassoon's 'Enemies' and 'The Rear-Guard':

> He stood alone in some queer sunless place
> Where Armageddon ends. Perhaps he longed
> For days he might have lived; but his young face
> Gazed forth untroubled: and suddenly there thronged
> Round him the hulking Germans that I shot
> When for his death my brooding rage was hot.
> ('The Enemies', ll. 1-6)

Groping along the tunnel, step by step,
He winked his prying torch with patching glare
From side to side, and sniffed the unwholesome air.
('The Rear-Guard', ll. 1-3)

Whether Owen also influenced Sassoon is less easy to determine. Sassoon himself writes that by July 1918 he was distancing himself somewhat from the war, and that in doing so he was following Owen's example:

I was developing a more controlled and objective attitude towards the War. To remind people of its realities was still my main purpose, but I now preferred to depict it impersonally, and to be as much "above the battle" as I could. Unconsciously, I was getting nearer to Wilfred Owen's method of approach. (*SJ*, 71)

As he suggests, it does not seem likely that this was in conscious imitation of Owen. Inasmuch as Sassoon *does* distance himself from the war, this was mainly brought about by the fact that in publishing his Statement, his personal stand against the war had come to a head. Also it should be borne in mind that during this period Sassoon had distanced himself from the war in a purely literal way as well: he was in England from April 1917 until January 1918, and was invalided home in July 1918, never to return to the front. For it is noticeable that when he is back among his men (as he was from February to July 1918), the angry voice also returns: in this respect poems such as 'Suicide in the Trenches' (February 1918) and 'I Stood with the Dead' (June 1918) do not really differ from his pre-Craiglockhart poems.

VIII

On 4 May 1918 the Battalion is on board a liner, being shipped from Palestine to France. On deck Sassoon quietly watches the men:

I like to see them leaning against each other with their arms round one another – it is pathetic and beautiful and human (but that is only a sexual emotion in me – to like them in those attitudes). Anyhow they are simple and childlike. (*DI*, 242)[36]

It has been suggested that Sassoon's compassion for his men "sprang from his vision of their individual beauty",[37] and that as such it was a sublimated expression of his homosexuality. And indeed, such poems as 'The Dug-Out' could suggest that Sassoon's concern for his men was at least partly due to the fact that he felt physically attracted to them:

> Why do you lie with your legs ungainly huddled,
> And one arm bent across your sullen, cold,
> Exhausted face? It hurts my heart to watch you,
> Deep shadow'd from the candle's guttering gold;
> And you wonder why I shake you by the shoulder.

In his diaries there are sparse references to these homo-erotic feelings, however, and Martin Taylor certainly exaggerates when he writes that "throughout the *Diaries* Sassoon enthuses about the young men who catch his eye".[38]

That Sassoon checked his latent homosexual feelings and sublimated them in the help and care for his men, is a reaction which was not uncommon:

> Of the active, unsublimated kind [of homosexuality] there was very little at the front. What we find, rather, especially in the attitude of young officers to their men, is something more like the 'idealistic,' passionate but non-physical 'crushes' which most of the officers had experienced at public school.[39]

But these passionate feelings were not felt by homosexual officers only. As Herbert Read's 'My Company' already showed, heterosexual officers could grow just as close to their men. Robert Nichols' 'Fulfilment' (from his 1917 volume *Ardours and Endurances*) is in this respect another typical example:

> Was there love once? I have forgotten her.
> Was there grief once? grief yet is mine.
> O loved, living, dying, heroic soldier,
> All, all, my joy, my grief, my love, are thine!

It would go too far, therefore, to suggest that the emotional impulse behind Sassoon's work is solely to be found in his homosexuality.[40] Though it is certainly likely to have played a part, the main inspirational source for Sassoon's war poetry is not to be found in the beauty of some of the young soldiers, but in his sense of responsibility for the men directly under his command.

As was the case in the *Lyrical Poems* section of *The Old Huntsman*, Sassoon's homosexuality is never openly expressed in the war poems: although in his diary he did admit to being in love with his fellow lieutenant David Thomas, he keeps quiet about it in the poems he wrote about him, 'The Subaltern', and the elegiac 'The Last Meeting'. The latter poem is Sassoon's earliest elegy, written in May 1916, and opens with a long description of a walk down the main street of the village where they were billeted when Thomas was killed. The poet visits the house where they stayed only to find no trace of his dead friend:

> Quite empty was that house; it could not hold
> His human ghost, remembered in the love
> That strove in vain to be companioned still.

He then heads for the woods, but though he senses the nearness of Thomas' ghost, the links have forever been severed:

> I know that he is lost among the stars,
> And may return no more but in their light.
> Though his hushed voice may call me in the stir
> Of whispering trees, I shall not understand.

In making his dead friend part of the mystical world of nature, a god, a ghost or a faun, Sassoon harks back to the favourite theme of his early poetry. This changes as the war progresses: the shift towards realism is also a feature of his later elegies. On 14 August 1917 Gordon Harbord, Sassoon's best hunting friend (the Stephen Colwood of *Memoirs of a Fox-Hunting Man*), was killed in France. Sassoon remembers him in 'Together', a poem written in Limerick in January 1918, where he enjoyed a few days hunting before returning to the front. It is a simple poem in a subdued mood, touchingly describing the emotions of the poet, who, riding home after a day's hunting, cannot believe that his friend is no longer with him:

> I shall forget him in the morning light;
> And while we gallop on he will not speak:
> But at the stable-door he'll say good-night.

What these elegies for close friends also show is that Sassoon's personal response to the war is completely different from the public protests on behalf of his men. He was lucky to survive the suicide missions in no man's land in March 1916, but once this personal anger had been vented in this initial, overstrung response, the brief career of Sassoon as Happy Warrior ended. The entry in his diary for 4 June 1918, when he was back at the front in France, sums up the difference:

> I was feeling jumpy and nerve-ridden and exasperated all day. It would be a relief to shed tears now [...] It is the result of working so hard and being worried with trivial details from morning till night. After all, I am nothing but what the Brigadier calls 'a potential killer of Germans (Huns)'. O God, why must I do it? *I'm not.* I am only here *to look after* some men.

IX

Sassoon's second volume of war poetry, *Counter-Attack and Other Poems*, was published by Heinemann on 27 June 1918, thirteen months after the publication of *The Old Huntsman*. In May 1917 Sassoon had been a platoon-commander with the Second Battalion R.W.F., recovering in a London hospital from a shoulder wound he had received at the Somme front. In June 1918 he was back in France, serving as a temporary Captain and in command of A Company of the 25th Battalion R.W.F. Nothing much seemed to have changed, but in the intervening months Sassoon had made his personal stand against the war, only then to decide – under the influence of Dr Rivers' treatment at Craiglockhart – that there was no point in continuing his protest and that the best thing for him to do was to return to the front.

Counter-Attack is dedicated to Robert Ross and contains thirty-eight poems, the earliest dating back to the time Sassoon spent in hospital in April 1917, while the latest poems were written in Limerick in February 1918, where he had been posted after reporting back for duty and was awaiting orders to return to the front. The surprising thing is that these momentous events are not reflected in the poems. In one of the most recently written poems, 'Suicide in the Trenches' (probably written in Ireland in February 1918), the outburst in the last stanza shows that the anger he felt towards the home front continued unabated:

> You smug-faced crowds with kindling eye
> Who cheer when soldier lads march by,
> Sneak home and pray you'll never know
> The hell where youth and laughter go.

But this anger does not seem to fit in with the fact that Sassoon, only a few months earlier while on leave in London, had allowed himself to be lionized as the 'famous war-poet' by some of the society-hostesses who were busily collecting money, socks and volunteers for the war effort. On 15 November 1917 Cynthia Asquith, daughter-in-law of H.H. Asquith, attended one of Mrs Sybil Colefax's many dinner parties:

> Just after we came up from dinner, two young men came – one very shy, the other to all appearances very much at his ease. The former was Siegfried Sassoon [the latter Robert Nichols]. He was in khaki: at first I only noticed his sticking-out ears and obvious embarrassment, but a closer scrutiny revealed great charm and a certain sweetness and grave strength in his countenance. I felt much drawn towards him, but had no conversation with him. Nichols, on the other hand, was twice introduced to me by the zealous hostess and we spent the remainder of the evening side by side. He was a thin alert face and is quick and agreeable to talk to – he expressed great admiration for Siegfried, both as poet and soldier. They both had shell-shock. For Siegfried, he claimed astonishing valour. They each read some of their own poems. Nichols raptly and passionately, as though absolutely carried away on the wings of

his own poetry and quite oblivious to his whereabouts, and Siegfried in a terse, laconic style – each manner was suitable to the particular matter.[41]

Sassoon never seemed to be bothered by the fact that five months after his passionate war protest he found himself reading his poems to a gathering of upper-middle-class ladies and gentlemen against whom some of his bitterest war satires had been directed in the first place. A young subaltern like Charles Carrington, who never identified with the plight of the private soldier to the extent that Sassoon did, admits in his memoirs that he got so fed up with London's middle-class society that he dressed up in a private soldier's uniform and went down to the East End, where he sought the company of the kind of men who reminded him of the camaraderie of his platoon.[42]

The fact is that Sassoon felt close to his men only as a soldier and as an officer responsible for his troops; as a poet or civilian he regarded middle-class society as his natural habitat. Whenever he was on leave in Britain, he was quite content in the company of his social equals without ever showing the least inclination to share the life of the common man.

X

By 1918 Sassoon's fame as a war poet had spread so far that his works were also published in America (American audiences had become more interested since the United States had joined the war in April 1917). The American sales of *Counter-Attack* were further boosted by an Introduction that Robert Nichols contributed to the first edition published by Dutton in December 1918.

As Sassoon recalls in *Siegfried's Journey*, Nichols had only met him a few times before he went with the British Mission (Ministry of Information) to America in 1918, lecturing on the war poets (*SJ*, 170). But what Nichols lacked in facts he made up in fiction, going over the top in a grand style. In the opening part of his Introduction, 'Sassoon the Man', he describes Sassoon as a tall man, with heavy jaw and aquiline nose, which together with "the fulness, depth and heat of his dark eyes gave him the air of a sullen falcon". He rounds off this section with some biographical information, in which he manages to get everything wrong: "He is twenty-eight years old; was educated at Marlborough and Christchurch, Oxford; was a master of fox-hounds and is a captain in the Royal Welsh Fusiliers". In December 1918 Sassoon was thirty-two years old, he was educated at Clare College, Cambridge, was never a master of fox-hounds and was then a temporary captain in the Royal Welch Fusiliers.

But Sassoon, usually a stickler for the truth as a poet and always inclined to belittle his own achievements as a soldier, never objected to this over-generous and mythical representation. In *Siegfried's Journey* he calls Nichols "an admirable impresario", adding that he was duly grateful for his performance and its results (*SJ*, 171). In the 1920s Nichols went to Hollywood.

Though Sassoon was one of the most successful soldier-poets, the overall impact of his poetry should not be exaggerated. A year after publication, the total number of copies printed for *The Old Huntsman* and *Counter-Attack* was 1,850 and 5,000 respectively. These totals are very modest in comparison with the sales figures of the home-front poet John Oxenham (1859-1941). In November 1915 he published his *All's Well!: Some Helpful Verse for These Dark Days of War*. In his foreword he explained why he chose this title, "out of eighty-six alternatives":

> Those who have so nobly responded to the Call, and those who, with quiet faces and breaking hearts, have so bravely bidden them 'God Speed!' – with these, All is truly Well, for they have equally given their best to what, in this case, we most of us devoutly believe to be the service of God and humanity.[43]

Oxenham's poems are so many variations on this theme: the war is fought for God, King and country, and all who perish – whether a gentleman or "a little chap" – are certain of a place in heaven. If Sassoon's satires are considered as an attack on this mighty home-front fortress, the conclusion must be that he failed: by 1918 more than 70,000 copies of *All's Well!* alone had been printed.[44]

XI

Most commentators agree that "Sassoon's best poetry is to be found in [his] powerful little satires. It lives by its passionate sincerity and honesty, but it is purely destructive".[45] When writing about the ranges of compassion achieved in war poetry, Jon Silkin claims that "the wonder is that Sassoon achieves neither compassion nor pity. Hardly, at any rate".[46] Modern critics were not the first to point out an apparent lack of pity in Sassoon's war poetry.

On 13 July 1918[47] John Middleton Murry published an anonymous review in the *Nation* of Sassoon's *Counter-Attack* (the same issue of the *Nation* printed Sassoon's 'I Stood With The Dead'). Murry begins by saying that

Mr. Sassoon's verses – they are not poetry – [...] touch not our imagination, but our sense. Reading them, we feel, not as we do with true art, which is the evidence of a man's triumph over his experience, that something has after all been saved from disaster, but that everything is irremediably and intolerably wrong.[48]

He goes on to claim that Sassoon's crude realism numbs rather than terrifies and that by simply piling up the horrors the particularity of each separate horror is lost:

There is a value in this direct transcription of plain, unvarnished fact; but there is another truth more valuable still. One may convey chaos of immediate sensation by a chaotic expression, as does Mr. Sassoon. But the unforgettable horror of an inhuman experience can only be rightly rendered by rendering also its relation to the harmony and calm of the soul which it shatters [...] It is on this that the wise saying that poetry is emotion recollected in tranquillity is so firmly based, for the quality of an experience can only be given by reference to the ideal condition of the human consciousness which it disturbs with pleasure or with pain.[49]

Much as Sassoon resented Murry's criticism, the fact remains that in his later prose success, *Memoirs of a Fox-Hunting Man*, he seems to have taken Murry's advice to heart: these 'memoirs' are based on the sharp contrast between the main character's pre-war existence and his war experiences.

However, in not allowing for the extraordinary conditions under which the war poems were written, and by simply dismissing them as not 'real' poetry, Murry's standards seem rather rigid; war poetry is a unique genre which cannot be judged by the traditional literary standards. No one would claim that these war poems are great poetry, but then they were not written to be judged purely aesthetically: Sassoon no longer believed in the poet as the creator of beauty; his overruling intention was to shock the home front into recognition (his use of the word "syphilitic" in 'They' is perhaps the best illustration of this *volte-face*), and this is the key-motive Murry completely disregards.

Also, in insisting on information about the poet's state of mind before the horrors occurred, Murry again misses the point: it was Sassoon's intention to portray the reality of war in a factual, objective way, not as the subjective impressions of an individual. Sassoon and Murry were on either side of the wide gap separating soldier-poets and home-front critics, and Sassoon was writing according to the soldiers' standards.[50]

For in acting as the self-appointed spokesman of the troops, Sassoon gave voice to many of the soldiers' grudges, one of their main complaints being that the home front knew nothing about the realities of the war. The need for such a spokesman is expressed in Gilbert Frankau's 1917 war poem 'The Other Side'. The poem is written in the form of a long letter in which a 'Major Average' acknowledges "a presentation copy of a book of war-verse, written by a former subaltern of his battery – now in England". The Major thinks little of the poems ("The same old Boy's-Own-Paper balderdash!"), which he thinks were simply written to please "the idiots at home". He then explains what he would like to do:

> Lord, if I'd half *your* brains, I'd write a book:
> None of your sentimental platitudes,
> But something real, vital; that should strip
> The glamour from this outrage we call war,

> Shewing it naked, hideous, stupid, vile –
> One vast abomination. So that they
> Who, coming after, till the ransomed fields
> Where our lean corpses rotted in the ooze,
> Reading my written words, should understand
> This stark stupendous horror, visualize
> The unutterable foulness of it all ....[51]

Frankau's major is, in fact, calling for the highly emotional, but at the same time realistic war poetry that Sassoon wrote, but which Murry condemned on purely literary grounds.

And yet, if these were Murry's standards, he was not always equally consistent in their application. When discussing Wilfred Owen's poems (the 1920 edition, with an introduction by Sassoon), he writes that: "The source of enduring poetry lies in an intense and overwhelming emotion. The emotion must be overwhelming, and suffered as it were to the last limit of the soul's capacity."[52]

This time there is no mention of the poet's initial calm and harmony, and as far as an overwhelming emotion is concerned: the driving force behind Sassoon's satires *is* an overwhelming emotion (it is this inconsistency in Murry's critical standards that makes one wonder if the fact that Sassoon had apparently so easily distanced himself from the stance he had taken in the 'Soldier's Declaration' that Murry had helped him compose, is not at least partly the reason for Murry's vigorous attack). In the same review Murry says that Owen revealed the secret of poetry when he wrote in the Preface that "the poetry is in the pity".

Which takes us back to the initial question: is it true that there is no pity in Sassoon's war poetry? This seems certainly to be the case with the satires Sassoon wrote in his role as the angry prophet. It is also true to say that there is little explicit pity in the poems he wrote from his concern for the soldiers. But is it not just the tone of voice of the poet, unmoved, and cold and pitiless as the war itself, that evokes pity in the reader? Is it to be expected that the closing lines of 'The General': "'He's a cheery old card,' grunted Harry to Jack / As they slogged up to Arras with rifle and pack / But he did for them both by his plan of attack", will be read as unemotionally as they are written? The fact is that although there may be little explicit pity in Sassoon's poetry, he does achieve pity, mainly by means of his favourite poetic device, juxtaposition. Although Jon Silkin recognizes juxtaposition as one of Sassoon's major strengths,[53] but he does not seem to allow for the extent Sassoon makes use of it.

In some of his most effective war poems, the two elements of a juxtaposition combine to produce a hidden meaning that suddenly dawns on the reader when he reflects on the poem. This is the case in 'Counter-Attack', which sets out as a descriptive poem, similar to 'A Working Party': an enemy trench has been successfully taken and "a yawning soldier" waits for the expected counter-attack, which is announced by a heavy artillery bombardment: "He crouched and flinched, dizzy with galloping fear / Sick for escape" (ll. 22-3). When the counter-attack begins the soldier is hit by a shell:

> Down, and down, and down, he sank and drowned,
> Bleeding to death. The counter-attack had failed.

Silkin is not impressed by these closing lines. In his opinion Sassoon uses "drowned" in l.38 in a crude attempt "to convey sensations of dying [...] through the analogy of drowning",[54] thereby forgetting that the drowning may be more literal than he thinks: in the first part of the poem Sassoon describes the dead in the trench as lying "face down-ward, in the sucking mud" (l.9) and the stanza ends with "And then the rain began, – the jolly old rain" (l.13). One is reminded of 'A Working Party', where the presence of the sniper who eventually kills the soldier is first suggested by the casual reference to "rifle-shots" in the first half of the poem.

What does work, according to Silkin, is that "His [the soldier's] death is juxtaposed with the failure of the counter-attack",[55] but this could be taken one step further. Sassoon knew that the contemporary reader when reading the last line would be reminded of newspaper reports about enemy attacks that had been successfully repulsed. The poem then suddenly becomes a forceful reminder of the individual tragedies that may lie behind such dry statements as "The counter-attack had failed".

Sassoon uses the same device to even more shocking effect in 'Died of Wounds'. The poem describes a badly wounded soldier whose screams keep the other soldiers in a hospital ward awake. The poet adopts a callous attitude; his wry comment on the soldier's screams, groans and sighs is that "he did the business well" (l. 4).

Next morning the soldier is dead, "And a Slight Wound lay smiling on the bed" (l.12). But in this simple poem Sassoon has provided a harrowing meaning to the empty phrase 'Died of Wounds', so familiar to his contemporaries from letters, newspapers reports and casualty lists.[56] Intent on driving home his message, Sassoon used this same device in 'The Hero', written a month after 'Died of Wounds'. In this poem a mother is told that her son had died a gallant death whereas in actual fact he had been a coward.

This poem was greatly resented by Bernard Freyberg, a hero of Gallipoli, who "thought the poem [...] caddish, as it might destroy every mother's faith in the report of her son's death".[57] Though Sassoon would undoubtedly have regretted each individual case in which this might happen, it was for him all part of his one-man attempt to disabuse the home front, and make them face up to the realities of war.

It should never be forgotten that Sassoon wrote his poems with this particular purpose in mind. The Poet/Prophet wanted the people at home to know what the war was really like, and in order to achieve this goal the poet was subordinate to the prophet. Above all, he wanted people to hear what he had to say, and, completely out of character, he made it his business to get a poem into a newspaper as soon as possible: "usually a finished poem which the poet thought good enough was almost immediately sent to a periodical and published there within a few days".[58] Characteristically, Sassoon did not send his poems to any of the major periodicals, instead preferring the pacifist *Cambridge Magazine*, "a penny paper for the internationally minded," then edited by C.K. Ogden.[59]

To say, then, that Sassoon achieves hardly any compassion or pity is simply not true. In the poems discussed so far, Sassoon in his role as prophet tries to shock the reader into pity. Pity may not be explicitly present, but the poem does intend to evoke pity in the reader. Yet there are also poems in which the compassion *is* explicit, but then the voice is not that of Sassoon the Prophet, but the personal voice of the poet himself. If only to show how far-reaching his compassion could be, there is the remarkable poem 'A Night Attack', not published until 1970, but written in July 1916. Back in a rest camp, the poet overhears some spiteful soldiers' conversation about the enemy: "The bloody Bosche has got the knock" (l.25), which puts him in mind of a body he has seen in "a squalid, miserable ditch",

He was a Prussian with a decent face,
Young fresh, and pleasant, so I dare to say.
No doubt he loathed the war and longed for peace,
And cursed our souls because we'd killed his friends

Michael Thorpe selects 'The Dug-Out' as one of Sassoon's most successful compassionate poems,[60] but while I would not want to argue about the compassion expressed in the poem, it is regrettable that the last three lines, in which the poet explains that "when you sleep you remind me of the dead", make the poem too explicit. Without these lines, the reader would have shared the soldier's "wonder", and with his understanding would come the realization that the dug-out is like a grave.

Murry's review in the *Nation* sparked off a short but sharp correspondence when the Morrells, Sassoon's Garsington friends, jumped to his defence. The following week the *Nation* published a letter to the editor written by Philip Morrell, in which he objected to Murry's "detraction of a gallant and distinguished author", while Ottoline wrote to Murry to say that Sassoon was in hospital with a head wound and that this negative review might well cause his death. Katherine Mansfield sided with Murry, calling Philip Morrell's letter an "abusive attack", whereas Virginia Woolf wrote to Clive Bell that she felt that the tone of Murry's article was "a little superior" and that she felt that Sassoon's poems were not without "some merit". In the end Sassoon acted as peace-maker, by sending a letter to Ottoline on 27 July in which he wrote that he wished he could do something "to make Murry happier". This gesture of forgiveness seems to have been smart politics on the part of Sassoon; as Virginia Woolf noted, Murry's attack led many other papers to publish favourable reviews of Sassoon's work. A reference in Sassoon's 1923 diary suggests that his conciliatory gesture had not been quite genuine and that four and a half years later he had neither forgotten nor forgiven.[61]

It is minor episodes like these that may create the impression that in 1918 everybody was talking and writing about Sassoon's war poetry. But the war poets were never widely discussed; the average man or woman in the street remained oblivious of these polemics and if they read any war books at all, it was far more likely to be Oxenham's *All's Well*, *The Vision Splendid* or *Hearts Courageous*,

Edith Anne Stewart's *Pilgrimage & Battle* or E.B. Osborne's *The New Elizabethans* rather than the war poetry of Sassoon, Nichols or Graves.

XII

Looking back on Sassoon's war poetry it could be said that after the initial stage of patriotic fervour the bulk of the poems were written by Sassoon the Prophet. His most famous war poems may be powerful satires, but these are not necessarily his best poems.

The largely descriptive poems such as 'A Working Party', 'A Night Attack', 'The Rear-Guard', 'Break of Day', 'Counter Attack' and 'Battalion-Relief', seem to me to be his most successful, though it could be argued that they largely succeed for historical-pictorial rather than literary reasons. It is in these poems that Sassoon used his 'picture-painting' qualities to full effect, giving the reader some idea of what trench-warfare was like. Emotionally-charged words are largely absent, and this allows the reader to let the poem sink in and work on his imagination. The poem thus elicits the response it was after without explicitly stating it, with the result that it makes a deeper and more lasting impression. Sassoon's most successful war-satires, such as 'Does It Matter' and 'Died of Wounds', operate in a similar way.

The poems in which the soldier-poet describes his own feelings usually clearly demonstrate his poetic shortcomings: it is not too difficult to sense the intensity of feeling behind the words, but the words themselves do not match up to this. What these poems reveal is that, though Sassoon's response to the war is always heartfelt and honest, he lacked the poetic resources to express the tremendous impact it had on him in equally powerful poetry.

In 'Banishment', written at Craiglockhart in 1917, shortly before he decided to go back to the front, Sassoon took stock of his situation:

> I am banished from the patient men who fight.
> They smote my heart with pity, built my pride
> Shoulder to aching shoulder, side by side
> They trudged away from life's broad wealds of light.
> Their wrongs were mine;and even in my sight

their first anthology, whereas a Modernist movement consisting of a number of rapidly changing coteries and factions published a wide variety of manifestos and programmes announcing a new poetic in numerous magazines.[5] This sudden outburst of activity was part of a process of readjustment, in which the world of letters tried to determine its new position.

In the course of the previous century a new readership had emerged; the process of industrialization had changed the fabric of society, and the rise of the middle classes meant that there was a new demand for a more popular art. Whether these needs could be met without compromising artistic integrity was one of the key-issues that separated the new movements:

> The democratization of culture through mass-education – even through the numerical growth of culture-hungry middle and lower-middle classes – was itself sufficient to make elites look for more exclusive cultural status-symbols. But the crux of the crisis of the arts lay in the growing divergence between what was contemporary and what was 'modern'.[6]

Their different ideas on this matter were reflected in the way both movements defended their points of view. From the start, the Modernists adopted a more intellectualist approach, attempting to devise a sound theoretical basis for their views. The Georgians, on the other hand, never got further than Marsh's rather vague 'Prefatory Note' to the first volume of *Georgian Poetry*, where he stated that the book was issued "in the belief that English poetry is now once again putting on a new strength and beauty".

All in all there existed a paradoxical situation in which the Modernist-coteries seemed disorganized, but were in fact all the time developing a new critical theory, whereas the Georgians, who gave the impression of a united movement, were in reality kept together by their shared enthusiasm for poetry and a vague belief that there was potentially still a wide readership for good poetry, rather than a unifying philosophy.

In this belief that good art could be appreciated by a large audience, as well as in other respects, the Georgians resembled the Pre-Raphaelites, as on a larger scale the whole conflict between

Georgians and Modernists mirrored the events that had taken place in the world of the visual arts in the nineteenth century.

III

In the fifth of his *Discourses on Art*, Sir Joshua Reynolds, the first President of the Royal Academy (1768-1792), drew attention to what he regarded as one of the main dangers of the popularity of the Academy's annual exhibitions:

> our Exhibitions, while they produce such admirable effects by nourishing emulation and calling out genius, have also a mischievous tendency, by seducing the Painter to an ambition of pleasing indiscriminately the mixed multitude of people who resort to them.[7]

Sir Joshua's warning words were soon forgotten. By the late 1840s, the newly-founded Pre-Raphaelite Brotherhood mounted an attack on the painting establishment represented by the members of the Royal Academy. The Academicians were accused of increasingly catering to the popular taste: Frederick Leighton's grand style neo-classicism, which gave shape to the Imperialists' belief that their civilization was a renaissance of ancient Greece and Rome, had been watered down by more populist painters such as Alma-Tadema, E.J. Poynter and Albert Moore, whose portrayals of the classic world breathed a distinct air of Victorian domesticity. These scenes found their contemporary equivalents in the all too often sentimental Victorian story-paintings by such Academicians as Edwin Landseer, W.P. Frith and Marcus Stone,[8] who were quite unrepentant about their popular successes. "If people only knew as much about painting as I do," Sir Edwin Landseer is quoted as saying, "they would never buy my pictures". The Pre-Raphaelites condemned populist practices and, championed by Ruskin, they tried to walk an artistic tightrope, believing that they could paint pictures according to their own artistic standards and still appeal to the general public. Theresa Thornycroft was taught these same values when she studied with Ford Madox Brown in the 1870s, and in her turn she passed them on to her son Siegfried. In *The Old*

Century Sassoon recalls how aware he was in 1907 of the high standards of Thornycroft craftsmanship:

> Could I carry on that tradition with my pen? I wondered, and should I ever write as good a poem as my mother's picture of *The Hours* [.....] For in that noble design I had always felt something of the poetry which I could never put into words; and in it I could recognize my kinship with the strength and simplicity of my mother's imaginations. (*OC*, 298)

Sassoon long continued to regard 'strength and simplicity' as the essential qualities of good art: it should be powerful and direct, without alienating the public at large.

In contrast to the Pre-Raphaelites, the Aesthetes and early Impressionists represented a more elitist viewpoint. When they appeared on the scene in the 1860s they proclaimed the artist's complete independence: the artist created beauty by selecting, not by simply copying Nature (as Whistler put it in his 'Ten O'Clock' lecture, Nature was the keyboard, the artist the musician: "To say to the painter, that Nature is to be taken as she is, is to say to the player, that he may sit on the piano"). The preferences of the populace were, of course, to be ignored altogether.

The Pre-Raphaelite cause failed because they were only united in their opposition to the Academicians. Their attempt to strike a balance between popular taste and artistic standards failed because there were no clearly stated standards to adhere to. The members of the Brotherhood gradually drifted off in different directions: Burne-Jones gave the industrialized world the slip and in his semi-mediaeval dreamworld, William Morris became a socialist pioneer, at the same time setting up a handicraft-workshop that ironically enough ignored the process of mechanization which had given birth to the working classes in the first place. But the Pre-Raphaelite failure found its most poignant illustration in the career of its one-time leader, J.E. Millais.

John Everett Millais (1829-1896) started as the brilliant young painter of such original canvases as 'Isabella' (1849), 'Ophelia' (1852) and 'Autumn Leaves' (1856) and a fierce opponent of the Academicians, but ended his career as President of that same Royal Academy, scoring huge popular successes with his 'Cherry Ripe' (1879), the colour reproduction of which was a bestseller, and

'Bubbles' (1886), the first painting to be used in an advertisement.[9] When he died, Arthur Symons (1865-1945), who three years later published his influential *The Symbolist Movement in Literature*, looked back on his career from the Aesthete's point of view. Headed 'The Lesson of Millais', Symons summed up what he believed to be the artist's position:

> The appeal of every great artist has been to the few; fame, when it has come, has come by a sort of divine accident, in which the mob has done no more than add the plaudits of its irrelevant clamour to the select approval of the judges.[10]

In view of this Pre-Raphaelite failure the contempt of the Decadent poets for the public taste and those artists who consciously set out to make what Symons called "the democratic appeal" was perhaps understandable, but in completely ignoring the question of a readership, thus ducking the poetry-populace issue altogether, they severed the link between artists and audience. Remembering Edward Dowson and Lionel Johnson, two fellow-members of the Rhymers' Club, Yeats regards their early deaths as a sad but inevitable consequence of this uncompromising attitude:

> You had to face your ends when young –
> 'Twas wine or women, or some curse –
> But never made a poorer song
> That you might have a heavier purse,
> Not gave loud service to a cause
> That you might have a troop of friends.[11]

But the Decadents were not the only ones to see the dangers of a popular literature. John Churton Collins (1848-1908) is now no more than a footnote in literary history,[12] but as a tireless campaigner for the teaching of modern literature and criticism at the universities, he both recognized the problem and suggested a possible solution. In 'The Present Functions of Criticism', the opening essay of his 1901 volume *Ephemera Critica*, he first emphasized the importance of the men of letters as a literary elite in words that echo Sir Joshua Reynolds' address to the Royal Academy:

As long as men of letters continue to form an intellectual aristocracy, and, stimulated by mutual rivalry, strain every nerve to excel, and as long as they have no temptation to pander to the crowd, so long will Literature maintain its dignity, and so long will the standard attained in Literature be a high one.[13]

He then goes on to say that the rise of a popular literature has become a major threat: commercial interests have become all important, and both editors and publishers have to cater, willy-nilly, for the popular taste. This has resulted in a critical climate that is one of a general "pleasantness":

Severity, we are told, is quite out of fashion [....] It is vain to plead that tolerance and charity must discriminate; that, like other virtues, they may be abused, and that in their abuse they may become immoral.[14]

What he is pleading for is, in Matthew Arnold's phrase, a disinterested criticism (disinterested both in the sense of unbiased as well as free from commercial pressures), and he was convinced that the universities were ideally suited for the all-important task of educating a new literary elite.

Ten years later Collins' gloomy predictions about the decline in literary standards had come true. Towards the end of the Edwardian era, English poetry was in a sorry state:

The popular poets [...] were not those who offered the complex qualities usually associated with good poetry, but those whose minds ran at the level of public expectation. Poetry was acceptable when it effectively versified Imperialist sentiments, the public school spirit, or patriotic fervour: otherwise it was unlikely to be widely read. The result was a low-charged literary atmosphere in which second-rate men grotesquely assumed the mannerisms considered appropriate to the position of public bard.[15]

This was the status quo that the Modernists and Georgians sought to alter. But whereas the Modernists followed the Decadent example in not concerning themselves with a readership for poetry, the Georgians were filled with a Pre-Raphaelite idealism, expressing a firm determination to re-educate the populace. In January 1912 Harold Monro, poet and publisher, launched his 'Poetry Review', contributing a preface in which he stated the periodical's creed:

> Time is ripe for the forging of a weapon of criticism, and for an emphatic enunciation of literary standards. Poetry should be, once more, seriously and reverently discussed in its relation to life, and the same tests and criteria be applied to it as to the other arts. This periodical will aim not so much at producing poetry as at stimulating a desire for it. We shall strive to create an atmosphere. We shall attempt to co-ordinate the bases from which poetry at last emerges.[16]

Monro thus set out to change the literary climate, convinced as he was that the public taste could be improved.

The Georgians and Modernists had a common enemy in the Traditionalists, whom both considered to be a Victorian remnant. The Georgians attacked the Traditionalists for their rhetorical and stilted style, instead advocating realism and a 'truth to life' approach that was reminiscent of the Pre-Raphaelite ideals. They insisted that contemporary speech become part of the poetic language and claimed that there was no such thing as a 'poetic subject': "all subjects can be poetical; but the poetical thing about them will always be, not *what* they are, but the way they come to us."[17] The Modernist poet, on the other hand, was interested in the form rather than the content of poetry:

> [He] tended to concentrate more on purifying poetic technique than upon truth to life or upon expanding the subject matter of modern verse. He was more or less single-mindedly devoted to good craftsmanship, and he found the poets of the centre [the Georgians] damnworthy not, usually, because they were realists, but because of what he considered their sloppy craftsmanship.[18]

The elder generation of literary critics did not distinguish between Georgians and Modernists, instead they described both in terms of a new generation of younger poets who threatened to destroy the civilized art of poetry.

In October 1916 the influential man of letters Arthur Waugh (1866-1943) reviewed *Georgian Poetry I* and *II* and Ezra Pound's *The Catholic Anthology, 1914-1915* in the *Quarterly Review* under the heading 'The New Poetry'. He regarded the new developments as wholly detrimental to the state of English poetry:

> It may be arguable that the poet should shovel the language of the mining-camp into his lyrics, but it is more than doubtful whether poetry will emerge [....] Poetry must possess beauty; beauty is the essence of its being; and it has never been the general experience that the language of the common crowd possesses either beauty or authority. When poetry proposes to confine itself to the commercial counters of speech, the first thing we should expect would be a failure in dignity and charm. When it sets itself to break loose from the traditions of structure and harmony, the next inevitable consequence would be the wastage of form and melody.[19]

In the end, the Traditionalists were no match for the combined Modernist / Georgian onslaught. They had continued their brand of poetry because it was popular but also because their poetic standards were never challenged. Soon after the emergence of the Georgians, several Traditionalists (in particular Henry Newbolt and Maurice Hewlett) started following their example – which in the long run had a negative effect on the Georgian cause in that it further tainted their innovative image. A few die-hards persevered with their rhetorical style, not realizing that amidst all the new poetry that was being written it began to sound hopelessly outdated: when Ezra Pound proclaimed the Imagiste poetic, following T.E. Hulme's dictum of a "hard and dry poetry" in recommending a sparse use of the adjective, William Watson spoke up nobly in its defence:

> Look not too coldly or too proudly down
> On this poor bondslave to a haughty Noun!
> Oft in his wallet hath he carried all
> His master's wealth. Oft hath this captive thrall,
> Marching before his lord with herald's blast,
> Won him salaams who else had noteless passed.[20]

'Bondslave', 'master', 'thrall', 'lord', 'salaam': forsooth the voice of a true Imperialist.

IV

It was the outbreak of the Great War that ended the age of active imperialism, thus effectively silencing the literary movement that was associated with it. That it marked the end of an era was not just something later historians concluded with the benefit of hindsight; it is a feeling that is already expressed in many contemporary writings. The death of the 27-year-old Rupert Brooke in April 1915 especially had a profound effect in intellectual circles. On hearing the news, Bertrand Russell wrote:

I am feeling the weight of the war much more since I came back here – one is made so terribly aware of the waste when one is here [in Cambridge]. And Rupert Brooke's death brought it home to me. It is deadly to be here now, with all the usual life stopped. There will be other generations – yet I keep fearing that some-thing of civilization will be lost for good, as something was lost when Greece perished in just this way.[21]

It was not until a year after the war that the nation began to realize the true magnitude of the war and its consequences:

The break with Victorian ethics, both moral and cultural, would have happened even if there had been no war. What the war did most was to expose the fearful hollow of 'authority'. It had put a premium on obedience. Obedience was the king's mystical due, the country's right, the generals' demand, the Church's everlasting exhortation, and Lord Northcliffe's constant clamour. It became a phobia. Deafened by so much journalistic patriotism, violated by slogans, and hypnotized by death and claptrap, a great population had resigned itself to the ecclesiastical political, and Press manipulators. When, after the war, these leaders continued to ask for blind obedience and didn't get it, there was at first consternation and then an intense fury. A new morality campaign was put into action. The forces of reaction swept to the colours.[22]

The Georgians were caught up in this reaction. The Traditionalist movement they had revolted against had disappeared and they were the natural heirs to the position of representatives of the native tradition. But this also meant a shift towards a more conservative position: from being the least progressive movement in the rebellion against the Edwardian Traditionalists, they now became their successors, and as such the new target of the Modernist opposition. This change did not take place overnight; for some years already the distinctions between the Georgians and the Traditionalists had been becoming somewhat blurred. And this was not only because the Traditionalists had moved in the direction of the Georgians; the movements had met half-way.

It was in effect an exact repetition of what had happened with the Pre-Raphaelites. A common enemy and a shared enthusiasm had for a time obscured the fact that the Georgians were an alliance rather than a movement with a clearly defined artistic creed, and it was inevitable that sooner or later the differences would surface. When Brooke published his patriotic *1914* sonnet cycle it was the culmination of a career that had taken him right across the political spectrum: from the young Fabian and neo-Pagan rebel of 1911 to the unofficial Poet Laureate of the Establishment in 1914,[23] thus becoming the John Everett Millais of the Georgians.

And he is not the only Georgian whose revolutionary convictions are to be doubted. John Drinkwater's status as an opponent of the Edwardian Traditionalists is equally questionable:

[I remember when] I first read Stephen Phillips's *Poems*. It was an experience never to be forgotten [....] I am sure [....] that 'Marpessa' is one of the most beautiful poems of the past forty years. Phillips was extravagantly praised by his contemporaries [...] but even such terms are less irresponsible than the contemptuous disregard of critics who hail the publication of a six-page pamphlet by some eminently constipated poet as an event of high literary importance. Alfred Noyes himself has in some measure been the victim of the same kind of caprice [...]

to-day it is not uncommon to find his name omitted altogether from discussions of modern poetry, which is absurd.[24]

In view of this it is hardly surprising that Arthur Waugh's kindest words in his 'The New Poetry' review were for Drinkwater; his "well-conceived and finely-written idyll" met with the critic's whole-hearted approval, and Waugh even suggested that Drinkwater might be able to bridge the gap between the old and the new.[25] In spite of his old-style poetry, Edward Marsh included Drinkwater in all five Georgian anthologies.

Defenders of the Georgian cause explain the Georgian decline by drawing a distinction between Georgians and Neo-Georgians, the latter being the poets who began to dominate the Georgian anthologies with the publication of the fourth volume, and later formed the nucleus of the anti-Modernists who published in the *London Mercury*: J. C. Squire (the editor), Edward Shanks, W. J. Turner and John Freeman. But as the examples of Brooke and Drinkwater show, this is at least partly a simplification: throughout his career John Drinkwater continued to write the kind of pastoral poetry that the Neo-Georgians were later criticized for.[26]

Also, it should not be forgotten that Edward Marsh remained firmly in control of the Georgian anthologies and that the decision to include the pleasantly pastoral poems in the two last volumes was solely his. Ultimately it was Marsh, the editor who had not shrunk back from including several controversial poems in *Georgian Poetry I* and *II* and some of Sassoon's fiercest war poems in *Georgian Poetry III*, who was responsible for the bland character of the later volumes. Partly this reflected the fact that most Georgian poets had run out of steam and were content to take up the position vacated by the Traditionalists, but it was also due to the fact that Marsh's desire to appeal to the general public gradually prevailed over his critical judgment.

Sassoon had not been the only one to complain about Marsh's choice of poems for *Georgian Poetry 1918-1919*. John Freeman (one of the Neo-Georgians) wrote to Marsh pointing out that the poems by him which Marsh had selected were in fact part of a sequence and that he would prefer these poems to be published as such. Marsh's answer is revealing:

I don't think you can want *only* to have the very small audience of people who have the insight, sympathy, and patience to study as a whole a series of poems which is not ostensibly or at all obviously a sequence and to do for themselves the elaborate work of piecing together. There must be a hundred who would appreciate and enjoy the poems as units, to one of the more strenuous kind of reader, and they are well worth appealing to. *Georgian Poetry* is meant for this general public.[27]

In his autobiography Marsh recalled "the most shocking remark" about Georgian poetry he had ever heard:

A young lion of the *Granta* [the Cambridge University undergraduate periodical] found difficulty in hitting on a "succinct formula in which to dismiss it"; but he had a shot. "Its main faults," he wrote, "are that it is facile, sentimental, socially and politically non-significant, *fit for people of all ages, and above all, popular.*" I gather from the phrase about social and political non-significance that the writer hailed from the Left; and I should have thought that the farther to the Left one was, the more one would wish the joy of poetry to be 'in widest commonalty spread.'[28]

By making poetry's popularity itself an issue, regardless of the fact whether a poem possessed any literary qualities that would make it good poetry, Marsh came dangerously close to reverting to the situation that had existed at the end of the Edwardian era and that had first led to the Georgian revolt. It meant the end of Harold Monro's ideal of re-educating the public; instead, Georgian poetry had succumbed to the demands of popular taste.

V

The regressive move in Georgian poetry after the Great War also underlined the extreme Englishness of the Georgians (yet another thing they have in common with the Pre-Raphaelites) as opposed to the far more European, if not to say global, outlook of the Modernists.

When Ezra Pound first settled in England in 1908, he had no sense of geographical and cultural borders separating the nations:

> An American like Pound came to *Europe*; and if he came to England, it was to one of the provinces of that larger cultural entity [...] what was precious about England was not what marked her off from the Continent but what bound her to the Mediterranean heartlands".[29]

T. S. Eliot showed a similar European outlook in his 1919 essay 'Tradition and the Individual Talent', which he began by saying that there was no real native tradition in English poetry, but only a European tradition which poets had to 'learn' (as he had done) in order to be able to further contribute to it. The essay was published shortly after the end of a European war; ten years earlier it could not have been written. By defining 'tradition' as a historical and aesthetic awareness that could be acquired through studying, Eliot was defining it in his own terms, terms that suited him as an outsider and enabled him to deny the existence of such a tradition in England. For there was a native tradition in that of the English pastoral, a native tradition that was constantly being adapted to the changing circumstances and closely linked with the sense of a national identity.

The post-war Georgian views on literature and nationality were the subject of a speech by John Drinkwater, read out posthumously at a meeting of the Royal Society of Literature of the United Kingdom in October 1937.[30] Drinkwater's speech is a defence of the isolationist position of the Georgians; his claim being that there is no need to read any literature but the national one:

> It is true that one country may have some familiarity with another's great creative writers through translations. And this is all to the good. Nevertheless, I do not believe that the international power of literature depends upon this kind of communication. I will go further, and rule out the knowledge that may come of foreign literatures by the simple process of learning foreign languages.

He then continues to attempt to prove his point with an argument that is baffling in its logic and extremely depressing in its display of ignorance about a historical perspective and the unique qualities of individual languages and cultures:

> I cannot read a word of Greek. I wish I could. My very scanty knowledge of the Greek classics is derived from a few translations, and yet because Shakespeare and Milton and Wordsworth have been a familiar part of my life for thirty years, I find myself when I stand upon the Acropolis responding with a quite clear-cut emotion to the essential significance of Aeschylus and Homer and Sophocles and Euripides. I know beyond question that in its fundamental aspects the life that I have drawn from my own poets is the life with which these Greeks illuminated the hearts and minds of the Athenian people.[31]

Drinkwater is in effect claiming that the only difference between nations and great writers is the language they speak and write in, and that there is therefore no harm whatsoever for writers to withdraw into their own native tradition.

Late-Victorian and Edwardian literature continued the English pastoral tradition in the work of George Meredith, the last of Hardy's Wessex novels, A.E. Housman's *A Shropshire Lad* (1896) and Edward Thomas's *The Heart of England* (1906). In the work of the Edwardian Imperialists it was the sense of a national identity that dominated. Fiercely patriotic, it celebrated the uniqueness of the British Empire and the English people in such works as Henry Newbolt's *The Island Race* (1898), William Watson's *For England* (1903), C.M. Doughty's *The Dawn in Britain* (1906) and Alfred Noyes' *Drake, an English Epic* (1906-08) and *The Enchanted Island* (1910). The Georgian revolt was directed against the Imperialists' patriotic jingoism, but at the same time Georgian poetry sought to continue the pastoral tradition: A.E. Housman was asked to contribute to *Georgian Poetry 1911-1912* and *Georgian Poetry 1918-1919* was dedicated to Thomas Hardy.

The 'end-of-an-era' feeling following the Great War had a profound effect on Georgian poetry. Unlike T.S. Eliot, who regarded the war as the final collapse of a European civilization – *vide The Waste Land* (1922) – the Georgians did not attempt to put it in a historical perspective, either on a European or a national level. Their reaction was one of withdrawal, an escape into a pastoral poetry tinted with nostalgia, and their attitude towards the outside world was characterized by a relapse into that inverted jingoism, the 'Little-England' mentality. Throughout the rest of their careers, England and islands became popular subjects for Georgian writers, as the number of titles that mention either England or islands testify: Vita Sackville-West's *The Land* (1926) and *The Dark Island* (1934), John Drinkwater's *From an Unknown Isle* (1924) and his anthology *A Pageant of England's Life Presented by her Poets: with a running commentary* (1934), Edward Shanks's *The Island of Youth* (1921) and *My England* (1938), A.G. McDonnell's *England Their England* (1934), W.W. Gibson's *Islands* (1932), Francis Brett Young's *The Island* (1944), Edmund Blunden's *English Poems* (1925), *The Face of England* (1932), *English Villages* (1941) and *Cricket Country* (1945) and Walter de la Mare's *Desert Islands* (1930) and *O Lovely England and Other Poems* (1953). Siegfried Sassoon's nostalgic *Memoirs of a Fox-Hunting Man* (1928) and *The Old Century and Seven More Years* (1938) can be regarded as his own contributions to this popular genre. The Modernists' reaction to this withdrawal was predictable, though it is noticeable that Ezra Pound's could at times sound equally nationalistic:

> the [English] language is now in the keeping of the Irish (Yeats and Joyce); apart from Yeats, since the death of Hardy, poetry is being written by Americans. All the developments in English verse since 1910 are due almost wholly to Americans. In fact, there is no longer any reason to call it English verse, and there is no present reason to think of England at all.[32]

Georgian post-war pastoralism manifested itself in different shapes and forms. Again a comparison with the Pre-Raphaelites suggests itself: turning away from the destructions that a mechanized age had brought, some sought an alternative reality, as William Morris had done in his handicraft workshop. Edmund Blunden may have turned away from the realities of urban life, but his nature poetry remained closely observed and realistic. In this respect he resembled some of the early Georgians, such as Walter de la Mare and W.H. Davies, who were true nature poets.

Others, on the other hand, escaped into a rural dream-world. In the early 1920s, Georgian poetry was referred to as the 'weekend-school of poetry' in that the poets worked and lived in the cities but rhapsodized on the beauties and pleasures of the countryside, without knowing much about it. They were an easy target for the critics, for, as Middleton Murry rightly pointed out in discussing Edward Shanks's contributions to *Georgian Poetry 1918-1919*, their poetry was devoid of content:

Mr Shanks's speciality is beauty. He is also an amateur of nature. He bids us: "Hear the loud night-jar spin his pleasant note." Of course, Mr Shanks cannot have heard a real night-jar. His description is proof of that.[33]

Shanks himself, who claimed to have coined the phrase 'weekend-poets', saw this poetry primarily as a social phenomenon:

in their nostalgic and sometimes almost invalidish preoccupation with landscape, the 'Week-end Poets' were very important as a social symptom. They were, as I meant to convey by the nickname, men whose centre of life was in the great towns and who did not like it. They were also conscious of living in an age when a profound change was coming over the England of the poets – and they did not like that either. The change had indeed got under way a hundred years before, but it was now going on with a dizzying and sickening rapidity [...] A country which had won the love of innumerable generations was slipping and sliding under their eyes like a dissolving view. [The poets'] efforts were almost feverishly devoted to recording what was going so fast before it should have gone altogether.[34]

The decline of Georgian poetry can at least partly be attributed to the severe losses the movement suffered during the Great War. Whereas amongst the Modernists the single Great War casualty was T. E. Hulme, the Georgian generation of pastoral poets was significantly depleted: it lost its greatest poets in Edward Thomas, Wilfred Owen, Isaac Rosenberg and James Elroy Flecker (though admittedly he was not a victim of the war but of tuberculosis), and poets of considerable promise in Charles Hamilton Sorley and Rupert Brooke.

The process of withdrawal was in itself not a tendency that restricted itself to the literary world: on the English musical scene there were many calls for a more English-oriented repertoire. But in considering the effects of the war on the fine arts it is important to remember that these were not hampered by the limited accessibility of a language, and had for many years been far more outward looking, willingly undergoing a foreign, mainly European, influence. Also, the worlds of both painting and music suffered fewer losses in the war. The introduction of the 'Official War Artists' scheme saved many painters on active service from front-line duty: C.R.W. Nevinson, William Rothenstein, Muirhead Bone, Paul and John Nash, and William Orpen were but some of the painters who at one stage became Official War Artists. Wyndham Lewis and Augustus John both received special commissions in the 'Canadian War Memorial Fund'.

As far as the musical scene was concerned, most of the young composers who were killed in battle had not yet made their mark;[35] it was the elder generation, Elgar, Delius (who lived in France), Holst (who Anglicized his name and dropped a 'von') and Parry, that still dominated the musical scene.[36] Still, young musicians in particular *did* complain about German music being played at London concerts. On 11 October 1916 the 'Pall Mall Gazette' published a letter by the then 25-year-old Arthur Bliss (who had lost his brother two weeks earlier):

> I do not know whether as a class musicians have been less affected (except financially) than other professions, but when straight from being wounded on the Somme I went into a London concert hall and heard a public vociferously applauding a German soloist, it gives me furiously to think [sic].[37]

But German music continued to be performed in London during the war years, mainly because it had been an integral part of the English concert repertoire for many years.[38] The fundamental difference between the situation in the fine arts and that in literature was that the cultural climate in the fine arts had been European for a considerable time, so that there was no possibility of simply reverting to a purely British alternative. But the pastoral tradition in literature had been such an essentially English phenomenon that a withdrawal into a nationalistic mode was always an option.

It is hardly surprising, therefore, that the end of the Georgians' revolt was also reflected in their attitude towards the Victorians. The often uncritical nostalgia that was the result of their dislike of contemporary conditions led many Georgians to take a milder and more sympathetic view of the Victorian era, whereas the Modernists and Bloomsbury Group continued to attack the smug and comfortable Victorian age. Lytton Strachey's *Eminent Victorians* (1918) purported to display the hypocrisy behind the facade of Victorian wealth and respectability; Edmund Blunden, who as a former war poet familiar with "those dreams from the pit" knew that a facade could hide hypocrisy but also sorrow or terror, warned against a too facile condemnation:

> I grant, these tall French windows, these smooth lawns,
> These monuments announce their quiet years;
> But who shall say what pale and anxious dawns
> Smote these? Be certain ere you risk your sneers.
> And of your charity admit that man
> Need not forever live in sharp distress;
> Admit, that you as often as you can
> Prefer to dance with happy thoughtlessness ...[39]

This mildness also characterizes the attitude of many 'elder' Georgians; they shunned polemics and generally behaved as Establishment poets, guardians of the native tradition who did not need to defend their literary views or proclaim new poetic creeds.

VI

Sassoon did not take an active part in the discussions on poetry as a popular art. As a war poet he had actually succeeded in striking a balance between the Georgian and Modernist position: on the one hand he had wanted to reach as large an audience as possible, but at the same time he had made no compromises, delivering his message in as shocking and provocative a way as he thought necessary. But as a Georgian poet he remained an outsider. In the Georgian anthologies he appeared predominantly as a war poet: in total seventeen of his poems were included in the third and fourth *Georgian Poetry* anthologies, and of these thirteen had the war as their subject. Though pleased with the huge sales of the anthologies, he was aware of the dangers of popular success; in June 1918 he wrote to E. M. Forster that "We Georgian Poets think such a lot of ourselves, just because Eddie Marsh has foisted 11,000 copies of our selected poems on to a crowd of people with a taste for verse".[40] The first year after the war – the year he was still in revolt against authority, campaigning for the Labour party and becoming the literary editor of the socialist *Daily Herald* – he maintained this critical stance, arguing in his letters to Marsh that Georgian poetry should not lose its critical edge.

In the 1920s Georgian poetry was increasingly identified with the Neo-Georgians and their leader, J. C. Squire. Adopting a far more aggressive and confrontational attitude than Marsh had ever done, Squire orchestrated a conservative backlash in the pages of the *London Mercury*, of which he was the editor. Though Sassoon and the elder Georgians may have shared his opposition to the Modernist tendencies, they were decidedly less reactionary in their views on poetry. Squire's conservatism became particularly obvious in his condemnation of what he believed to be vulgarity and bad taste in modern poetry. In a review of Aldous Huxley's volume of poetry *Leda* (1920) he referred to Rupert Brooke's 'A Channel Passage' as the starting point of this unfortunate development:

> Rupert Brooke began precisely as Mr. Huxley began: he went as far as he could (decently) and showed love competing with the retchings of sea-sickness. The second-rate stay in that frame of mind and course of art. They go on trying to be shocking until they tire of being ignored. But writers of real genius learn in time that everybody knows quite as much about eructations, excrements, bad smells and base desires as they do: and that people read poetry for the sake of beauty and for an appeal to the highest of appreciation and aspiration that is in them.[41]

Squire's implications are obvious: Brooke had of course not been "second-rate"; he had seen the error of his ways and progressed to writing 'real' poetry in the shape of the morally uplifting *1914* sonnet cycle. But in stating that poetry was read for its beauty and edifying qualities, Squire proclaimed a view on poetry that had been held by the Edwardian Traditionalists[42] but had been refuted and attacked by the Georgians in 1912-13. Their desire for a realistic poetry had convinced the Georgians that beauty was not an essential ingredient of good poetry. The war poets had reached this conclusion the hard way, as Sassoon's example illustrates, but elder Georgians who had not fought in the war, such as Masefield, W.W. Gibson and Abercrombie, had reached the same opinion.

Lascelles Abercrombie (1881-1938) – who in the 1920s embarked on an academic career and became in his critical writings, albeit belatedly, the Georgian theorist – came to define poetry in terms of the conveying of an experience; according to him poetry was "the art or system of contrivances whereby experience can be transferred whole and unimpaired, in all its subtlety and complexity, from one mind to another."[43] This definition emphasizes the position of Georgian poetry as part of the native English tradition, going right back, as it does, to Wordsworth's "emotion recollected in tranquillity". Abercrombie also distanced himself from the Modernists' intellectual approach, insisting that "the poet is a *maker*, and not a critic or philosopher" and that poetry originates on a non-intellectual level: "verbal thought has nothing to do with it. It is as experience – imaginative experience – that poetry begins."[44]

Sassoon's ideas about poetry largely corresponded with Abercrombie's. He hardly ever expressed any theoretical views on poetry, undoubtedly yet another result of a brain that did not take to abstract-ions. But on 16 March 1939 he delivered the Arthur Skemp Memorial Lecture in the University of Bristol.[45] In this lecture, entitled *On Poetry*, Sassoon gave a rare insight into his poetic beliefs. His opening remarks clearly suggest that he felt acutely uncomfortable in his role of lecturer at a university, for he begins by saying that, rather than a lecture, he will call his talk "the diffident divulgement of a few personal opinions", adding that his opinions are *personal* and not *professional*, because "poetry *is* an essentially personal experience" (6). He then begins by stressing the importance of craftsmanship, for poetry can only communicate if the poet possesses the necessary technical skills: "a man may be born a poet, but he has to make himself an artist as well" (6-7). A poet has to master his craft to the extent that technique becomes an *instinctive* rather than a *conscious* part of poetical composition. Sassoon's presentation of the creative process also emphasizes its non-intellectual, instinctive nature. He makes a clear division between an intellectual and a non-intellectual component by stating that poetry originates in the subconscious mind, and that the intellect comes in later "with his critical suggestions and luminous emendations" (8).

It comes therefore as no surprise that for Sassoon the best poetry is as non-intellectual as the process that brought it about. For him poetry is most moving and memorable when it speaks the simple language of the heart. This is what he calls *direct utterance*, which he then goes on to define as

> a full and living voice, seemingly natural, though often using the language of a personal poetic idiom. I mean the true vocal cadence of something urgently communicated – the best words in the best order – yes – but empowered also by sincerity and inspiration. (11)

He then comes to what he calls "dangerous ground": modern poetry. It is a subject he would have preferred not to discuss, but as "an old-fashioned defender of direct utterance, I am obliged to say something about those contemporary innovations which flatly contradict what I believe in" (11). Sassoon did not like Modernist poetry, but he was always careful not to condemn Modernism outright. Diffident about his own poetic achievements and intellectual abilities, he was always keenly aware of the Modernists' intellectual superiority (his 1920 diaries show that he usually felt completely out of his depth in the company of T.S. Eliot or Wyndham Lewis), and therefore did not feel qualified to judge. But in his desire to avoid controversial remarks, he goes to extraordinary lengths. He begins by saying that "clever, innovative verse" has been written by "a lot of people born since 1900 or thereabouts" (11). The vagueness seems intended to suggest that Modernist verse was only written by a new generation of poets, but the leaders of the movement, Wyndham Lewis (born 1884), Ezra Pound (born 1885), T. S. Eliot (born 1888), and Edith Sitwell (born 1887) – she being the only 'Modernist' poet Sassoon mentions by name – were all his near contemporaries. He then goes on to say that he has "wrestled" with vast quantities of Modernist verse and that he has found in it "considerable ingenuity, verbal audacity and compression of ideas," but that he is constantly discouraged by its "ambiguity, euphuistic indirectness, and a sort of dehumanizing logic" (12). He is more ouspoken in his condemnation of the dogmatic poetic theories of Modernist critics:

> advanced critics tell us that a poem must 'have its own internal logic'; and they insist that it is a vice to be tuneful, romantic, or enthusiastic. Pedantry and puritanism have been very busy lately inventing strait-waistcoats for the lyric muse. One might almost put it that a few dreary-minded and superior persons have been indoctrinating their own dreariness on the young experimentalists of our thought-riddled and mechanistic age (12).

According to Sassoon, modern verse has become more and more technique-conscious. As part of this development, he has noticed a tendency to apply the terminology of music and the graphic arts to poetry. This is a form of criticism he rejects without reservation: "that sort of thing very easily degenerates into aesthetic twaddle [...] If we are going to mix up the arts in this way, why not apply the design of an internal-combustion engine to a symphony?" (13). He also does not believe in political poetry ("Can there really be such a thing as a Marxist Muse?"), proving his point not by discussing any of the poems of the Auden-generation, but by reminding his audience that Swinburne ("a lord of language") in his 'Republican' verse fails to move the reader, whereas his lyrics and elegies have a timeless beauty and eloquence. Considering Swinburne's status in the 1930s, one may well doubt whether Sassoon's audience found this a very persuasive argument.

This view of politics in poetry must have come as a surprise to an audience that knew Sassoon mainly as the highly political war poet of the Great War, but Sassoon restricts himself to his personal views on poetry, without ever referring to, or quoting from his own work. His final remark about political poetry is that its only suitable form is the satire, which could be interpreted as a guarded defence of his own work, although even then it remains a fact that some of his bitterest war protests are not satirical at all.

In the last part of his lecture Sassoon returns to his own concept of poetry, which is largely an adaptation of his mother's views on painting. Referring to himself as a "submissively visual writer" (19), he stresses the importance of the mind's eye: "Thinking in pictures is my natural method of self-expression," but he then adds a very Georgian proviso in stating that visual imagery had to be employed sparingly: "Simplification of visual imagery is essential to the best poetry. Strength and simplicity always go together" (25). Later he was to refer to this restriction as "controlled visualisation" (*M*, 208), which he considered an essential requisite for good poetry: too many images and pictures would confuse the reader and spoil the poem's communicative effect. In his conclusion he juxtaposes his mind-sight, the visualizing power of his imagination, with the intellectual effort of contrived thought:

> And that is where imagination, when instinctively controlled, gets the better of contrived thought. For mind-sight eliminates what is inessential, and achieves breadth and intensity by transmuted perception. (25)

On Poetry is the nearest Sassoon ever came to writing a poetic manifesto. A week after giving the lecture, he reported to Max Beerbohm that afterwards he had been "loudly applauded by a large audience, many of whom had overheard it only in patches, owing to the perfidious acoustics of the sumptuous hall in which it was delivered" (*LMB*, 77). Whether the acoustics were wholly to blame for his inaudibility is doubtful: Sassoon was never a gifted public speaker and his diction tended to be flat and fading. That the applause might not have been an indication of support for the contents of his lecture is something that will not have bothered him. Like other Georgian poets, such as Walter de la Mare, Ralph Hodgson and Edmund Blunden, Sassoon preferred to stay out of any literary debates, quietly going his own way in steering a middle course between Squire's conservatism and Eliot's Modernism. During most of the 1920s his silence was also caused by the fact that he was too busy trying to find a new poetic voice. But in his outspoken preference for a sincere, vigorous but essentially simple poetry that would thus be accessible to the general reader he did remain faithful to one of the main Georgian ideals.

CHAPTER 4

SATIRICAL INTENT

I

Siegfried Sassoon did not thrive on inner conflicts, neither as a man nor as a poet. The years immediately following the Great War were among the bleakest in his life. His war poetry had made him a minor celebrity, but in 1919 he began to regard this reputation as a burden: he felt, rightly or wrongly, that expectations were high and this put him under considerable pressure. But more important were the inner conflicts: the conviction that he was a poet, the realization that he had neither a poetic voice nor a subject to write about, the desire to win praise and recognition, and the fear that he would fail and disappoint his readers, left him in a state of apathy. A combination of anger and compassion had been the driving force in his war poetry, but with this force gone, Sassoon relapsed into his pre-war indolence and diffidence.

When looking back to these years towards the end of his life, the tone becomes apologetic: "One thing is that, as I always tell people, I was never a *professional* writer, and in some ways a complete amateur. In 1919 I was still in the 'Lower Fifth', and the next six years were spent in trying to get into the 'Upper Sixth'" (*L.C.*, 13). Claiming that he was not a professional writer may seem a bit odd for somebody who always considered himself a poet, and at the time, apart from an annual allowance, depended for his income on his writing.[1] But it is a fact that Sassoon's post-war career as a poet is that of a gentleman-poet rather than that of a professional writer: he never aspired to a life as a professional man of letters and always remained essentially an amateur. As such it is only logical that he appears as Siegfried Victor[2] in Wyndham Lewis's *The Apes of God* (1930), that rambling, epic condemnation of an amateur age in which self-advertising writers only dabbled in the arts and serious artists (like Lewis) were ignored. Sassoon was different in that he always shunned the public eye: *all* his post-war volumes appeared first in privately printed editions and often it was not until several years later that a selection of these poems was published in a trade edition. And it was not only in practical matters that he reverted to this pre-war situation.

II

Sassoon's first post-war volume, *Picture Show*, was published in June 1919 in a private edition of two hundred copies printed at the Cambridge University Press. Only one hundred and fifty copies were for sale (at a guinea each), the remaining fifty were for the poet, who sent them to friends and relatives. No British trade edition ever appeared, though an enlarged American trade edition was published by Dutton in 1920. The book's contents illustrate his lack of direction, because unlike his other volumes it is rather a mixed bag: war poems, satires, love poems and the ruminative poetry that was to dominate his later volumes.

The title itself sounds promising: for a visual poet like Sassoon it seemed an innovative and yet logical choice to use the new popular art form of the cinema as a source of inspiration. But these expectations are immediately disappointed in the title poem, which reveals that quite the opposite had happened. Instead of new elements enriching his poetry there was a relapse into his pre-war style:

> And still they come and go: and this is all I know –
> That from the gloom I watch an endless picture-show,
> Where wild or listless faces flicker on their way,
> With glad or grievous hearts I'll never understand
> Because Time spins so fast, and they've no time to stay
> Beyond the moment's gesture of a lifted hand.

The opening line is particularly unfortunate: the monosyllables create a dull and monotonous rhythm which is even more emphasised by the rhyme words, whereas the 'announcement' in the second half is completely superfluous. But it is the poetic persona that is the most striking; in his role of the powerless onlooker, Sassoon has in effect reverted to the persona of his pre-war poems. To compare these lines with the opening lines of 'Goblin Revel' (written 1909-10)

> In gold and grey, with fleering looks of sin,
> I watch them come; by two, by three, by four,
> Advancing slow, with loutings they begin
> Their woven measure, widening from the door

is to notice that the speaker's roles in both poems are identical and that the tones also show a remarkable similarity. The fundamental difference between the two poems is, however, that in the early poem the experience is purely imaginative, whereas in 'Picture Show' Sassoon attempts to describe a reality: a recurring dream he had in which he saw the faces of those who were killed in the war. His inability to express this in a more powerful poetry is indicative of the lack of progress he had made.

The introduction to *Picture Show* stated that the poems in the volume were written after January 1918. It is not surprising, therefore, that the book still contained some war poems: among the thirty-four poems Sassoon retained in the *Picture Show* section of the collected edition are seven war poems, five about war recollections, and a war satire on a biblical theme.

In 'To Leonide Massine in "Cleopatra"' Sassoon tried to distance himself from his war memories. Watching Massine, the principal dancer in Diaghilev's Russian Ballet, in his dying scene the poet is reminded of all the real deaths he has witnessed:

> You die but in our dreams, who watch you fall
> Knowing that to-morrow you will dance again.
> But not to ebbing music they were slain
> Who sleep in ruined graves, beyond recall;
> Who, following phantom-glory, friend and foe,
> Into the darkness that was War must go;
> Blind, banished from desire,
> O mortal heart
> Be still, you have drained the cup; you have
> played your part.

Again this is a poem that fails, partly through over-elaboration (the contrast between the stage death and real deaths is clear enough to render the second line unnecessary), but also because the description of the soldiers marching is over-dramatic, and the ending, whether consciously or unconsciously echoing A.E. Housman's 'Be still, my soul, be still' (*A Shropshire Lad*, XLVIII), is cliché-ridden and fails to move. In the other poem dealing with the after-effects of the war, Sassoon does not manage to strike a convincing note either. 'Memory' (written 1 February 1918) heralds what was to become the underlying theme of the Sherston memoirs, how the war had destroyed his pre-war existence:

> But now my heart is heavy-laden. I sit
> Burning my dreams away beside the fire:
> For death has made me wise and bitter and strong;
> And I am rich in all that I have lost.

Apart from the first line, which is again reminiscent of A.E. Housman ("With rue my heart is laden / For golden friends I had", *A Shropshire Lad*, LIV), the thing that strikes the reader here is the way the poetry fails to support the contents: though he poet claims to have gained both strength and richness, the lines express a wistful and sad mood, rather than a vigorous and enriched one. The concluding lines illustrate Sassoon's inability to convey heartfelt emotion:

> O starshine on the fields of long-ago,
> Bring me the darkness and the nightingale;
> Dim wealds of vanished summer, peace of home,
> And silence; and the faces of my friends
> (ll. 12-15)

One can only agree with Michael Thorpe when he says that the poem epitomizes Sassoon's poetical weaknesses with its "style that produces an effect of remoteness and artificial feeling".[3]

It is a relief to find that Sassoon could still write in the crisp, concise style of his war poetry: 'Devotion to Duty', though written in February 1919, can well be counted among his most effective war satires. In the first two stanzas the reader is subtly wrong-footed; the King reading a "G.H.Q. dispatch" reporting the death of an officer killed in action who in his final moments managed to gain "our first objective" and whose "fine example most effectively sustained" the spirit of the troops, is automatically taken to refer to George V mourning the death of yet another hero who laid down his life for his country. In the last stanza follows the cruel twist: "He gripped his beard; then closed his eyes and said / 'Bathsheba must be warned that he is dead'". In 'Ancient History' Sassoon reverses the process: instead of using a contemporary setting for a biblical story, he uses a biblical setting for a contemporary viewpoint. Casting Adam in the role of a social-Darwinist, he portrays him mourning the death of Cain. Abel had been a born loser, "a lover with disaster in his face", but Cain was the grandest of them all, "Hungry and fierce with deeds of huge desire". Adam comes to the very post-Great War conclusion that power corrupts and that even God is prone to favouritism: "*'God always hated Cain'*".

Many of the poems in *Picture Show*, both the war and the non-war poems, refer to sleep and dreams. This new theme in Sassoon's poetry was a direct result from the neurasthenia-treatment he had received at Craiglockhart War Hospital in 1917. His doctor there had been the psychologist and anthropologist W.H.R. Rivers (1864-1922), who became a personal friend and counsellor and who was, according to Rupert Hart-Davis (Sassoon's friend and literary executor) "his chief father-figure".[4]

Rivers had been one of the first in England to accept Freud's dream theory, and he made active use of dream-interpretation in his treatment of shell-shocked officers at Craiglockhart. In March 1917 he read a paper to the Edinburgh Pathological Club entitled 'Freud's Psychology of the Unconscious'. In it he confirmed Freud's earlier findings, and stated that "specific symptoms could be linked with specific traumatic events, and that once the memories were recovered the symptoms disappeared".[5]

After his treatment at Craiglockhart, Sassoon had become convinced of the importance of self-analysis; in 1966 he referred in a letter to "the quest for 'autognosis' which I derived from Rivers" (*L.C.*, 13). The many times dreams are mentioned in *Picture Show* suggest that Sassoon felt a therapeutic need to incorporate his dreams into his poetry, but what the dream-poems also show is that he makes a wider use of the term, applying it both to dreams and thoughts:

> I dreamt I saw a huge grey boat in silence steaming
> Down a canal; it drew the dizzy landscape after.
>
> ('Miracles', ll. 1-2)

> Last night I dreamt an old recurring scene -
> Some complex out of childhood; (sex, of course!).
> ('Prelude to an Unwritten Masterpiece', ll. 6-7)

> You've said it all before: you dreamed of Death,
> A dim Apollo in the bird-voiced breeze.
> ('Limitations', ll. 11-12)

> I quaked uncomforted,
> Striving to frame to-morrow in a dream
> Of woods and sliding pools and cloudless day.
> ('To a Very Wise Man', ll.11-3)

> Waiting for sleep, I drift from thoughts like these;
> And where to-day was dream-like, build my dreams.
> ('Falling Asleep', ll. 11-12)

The fourth and fifth quotations do not seem to refer to genuine dreams, rather they describe day-dreams, thoughts or images he tried to impose on his thinking or his dreaming, in order to control his thoughts and prevent disturbing memories from creeping up on him. He gave a vivid picture of this mental process in an earlier war poem, 'Repression of War Experience', written in the summer of 1917 and published in *Counter-Attack*, which also shows that it was part of a therapy he had been taught at Craiglockhart:

> Now light the candle; one; two; there's a moth;
> What silly beggars they are to blunder in
> And scorch their wings with glory, liquid flame -
> No, no, not that, - it's bad to think of war,
> When thoughts you've gagged all day come back to
>   scare you;
> And it's been proved that soldiers don't go mad
> Unless they lose control of ugly thoughts
> That drive them out to jabber among the trees.

This poem is one of the first to show Dr Rivers's influence; 'Repression of War Experience' was the title of a lecture he had delivered earlier in 1917.

That the scourge of the war-enthusiasts had buried the hatchet is best illustrated by the last poem in *Picture Show*, Sassoon's anthology piece 'Everyone Sang' (it was with this poem that he was included in his favourite anthology, *Palgrave's Golden Treasury*). In *Siegfried's Journey* he recalls that

> 'Everyone Sang' was composed without emotion [...] Many people, by the way, have interpreted the poem as referring to soldiers singing while on the march, so I take the opportunity of stating that no such idea was in my mind. (*SJ*, 141)

In fact the singing is a reference to the social revolution Sassoon hoped to be at hand. But in sharp contrast to his war poetry, he does not seem   particularly bothered by the fact that the poem is misunderstood. The irony in the fact that the rebel war poet's one stock anthology piece should be a poem supposedly celebrating Armistice escapes him altogether. It was the recognition and the confidence it gave him that were far more important to him at this stage.

One of the older men who did a lot to further Sassoon's career in London, and whose advice he was always eager to hear, was the journalist and art critic Robert Ross, one of the few friends to remain loyal to Oscar Wilde in the 1890s. Sassoon first met him at the Gosse's in 1915, and it was Ross who had encouraged the soldier-poet to develop the satirical side of his war poetry. Ross remained a close friend and confidant until his sudden death in October 1918. The 'Elegy' Sassoon wrote as a tribute to his friend is generous in spirit, but an otherwise disappointingly impersonal poem. It resorts to stereotype images ("But loyal love has deathless wings / That rise and triumph out of night") and Sassoon makes no attempt to strike a more intimate note, never once referring to his individual feelings or memories. What Sassoon appreciated above all in Ross as a friend were those qualities that were also applicable to himself, generosity and loyalty. Also, though it would be wrong to suspect an intentional pun in the the line "And death has found you, kind and gay" (at the time the word had not yet acquired its more recent meaning), Ross was one of the few people with whom Sassoon openly discussed his homosexuality.

Ross's chambers at 40 Half-Moon Street were a favourite meeting place for homosexual literary men,[6] but Oscar Wilde's experiences had taught Ross that discretion was of the utmost importance. In 1913 Ross himself had been the victim of a hate campaign by Lord Alfred Douglas and his right-hand man T.W.H. Crosland. Douglas had referred to Ross as "the High Priest of all the sodomites in London" and had actively persecuted him, in an attempt to find incriminating evidence. Ross avoided arrest through the help of Edmund Gosse, who had asked his 'friends in high places' to intervene on Ross's behalf. In June 1914 Ross took Crosland to court, claiming that he and Lord Alfred Douglas (who was abroad at the time) had conspired to bring charges against him for having "committed certain acts". Crosland was acquitted, but when Lord Alfred Douglas returned to England in October he was arrested and also brought to trial. Edmund Gosse and H.G. Wells appeared as witnesses for Ross, but the case finally collapsed through lack of evidence. Douglas was discharged and Ross was left financially ruined. Gosse again helped him out by starting a public subscription to help him pay the legal costs.[7] Sassoon first met Ross a year after this episode came to an end, and he took it as a warning.[8] He was shocked to hear about Douglas and Crosland's disgusting behaviour and abruptly stopped sending poems to Douglas's *Academy*. In 1966 he referred in a letter to Crosland and Douglas's "malignant persecution" of Robbie Ross, adding that this had "undoubtedly hastened his death" (*LC*, 21).

It is no coincidence, then, that the beloved in the six love poems in *Picture Show* is never described. Sassoon met the young artist Gabriel Atkin in December 1918. It seems to have been his first homosexual affair, but in all his writings Sassoon remains reticent about its intimate details. Though he later became more open and outspoken about his homosexuality, it must have been a great anxiety to him, especially in the light of his Victorian upbringing. What is clear is that he never felt comfortable with the physical and passionate side of homosexual love. In his references he resorts to a Victorian vocabulary, writing about "lust" and his "animal instincts" as if he somehow felt that he was doing wrong.

Love poems are a very late arrival in Sassoon's *oeuvre*, but unfortunately they do not bring a new freshness and individuality to his style. Though they are the record of what must have been some of his most personal and intense experiences and emotions, they are written in the romantic and impersonal style of his pre-war poetry. The first four poems recall the happiness of the first months of their affair, but in 'The Imperfect Lover' the mood changes:

> But I've grown thoughtful now. And you have lost
> Your early-morning freshness of surprise
> At being so utterly mine: you've learned to fear
> The gloomy, stricken places in my soul,
> And the occasional ghosts that haunt my gaze.

Sassoon fails to express these highly personal feelings in an equally personal idiom. Instead, he rehashes by now all too familiar phrases: the Meredithian 'early morning'; two favourite words 'gloom' and 'ghosts' which through over-use have become empty phrases that do not evoke any response in the reader; and the maudlin 'stricken places in my soul', which almost begins to sound insincere. Sassoon always claimed that he needed personal experiences to write about; this claim is not borne out by these love poems, and though one can have sympathy for his reticence on the subject of homosexuality, this does not excuse their overall flatness.

The most personal lines are to be found in what is not a love poem at all. 'To a Childless Woman' is addressed to a barren woman whom the poet watches in a chapel, but the concluding lines can only be interpreted as a veiled reference to Sassoon's homosexuality:

> I too have longed for children. Ah, but you must not weep.
> Something I have to whisper as I kneel beside you...
> And you must pray for me before you fall asleep.

Though the poem is set in a chapel, the speaker shows no great faith in the Christian God. As in the two biblical satires, his attitude remains one of scepticism: watching the woman at prayer he does not seem to believe that divine intervention can alter a physical reality: "What mercy can He give you? – Dreams of the unborn / Children that haunt your soul...?"

This rejection of religion is particularly interesting in connection with a poem in which Sassoon faces up to yet another inner conflict. In 'Limitations' he attempts to reconcile the man who enjoys his childhood memories and the poet who does not consider these an original subject for his poetry:

> You've got your limitations; let them sing,
> And all your life will waken with a cry:
> Why should you halt when rapture's on the wing
> And you've no limit but the cloud-flocked sky?...
> But some chap shouts, 'Hey, stop it; that's been done!'–

What these lines show is a fundamental blind spot in Sassoon's self-criticism: his apparent inability to distinguish between subject and style. He stops short at making his childhood a poetic subject because he feels "that's been done". It does not seem to have occurred to him that it was not the subject, but his treatment of that subject and more particularly the poetic language he used in dealing with that subject that lacked originality. Ten years later his childhood *did* become an important subject in his poetry, but by then it had been set in the larger framework of his religious pilgrimage. For the moment, Sassoon concluded that the lyrics in *Picture Show* were on the whole unsatisfactory. He made no further attempts at writing in this vein, instead he turned to satirical verse, perhaps thinking that his war poetry had shown his competence in that genre. But his reasoning proved to be completely erroneous for instead of revealing some of his strengths, his satirical verse was to show up some of his worst poetic and intellectual weaknesses.

III

Satirical poems were greatly in vogue during the 1920s. Most appeared anonymously in the many literary magazines, to which Sassoon also offered an occasional contribution (though few of these poems were ever reprinted). Satire was a popular weapon in the polemics between Neo-Georgians and Modernists. The older Georgians, Sassoon included, did not really take part in this and were rarely a target. The two long satires that are usually taken to be ridiculing the Georgians are not directed against the original Georgians at all. Osbert Sitwell's 'The Jolly Old Squire or Way Down In Georgia' (1922) is, as the title indicates, an attack on J.C. Squire's *London Mercury* group (the Neo-Georgians) and Roy Campbell's 'The Georgiad' (1931) savages all those who ever incurred Campbell's displeasure – which is almost everybody – but is mainly directed against J.C. Squire, the effeminate 'Bloomberries', and especially against Vita Sackville-West and her husband Harold Nicolson.

Sassoon's *Satirical Poems* were published by Heinemann on the 29 April 1926 in an edition of 2000 copies. In the intervening years he had written very little. His collected *War Poems* were published by Heinemann in October 1919 in an edition of 2000 copies (a second edition of 1000 copies followed in January 1920). The trade editon of his satirical verse was preceded by two privately printed satirical volumes, *Recreations* (printed March 1923 in an edition of 75 copies) and *Lingual Exercises* (printed February 1925 in an edition of 99 co-pies). Sassoon preserved all the poems from *Satirical Poems* in his collected edition, adding four later ones; as in the case of his early poetry, the reason must have been that he wanted to record his development. The poems themselves are far from impressive. In returning to satirical verse and thinking that his socialism in peace-time would be as effective as his anger and compassion in war-time, Sassoon made a fundamental error of judgment; he should have heeded E.M. Forster's advice, who told him in 1919:

> Use society until you think it's using you, when drop it. As to satire, for God's sake only write it if it amuses you or if savage indignation impels you: the satirical *habit* means slow death of the most ignoble kind.[9]

Sassoon's response to the war had been sincere and deeply-felt, he had had first-hand knowledge of the men and conditions he was writing about, and he had used a simple and direct language to achieve his aims. But his socialism was only skin-deep; he knew very little about politics and the issues that were being discussed, and as a writer he moved in comfortably middle and upperclass circles, having no direct contact with the people for whom he 'fought'. As for the poetic language he used, it was so artificial and stylized that it was likely to isolate him from, rather than appeal to, a working-class audience.

What he attempted to do, was to become a sort of Henry James or Max Beerbohm, perceptive and critical observers of the privileged social circles they moved in. But in his war poetry he had not been an observer but a participant: it had been anger that had provided the sting, but personal experience that had given his satires credibility and authority. As a satirist of the establishment, on the other hand, he was no more than an observer: he lacked the ability to empathize and analyse, and he did not have the penetrating insight that was required for a really effective debunking. His attempts at social satire are no more than attempts to ridicule by using complex language and exaggerated poetical devices, especially alliteration.

On Empire Day (24 May) 1924 he attended the official opening of the British Empire Exhibition at Wembley (the first great national event to be broadcast by the BBC). In 'Afterthoughts on the Opening of the British Empire Exhibition' he attempts to take a satirical view of the occasion, but gets no further than an exercise in poeticizing: the events in the morning are described as "That ante-noontide ceremonial scene" and the rest of the poem is marred by an excessive use of alliteration

> Ebullitions of Empire exulted. I listened and stared.
> Patriotic paradings with pygmy preciseness went by.
> The band bashed out bandmaster music ...

Characteristically unable to take an impersonal view, there are moments when Sassoon's forced and poeticized descriptions backfire and he unwittingly pokes fun at himself as the eager but impotent satirist:

> Resolved to satirize Hotels-de-Luxe,
> Shyly I sift the noodles from the crooks
> Beneath whose bristly craniums a cigar
> Juts and transmutes crude affluence to ash.
> ('The Grand Hotel', ll. 12-15)

As far as satire is concerned this is reminiscent of Sassoon's Masefield pastiche 'The Daffodil Murderer', in that he is trying very hard to create a humorous effect without succeeding in doing so. But the weakness of these poems does not lie only in his feeble satirical skills.

Sassoon may have attempted to cast himself in the role of the socialist satirist taking a critical view of the upper middle-class world from the inside, but ultimately that was a role that did not suit him at all. His heart was not in it; he was by nature an outsider, a man with reclusive tendencies who never really belonged to any group or movement. Even his war protest had been an individual action; at no time had he tried to mobilize the opposition and become the leader of a concerted action against the continuation of the war.

His involvement in *Clarté*, a post-war pacifist movement founded and led by Henri Barbusse with the aim of uniting French and English intellectuals in their opposition to militarism, was short-lived and unsuccessful. He lacked genuine interest and felt no desire to take over the torch from the older generation. To wash his hands of it he wrote to *Clarté*'s English secretary Douglas Goldring that there was no point in going on unless the movement was actively supported by H.G. Wells and G.B. Shaw.[10] In his memoirs he writes in typical self-disparagement that another reason for his break with *Clarté* was that he did not have "the ghost of a notion what it was all about" (*SJ*, 169).

The most interesting thing about these 'satires' is that they were written by a man who has decided that as a committed socialist and aspiring intellectual he has to disapprove of the life he is leading, so that these poems are partly an attempt to convince himself of this fact. Ultimately, then, he is satirizing his own life-style, writing poems about cricket, fox-hunting, museums, the theatre and music, in an attempt to persuade himself that these are things he does not really care for. He fails, as he has to admit to himself amid the pompous splendour of a Bavarian palace:

> My sympathy for Soviets notwithstanding –
> (Dare one deplore the dullness of Democracy?)
> I am touched, I am enticed, by super-lavish
> Expense; half-cultured coxcomb Kings commanding
> In palacefuls the trappings of Autocracy,
> With all their country's coffers ripe to ravish.
> ('Fantasia on a Wittelsbach Atmosphere', ll. 22-7)

As with the *Lyrical Poems* in *The Old Huntsman* which were not lyrical at all, so these satires are no satirical poems. Most of them are no more than unsuccessful exercises in witty observation. Below the surface level these poems stop being witty and satirical altogether; in most of them the poet himself is present as the observer, and the pervading atmosphere in the poems in which he describes the people in his own little world, such as 'The Grand Hotel', 'The Blues at Lord's', 'Reynardism Revisited', 'The London Museum' and 'The Turner Rooms', is one of estrangement, one gets the sense of a man who is writing about a society he no longer feels part of.

Sassoon gathered material for his satirical poems in his diaries, and these unadorned, factual descriptions are more effective than any of the poems he wrought out of them. Unlike the young Evelyn Waugh in *Decline and Fall* (1928) and *Vile Bodies* (1930), he failed to realize that the high society he was satirizing was itself often behaving so ridiculously that it needed a 'dead-pan', and not a baroque portrayal. A brief description of a Lady Cunard dinner party at an expensive Monte Carlo restaurant is enough to set the imagination going: "The noise of the band (quite near the table) was terrific, and shouting was the only medium by which 'polite conversation' could be carried on" (*D3*, 103). Reading these passages in Sassoon's diaries makes one regret that he never attempted using this material in a novel:

This afternoon Frankie Schu [Schuster] had a tea-party. Three middle-aged ladies – Mrs Brinton (formerly Mrs Willie James), Lady Alwynne Compton-Vyner, and Lady Eva Wemyss, a jolly, fat cosy old thing, dressed anyhow, with stuffed-sawdust legs, who lives near here with her mother, Lady Cowley, an aged gambler, who is apparently impervious to bereavement. "When I told her that X was dead," said Lady Eva, "she never even looked up, but just went on playing patience" [...]

Lady Alwynne Compton-Vyner, in an effort to make the conversation sparkle, quoted the Nice newspaper which announced the arrival of [the second Duke of Westminster's] yacht – "The Duke of Westminster, *brother of the Prince of Wales*". She said it was one of the funniest things she'd ever read! "Ha ha; hee hee!" (We all laughed automatically.) Mrs Brinton capped this with an "excruciatingly funny story" about someone in Monte Carlo who went up to Lady Hawtrey and said "How are you, Lady Tree". (Roars of laughter from Schuster.)[11]

This more natural style of the diaries was one Sassoon never achieved in his satires; the desire to create a humorous effect led to a kind of verse that was mannered and over-written.

Placed in the wider context of his collected poems, the satirical poems show that basically they were a wrong turning, that Sassoon initially still believed himself to be a minor prophet whose duty it was to comment on the rights and wrongs of society and to be actively involved in improving the world. The poems are an unintentional illustration of his gradual realization that it was impossible for him to dedicate himself whole-heartedly to the socialist cause, for the simple reason that it went against the grain: "For the fox-hunting man was irrepressible, and the superficially adopted Socialism – though generous in impulse and intention – required more than corduroy to conceal its inadequate repertoire" (*SJ*, 135). Instead of focusing on the outside world, Sassoon gradually turned inwards, concentrating on his inner conflicts, finding out about and coming to terms with his own limitations, and admitting to himself that in his prophet role he had been in danger of overreaching himself.

On the title page of the privately printed *Lingual Exercises* he had quoted some lines from Psalm cxxxi:

> I am not high-minded; I have
> no proud looks. I do not exer-
> cise myself in great matters
> which are too high for me.

The mid-1920s mark the period when he came to the conclusion that neither socialism nor intellectualism suited him. In December 1925 he wrote to a friend that

> I have done with verbal gymnastics in future. Being smart don't suit me, really. But it was a phase which had to be worked out, & now I can be as simple, sensuous, & passionate as I please.

Towards the end of his life he suggested that he regarded these poems as preliminary studies, exercises in which he tried to master the art of writing poetry:

> *Satirical Poems* was an exercise in learning to use words with accuracy (the *content* was only playing a mental game without deep seriousness), and these years were a process of getting the war out of my system. (*LC*, 13)

His saying that the content of the poems was negligible is clear proof of the fact that it was his poetic development rather than the poems' individual qualities that accounted for their inclusion in the collected edition. He thus did not subscribe to the view that a collected edition contains those poems by which a poet wishes to be remembered. Though he did not add an introduction to his *Collected Poems*, it is clear that had he done so it would have echoed the concluding paragraph of the 'Preface' of the collected edition of his fellow-Georgian, Lascelles Abercrombie:

> The poems and plays are reprinted almost without alteration. This does not indicate any complacency on my part; it merely indicates a very positive conviction that they must take their chances as they were written, under the impulse in which they originated. Who can see their faults better than I can? But even if I could correct their faults, it would almost certainly be by introducing something worse – disharmony of mood and spirit.[12]

IV

The last of Sassoon's satirical efforts was published by Duckworth on 15 May 1931. What had provoked him into writing these fourteen parodies under the pseudonym Pinchbeck Lyre were the poems and popularity of his exact contemporary Humbert Wolfe (1886-1940).

Wolfe, a senior civil servant at the Ministry of Labour (where the poets F.S. Flint and Richard Church were among his subordinates), started his prolific career as a poet, satirist and critic in 1920 with the publication of his *London Sonnets*. All through the second half of the

1920s Wolfe continued to be widely read, though many writers and critics did not share the public's enthusiasm (he had been one of the targets of Roy Campbell's 'The Georgiad' and Wyndham Lewis's 'One-Way Song').

Wolfe's poetic voice was outdated and rhetorical, an echo of the late nineteenth-century poetry of Oscar Wilde and William Watson. His entry in the *DNB* manages to say that his style was old-fashioned in the nicest possible way:

> He wrote defying contemporary trends, had an urgent belief in goodness and beauty, and, in a disillusioned age, was unashamed of idealism and pathos. Inevitably, then, he invited attack, which made him suffer.

Critics were indeed not kind to Wolfe. His 1926 volume *Humoresque* was dealt with by Edgell Rickword in *The Calendar of Modern Letters*:

> his attempts to stylize the banal are frustrated by an ingrained banality of style. The obvious may yield exquisite fruit, if culti- vated with....devotion and intelligence [....] But, when the expression is anything less than consummate, there is obvious- ly nothing there to break the hideous fall.

Five years later Rickword dismissed Wolfe's *Snow* in a brief review under the heading 'High-Sounding Nonsense'.[13]

Sassoon was equally irritated by Wolfe's verses. Writing to his friend Max Beerbohm in July 1931 he asked "Did you like *Pinchbeck Lyre*? Unkind; but the result of much piffle-provocation" (*LMB*, 17). He was probably particularly irritated by Wolfe's self-importance: one of Wolfe's idiosyncracies is his obsession with the poet's power to immortalize his beloved - which in Wolfe's case all too often means that he starts writing about the poet, i.e. himself.

This is one of the themes of Sassoon's parodies, as in 'Conundrum':

> Which must be most immortal, which of us twain? –
> I, casting clustering assonances at you
> (And scribbling on my shirt-cuffs in the train),
> Or you, the ultimate indelible statue?

Wolfe's volumes *Humoresque* (1926) and *This Blind Rose* (1928) appear to have been the main sources of material for the Pinchbeck Lyre poems. Sassoon faithfully copied some of Wolfe's stylistic oddities: a liberal use of French words, no capitals at the beginning of lines, many hyphenated compound adjectives and nouns, and when Wolfe uses proper names and nouns as verbs, as in a poem entitled 'June unjuned', Sassoon counters with an equally inspired "Vasco da Gama / who Columbussed beyond horizons and found them profitless" ('Largesse').[14]

For those familiar with Wolfe's verse, the parodies were easily recognizable and not unfunny. But what they unintentionally also show, is that Wolfe's typical style, with its abundant use of alliteration, assonance, compounds, and archaic and complex language, is uncomfortably similar to Sassoon's own.

One of Wolfe's most irritating habits are the many authorial 'asides', bracketed comments that interrupt the flow of the poem. They occur frequently in the Pinchbeck poems, but Sassoon does not seem to realize that they are also an annoying feature of his own poetry, both of his satirical and serious verse.[15] Though he does succeed in ridiculing Wolfe's style through sheer exaggeration, the fact remains that his own poetry never completely lost an unfortunate tendency to lapse into the rhetorical devices he ridiculed in the Wolfe parodies.

'*Poems* by Pinchbeck Lyre' was never reprinted and not included in Sassoon's collected edition. Among his satirical verses they are definitely not the worst, but in spite of Humbert Wolfe's concern with poetic immortality his verses did not survive him and with their disappearance the Pinchbeck Lyre parodies lost their *raison d'être*. Neither did they mark a stage in Sassoon's poetic development, for in the mid-1920s Sassoon had at last found both the theme and the poetic voice that were to dominate his post-war poetry.

CHAPTER 5

THROUGH THE WICKET GATE

I

In October 1923 Sassoon noted in his diary that he had "decided to call my next book (love and lyrical poems) 'The Heart's Journey', and publish it in October 1926 (after my fortieth birthday)". In fact it was not published until 1928, but that he decided on a title for a volume that apparently was to mark the start of a new 'life-begins-at-forty' phase as early as 1923, suggests that he was dissatisfied with his existence and felt that it was time for a fundamental change. Ever since the end of the war he had lived in a state of mental turmoil; all the contradictory elements in his personality had collided and made inner peace and stability impossible. He was habitually in two minds about everything. Living in London in the early 1920s, he wanted to be a Labour Movement intellectual, and as such he thought he ought to give up hunting and polite society. Yet he found it impossible to do so, although, as a poet and aspiring intellectual, he became increasingly critical of his former hunting friends:

> They are the product of a stupid environment [....] They refuse to face the problems of human existence, and say 'Perhaps we aren't meant to know'. Such people...are known as 'the backbone of the country'. The creative and original people are ahead of society, so they are really outside the body of which upper-middle-class stupidity is the 'backbone'. (*D2*, 111)

Yet the idea that as a self-respecting man of letters he could no longer associate himself with this ignorant lot all too often induces a more wistful mood, in which he views the racing world in a different light:

> I know well enough that horsemanship is less important than the art of poetry, but my love of horses is deeply rooted, and I

had an exiled feeling. Viewed from the detachment of to-day, the sportsmen and the countrified people in their comfortable clothes produced an impression of contentment which I envied. (*D3*, 226)

Sassoon was struggling to live up to his own ideas of what a man of letters should be like. He had convinced himself that the serious writer forgoes the pleasures of life and suffers for his art, the problem in his own case being that in spite of this self-imposed restraint he did not produce any work of artistic merit. But he also seems to have been affected by the idea that man of letters and intellectual were roughly synonymous terms. As his criticism of the hunting fraternity shows, it gave him feelings of superiority that also caused problems in other areas of his social life.

After his affair with Gabriel Atkin, he had several other young friends, but these relationships were often hampered by Sassoon's pride and arrogance. About one of these young men he writes that he resents being criticized by him:

The fact is that I am affectionately disposed towards him, but I do not respect him as an intellectual equal. I am intensely proud of my prestige as a 'man of letters' – the fact that Hardy and Hodgson and de la Mare and all the rest of them accept me as one of their clan. It is a pride I have often resented in Bob Nichols, when he patronises inferior writers and society women – adopting an overbearing attitude towards them in conversation. (*D2*, 275-76)

This illustrates one of the basic dichotomies in Sassoon's character: though kind and modest, he was at the same time a proud man. The critical tone of intellectual superiority was the result of frustration rather than conviction: his desire to become an intellectual man of letters was not only thwarted by his natural diffidence and his dissatisfaction with the quality and quantity of his poetic output, but also by his disconcerting experiences in London's literary world, for he never felt less intellectual than when in the company of intellectuals. Again it was his inability to cope with abstract concepts that caused him to be left behind in philosophical debates:

I listened to a philosophical discussion between Bertrand
Russell and George Santayana. As far as I can recollect, they
were investigating the reality of Reality, or something
equivalently beyond my powers of comprehension. (*SJ*, 127)

Taking part in an intellectual discussion was essentially a humbling
experience for him, one that made him only too aware of his
intellectual limitations:

I seem incapable of exercising my mind on abstractions. My
interests all derive from concrete experiences. My life is only a
series of pictures, punctuated with groans and guffaws.
Incapable of formulating theories or constructive ideas, I
blunder past panoramas of sensuous impressions which rush
toward me and occasionally take shape at the point of my pen.
My 'ideas' are merely emotional or introspective ejaculations.
My memory a museum of departed passions! (*D3*, 148)

This somewhat purple passage was written in the early summer of
1924, which is the period when Sassoon finally made up his mind
what to do. He had come to realize that it was not just his poetry, but
his whole life-style that had been wrong. Meeting Osbert Sitwell in
the street, he tells him that: "I like reading people's books. But I find
that knowing literary people personally leads to disaster. I like to be
aloof – to watch people..." (*D3*, 140). The turning point in Sassoon's
post-war career is this moment when he decides to give up trying to
belong to any group or movement and to simply follow his own
instincts. Realizing that he did not feel completely at home in either
the world of the Edwardian sportsman or that of the London man of
letters, his solution was essentially to withdraw from both.

He also knew there was no going back to his pre-war life. Though
still very close to his mother he thought her almost embarrassingly
old-fashioned. He felt he could not take Gabriel Atkin (their affair
had gradually subsided into a close friendship) to meet his mother,
because they stood on either side of the Traditionalist/Modernist
divide: "G. represents green chartreuse and Epstein sculpture. Mother
is G.F. Watts and holy communion" (*D2*, 72). For the moment, his
visits to Weirleigh, his childhood home, had also lost their appeal:
"The place is saturated with intimate associations, but they grow

weaker, and I more detached from them, every time I go there" (*D3*, 174). In his letters and diaries he refers to this as an "Enoch-Ardenish feeling" (*D3*, 95),[1] and this estrangement from his past closed off a return home as an option.

Two men seem to have played a vital role in the fundamental change of course Sassoon eventually decided on. In his 1922 diary he noted that W.H.R. Rivers, his admired friend and former doctor, was "neither sporting, nor Bohemian, nor eccentric, nor 'Socialist', but merely human and clear-headed and wise" (*D2*, 110), and it is clear that these are the qualities and the independent attitude that now represent his ideal. Rivers' sudden death later that year came as a terrible blow to him. But an even more important influence on Sassoon's life and work was his friendship with the poet Ralph Hodgson. Though a contemporary literary survey has little else to tell about him than that he was "a leading authority on bull terriers",[2] he was in fact very much a thinking poet, who spent whole evenings expounding his thoughts and ideas on a wide variety of subjects to a spellbound Sassoon.

Ralph Edwin Hodgson (1871-1962) never liked to talk about his youth. He was born in a poor family in county Durham, but his father died when he was still a boy and he was brought up by friends in Surrey. In his teens he travelled to America, but returned to London in the early 1890s to start work as a black-and-white artist for papers and magazines. In 1913 he founded 'The Sign of the Flying Fame' (together with Claud Lovat Fraser and Holbrook Jackson), a publishing house that produced poetry in beautifully designed chapbooks and broadsides. His first volume of poetry, *The Last Blackbird and Other Lines*, was published in 1907, but it was with his second volume, *Poems* (1917), that he established his reputation as a poet.

It was this volume that contained 'The Song of Honour', a long poem that won him the Polignac prize in 1914 and which A.E. Housman called one of the best poems written in the twentieth century. Sassoon also greatly admired this poem, in which the poet attempts to interpret a mystical experience, a moment of vision in which he saw in nature a manifestation of spiritual splendour. Hodgson's attitude is best understood through 'The Mystery', in which God takes the poet by the hand and gives him a rose from a red rose tree:

British universities, as Churton Collins had recommended, they usually chose to go abroad. Lascelles Abercrombie was the only Georgian to build up an academic career in England; Edmund Blunden, Robert Nichols and Ralph Hodgson all accepted academic posts in Japan in the 1920s. Sassoon's lack of formal training made an academic career a virtual impossibility, and so he was extremely lucky when on the death of his aunt Rachel in 1927, he inherited £30,000.

Rachel Beer was Alfred Sassoon's younger sister. After his family's excommunication, she had continued to pay them secret visits at Weirleigh. In 1887 she too committed the mortal sin of marrying outside the Jewish faith. Her husband Frederick Beer was the son of a German Jew, who had made a fortune on the London Stock Exchange. On his death he left his son two papers, *The Observer* (which he had bought in 1870) and *The Electrician* as well as an annual income of £20,000. But Frederick Beer's poor health prevented him from taking an active interest in journalism and so his wife took over his duties from him: Rachel Beer became editor of *The Observer* and bought the *Sunday Times* in 1893.

She could never accept the fact that her husband would not recover and Sassoon poignantly records how in 1897, when she bought him a cricket bat, she ordered a complete cricket outfit for her husband ("stumps and all"), although at the time he was a permanent invalid who never left his bedroom (*OC*, 97). By that time it was increasingly obvious that her nerves were suffering under the strain. Her behaviour became more and more erratic: she asked all publishers to send her review copies for the *Sunday Times*, but hardly ever opened any of the parcels. In 1899 she sent her cousin Siegfried a *Bibliography of the World's Municipal Literature* as a Christmas present; he was thirteen at the time. When her husband died in 1903 she broke down completely and was placed in the care of the Commissioners of Lunacy the following year. The papers were sold and Rachel retired to a house in Tunbridge Wells, not far from Weirleigh. Theresa Sassoon and her children continued to visit her there. In 1924 Sassoon was told by his mother that his aunt was not supposed to live much longer. He noted in his diary:

> This means, I suppose, that we shall be inundated with 'poor' Auntie Rachel's money within a year or two. (We have been waiting for it about twenty years!)

Hope it won't interfere with my efforts to live austerely and simply. Must try and forget about it. It will bring me no peace that I can't attain on my present income. (*D3*, 124)

But his aunt lived on for another three years. When Sassoon finally did receive his inheritance, in 1927, the desire for an austere and simple life had lost much of its appeal.

II

In the summer of 1924 Sassoon went for a driving tour through England and Wales. On 27 August he was in Llansantffraed where he visited the grave of Henry Vaughan. He later said that the poem he wrote that day to commemorate the visit, 'At the Grave of Henry Vaughan', was the first written in his new poetic voice.[4] Free from the restraints that his aspirations to conform to his idea of a man of letters had placed upon him, he had decided to follow his religious instincts and embark on yet another "quest for 'autognosis'", one that would last the rest of his life. The Heart's Journey, then, would be an inward journey, a quest for self-knowledge, an exploration of the essential self: the soul. It marks the beginning of the poet's retreat from worldly affairs.

Sassoon was almost forty-two when *The Heart's Journey* was published in August 1928. The book is a great improvement on its immediate predecessors, *Picture Show* (1919) and *Satirical Poems* (1926) in that it has a personal and unifying tone, a tone that was to recur in all the volumes of poetry that were to follow. It contains thirty-five poems, written between 1918[5] and 1927. The new poetic voice is very soft and unobtrusive; unlike the voice of his war poetry it makes no direct appeals. The reader overhears rather than that he is being addressed. It is intensely sincere and intimate, but the mood is fragile; the poetry has very little power and depends almost completely on the reader's empathy. It was by its very nature a poetry that could only appeal to the very few. This only made the process of publishing all the more painful. Geoffrey Keynes,[6] who got to know Sassoon in the early 1930s and helped him prepare some of his later volumes, recalled that

Sassoon had ambivalent feelings about publishing his poems. While publication seemed to be an invasion of his privacy, he disliked being ignored. He knew that his poems were old-fashioned in form, at a time when Eliot (whom SS always referred to as 'Towering Tom') held the favour of the critics, but he believed in his own quiet Muse and was very sensitive to criticism.[7]

Bernard Bergonzi is obviously one of the critics who have little time for it: "the bulk of his later poetry, sententious or laxly pastoral, is carefully written and overpoweringly dull."[8] This may seem an unfair and curt dismissal, but it is a fact that this modest and personal poetry lays itself wide open to such a charge. The journey into his own past which Sassoon was undertaking was in essence not all that different from that of T.S. Eliot in *Four Quartets*: both poets turned away from the world in search of spiritual strength. But the extreme limitations of Sassoon's poetry stand out in comparison. By the time he came to write *Four Quartets* Eliot had changed his mind about the position of the poet and had become more concerned about his audience. In 'The Music of Poetry' (1942) he wrote that "while poetry attempts to convey something beyond what can be conveyed in prose rhythms, it remains, all the same, one person talking to another". He then went on to say that "Every revolution in poetry is apt to be, and sometimes to announce itself to be a return to common speech",[9] thus proclaiming a viewpoint that had been defended by the Georgians and vilified by the Modernists.[10] Both *Murder in the Cathedral* and *Four Quartets* mark Eliot's "growing preoccupation with what he had called the 'social usefulness' of the poet that he should adopt the tone of someone addressing an audience, speaking out loud rather than to himself".[11]

Sassoon had reached the heights of 'social usefulness' in his war poetry, but in the poetry he wrote to chronicle his spiritual pilgrimage this position was completely reversed. Though he remained true to his dictum of simplicity in poetry, the idea of a readership played no part whatsoever in its conception; he is completely self-absorbed, disregarding the idea of social usefulness. If this was to be the position of 'prophetic aloofness' that he and Hodgson agreed on as the ideal position for the poet, then it is strange that the prophetic element in this poetry is largely absent. The tone of most of the poems is strictly personal; no attempt is made at widening his scope into an investigation of the human condition. The true prophetic outlook in this respect is Eliot's; many of the ideas he puts forward in 'East Coker' are almost exactly the same as Sassoon's, but Eliot presents these ideas – the need to be in harmony with nature, humility as the only true wisdom and the importance of childhood – as essential to human happiness and understanding. Sassoon's observations, on the other hand, are all part of his self-analysis and are never presented as a general statement on human life. In comparison with Eliot's handbook the record of Sassoon's spiritual journey reads as no more than a case-study.

III

The Heart's Journey opens with an invocation to the Muse, though on this journey the poet's Muse will not be some outside spirit, but his own soul; at the very outset this shows the self-centred nature of this poetry. 'Song, be my soul' is an early poem, written in October 1923, in which Sassoon announces the first phase of his pilgrimage, a return to his childhood:

> Song, be my soul; set forth the fairest part
> Of all that moved harmonious through my heart;
> And gather me to your arms; for we must go
> To childhood's garden when the moon is low
> And over the leaf-shadow-latticed grass
> The whispering wraiths of my dead selves repass.

One of the aims of this return is to discover the origins of the contradictory elements in his character:

> In me the cave-man clasps the seer,
> And garlanded Apollo goes
> Chanting to Abraham's deaf ear.
> In me the tiger sniffs the rose.
> Look in my heart, kind friends, and tremble,
> Since there your elements assemble.
>   (VII, ll. 7-12)

And he also realizes that the spiritual journey he is about to undertake is one he will have to go alone:

> Alone ... The word is life endured and known.
> It is the stillness where our spirits walk
> And all but inmost faith is overthrown.
> (XI, ll. 8-10)

The "inmost faith", the self-knowledge, introduces the religious element; now that he has turned his back on the world the search for the unknown self has become the search for a religious belief. Sassoon's habit of over-using certain words is immediately noticeable. In his war poetry it was words such as "stumbling" and "groping" and in his nature and lyrical poetry "gloom" and "glade"; these words still occur frequently, but "Elysian" and "Paradise" are new favourites which illustrate the religious concern. This religious theme is further expanded in 'Farewell to a Room', where Sassoon describes the room he has lived in for five years as a part of himself: "You tranquil-toned interior, void of me / seems part of my own self which I can see". In the final lines of the poem, Sassoon calls his room a "Cell", thus comparing himself with a monk and ultimately implying that the heart's journey is a pilgrimage.

This idea is strengthened by Sassoon's description of the destination of his journey as a Paradise or Elysium. In April 1925 he writes in his diary about "an inward sense of homesickness for that land where I would be – that Elysium, forever deluding me with its mirage in the desert of my frustrated and distorted desires" (*D3*, 235). This Elysium is described as "ultimate spring", and, as in Sassoon's early poetry, spring is associated with youth. Thus, in III:

> As I was walking in the gardens where
> Spring touched the glooms with green, stole over me
> A sense of wakening leaves that filled the air
> With bodings of Elysian days to be.
>
> ...
>
> It seemed I stood with Youth on the calm verge
> Of some annunciation that should bring
> With flocks of silver angels, ultimate Spring
> Whence all that I had longed for might emerge.

Michael Thorpe has rightly described the poems in *The Heart's Journey* as "*preparations* for the journey: setting the house in order, checking its contents, deciding what will be needed and what can — and must — be left behind".[12] One of the things that must be left behind if he wants to return to his childhood state are the intellectual aspirations he once held. From now on he no longer writes about "intelligence" but about "wisdom", and for him "wisdom" is not the knowledge of experience accumulated in the course of one's life but the quietist's humility and acceptance of all that is. These are the elements he found in the work of the seventeenth-century Devotional poets, George Herbert, Thomas Traherne and, especially, Henry Vaughan. The poem he wrote at Vaughan's graveside is that of the apprentice thanking his master for the important lessons he has been taught:

> Here faith and mercy, wisdom and humility
> (Whose influence shall prevail for evermore)
> Shine. And this lowly grave tells Heaven's tranquillity.
> And here stand I, a suppliant at the door.

For Sassoon, the importance of childhood lies in its innocent enjoyment of life, its naive expectancy, and in the child's nature being uncorrupted by worldly experience. He had left his man-of-letters' desires and ambitions behind him and now only desired to return to this state of grace, so perfectly expressed by Vaughan:

> Dear, harmless age! the short, swift span,
> Where weeping virtue parts with man;
> Where love without lust dwells, and bends
> What way we please, without self-ends.
> An age of mysteries! which he
> Must live twice, that would God's face see.[13]

Sassoon echoes this view in *The Heart's Journey* XII, where looking at the stars, unchanged since his youth, he regrets "Our loss of this loved heritage of light". This association of youth with light is part of a fundamental juxtaposition that underlies all this poetry. Youth is associated with light, morning, spring, innocence and intuition; this is juxtaposed with adulthood, darkness, night, autumn, experience and unwisdom.

In the poems that follow Sassoon takes stock of his present situation and desires, of his need to be in harmony with nature ('Strangeness of Heart', XIII), how his main sources of comfort are music (XIV) and the wisdom he finds in the works of great poets ('Grandeur of God', XV).

IV

In *The Heart's Journey* Sassoon does not yet embark on his pilgrimage; he is still the suppliant pleading for his soul's release, that it may leave behind the prison of age and knowledge:

> O inwardness of trust, – intelligence,–
> Release my soul through every door of sense:
> Give me new sight; O grant me strength to find
> From lamp and flower simplicity of mind.
> ('A Midnight Interior', XXIV, ll. 11-14)

The homely epithet and the symbolic use of the light and dark are dominant symbols in what I consider Sassoon's most important post-war volume, *Vigils* (1934-35).[14]

By the time *Vigils* was published, Sassoon had also withdrawn from the world in a more literal sense. The period 1928-1933 had been an eventful one in his private life. In 1927 he had first met the Honourable Stephen Tennant at one of Osbert Sitwell's dinner parties. Spoilt, privileged and extremely effeminate, Tennant (1906-1987) was completely enamoured of his own beauty, and narcissistic comments on his enchanting features are a favourite theme in his diaries ("You were beautiful this evening, Stephen, your hair and skin were lovely, your eyelashes have grown, your eyes were very blue with just a *soupçon* of *'bleu argente'* on the lids").[15]

When Sassoon first met him he was in his early twenties and widely known as a society beauty. Middleclass homosexuals such as Sassoon, Cecil Beaton and E.M. Forster all fell under the spell of this beautiful child, partly because they admired the way in which a true aristocrat like Tennant flaunted his homosexuality without ever being disconcerted by the hostile reactions that his extravagant behaviour sometimes elicited.

Sassoon fell madly in love with Tennant and courted him with gifts and compliments. The reticent soldier-poet and the ethereal socialite made an odd couple, though they did have many things in common: both had been brought up by an over-protective mother, both had lost a brother in the war and both their mothers had for that reason become involved in spiritualism. They also shared a love for art and literature, especially the Russian ballet and the writings of Walter Pater.

Tennant was arguably the love of Sassoon's life, though there is no evidence to suggest that their affair was ever consummated.[16] At first they were very happy together, because Sassoon was as eager to give love as Tennant was keen to receive it. Tennant's health was always poor, among many other ailments he suffered from tuberculosis, and his doctors prescribed frequent rest cures. Tennant and Sassoon experienced their happiest times together as invalid and nurse in Haus Hirth, a pension in the Bavarian Highlands during the winter of 1928-29 and on a trip to France and Italy from November 1929 to May 1930. Sassoon's poem 'In Sicily', written for Stephen and published in *Vigils*, is the only reminder in his *oeuvre* of these glorious days.

The last three years of their affair were desperately unhappy for Sassoon. They returned to Wilsford, Tennant's country estate in Wiltshire, in May 1930. Tennant's health soon suffered another relapse, which made him retire to his bed. Sassoon moved in to act as his faithful nurse and companion. The fact that he almost immediately began to discourage visits from Tennant's friends may well have been done with the best of intentions, but it also suggests a possessive streak in Sassoon's character that is reminiscent of Theresa Sassoon's possessive love for her husband. Tennant soon grew tired of Sassoon's constant presence and announced that he would prefer to employ a professional nurse. Undeterred, Sassoon rented a house near Wilsford in October 1931 so that he could still be near to his loved one.

What he did not realize was that for Tennant the magic of their relationship had gradually disappeared. For two more years Sassoon refused to be put off. He kept himself informed of Tennant's condition, and when he lost confidence in the doctors that were treating him, he asked his close friend Sir Henry Head to go and see the patient. Sir Henry recommended that Tennant be moved to the Cassell Hospital for Functional Nervous Disorders in Penhurst, Kent, not far from Weirleigh. From there, Tennant dictated a letter to Sassoon in May 1933 in which he finally told his former lover that he did not want to see him anymore.

While still recovering from this blow, Sassoon was introduced to Hester Gatty at the Wilton Pageant on 5 June. Their mutual friend Edith Olivier described her as "exquisite [...] and very much like Stephen".[17]

Hester Gatty (1905-1973) was the daughter of Sir Stephen Herbert Gatty, a distinguished lawyer and judge, and a niece of Mrs Juliana Ewing, author of popular Victorian children's stories. She had a very sheltered upbringing (according to her son she could not even boil an egg at the time of her marriage),[18] and spent much of her childhood at her parents' estate in the Isle of Mull. Her interest in literature and the arts was never more than that of a dilettante, but the was a member of The Scratch Society, which privately published small volumes of its members' verses. Sassoon met her again in September and a month later he wrote to Geoffrey Keynes to announce his engagement: "we were 'made for one another', as the saying is".[19]

V

In spite of his hectic private life Sassoon was aware of the political developments in Europe. The Great War had come as a total surprise to the ignorant young man he had been in 1914. But in the early 1930s he was better informed and quick to realize that European peace was yet again under threat. In 1933 he published *The Road to Ruin*, a slim volume of eight poems in which he once more adopted the prophet-role, warning his readers about the devastating effect another war might have. The poems themselves have little merit; the two most interesting being 'A Premonition' and 'An Unveiling'. In 'A Premonition' the speaker's ghost visits the National Gallery after a gas-attack has wiped out the population, only to find that the timeless achievements of man's creative powers are not proof against man's destructive capabilities:

> The claim
> Of Art was disallowed. Past locks
> And walls crass war had groped, and gas
> Was tarnishing each gilded frame.

'An Unveiling' is written in the style of his hard-hitting Great War satires, cleverly updated to drive the message home. Survivors of the gas attacks have gathered to commemorate the dead. The President's oration ends:

> We honour here' (he paused) 'our Million Dead;
> Who, as a living poet has nobly said,
> 'Are now forever London'. Our bequest
> Is to rebuild, for What-they-died-for's sake,
> A bomb-proof roofed Metropolis, and to make
> Gas-drill compulsory. *Dulce et decorum est...*'

The echoes of Brooke and Owen serve as a reminder of how little has been learned from the Great War.

Sassoon himself made no further attempts to make his voice heard as a warning prophet after the publication of this volume. In December 1933 he married Hester Gatty in Christchurch, Hampshire, after a courtship of only six months. When they returned from their honeymoon the couple moved into their new home, Heytesbury House, near Warminster in Wiltshire in May 1934. During these months Sassoon was uncharacteristically carefree and happy. A slightly bemused T.E. Lawrence, who visited them at Heytesbury House in July 1934, reported on his visit to Geoffrey Keynes:

> All visitors there intrude, as yet, I think. He and she are like children alone in the world. The huge house, which they are furnishing for a song in memory of the mansion style: the gardens, so lavishly kept up, the quiet sun-impregnated park: the two laughing strangers running about it, making pretence to own it. Yes, Heytesbury was rather like one of the great villas of Roman Britain, after the Legions had gone.
>
> S.S. looked abnormally happy. Much of his hesitant diction has been forgotten. He speaks easily, and is full of private jests. He looks so well, too. I was told that he captains the local cricket team, and the village postman (having exhausted the war books) is going on to his poetry.[20]

The strange and ominous simile comparing Heytesbury House with a villa in post-Roman Britain and the description of Sassoon as being "abnormally happy" clearly suggest that Lawrence did not expect Sassoon's blissful mood to last very long.

The writer Dennis Wheatley had been billeted at Heytesbury House as a young subaltern in August 1916, and though his fellow-officers and he had enjoyed the park and the garden, "the great disadvantage of the place, as far as we were concerned, was its isolation".[21] That isolation was, of course, part of the appeal for Sassoon.

Though he kept a keen eye on the developments in the world he had no longer any desire to take part in them. For in *Vigils* he again and again rejects 'the world', which for him is the man-made world, as opposed to Nature and Heaven. The title itself is crucially important to understand the mood of the volume. Not only does *Vigils* refer to the nocturnal hours of quiet and solitude when the lonely pilgrim continued his inward journey, "Lone heart, learning / By one light burning / Slow discerning of worldhood's worth" ('Vigils', ll.1-3), it also reflects the total disillusionment the poet feels with the world.

As was discussed in the first chapter, Sassoon considered his poetry to be his real autobiography. And when he compiled his *Collected Poems* in 1961 he took care to mark the several stages in his development. It is important to notice the sharp contrast between the "morning-minded" young poet of the *Lyrical Poems 1908-1916* and the disillusioned mature poet of *Vigils*. The underlying juxtaposition of *The Heart's Journey* has been expanded to include his whole *oeuvre*: it is the contrast of light and dark, of youth and adulthood, of expectation and disillusionment.

One of the things Sassoon relates in *Vigils* is what his pilgrimage has so far taught him. He confirms that solitude and stillness are the required conditions for the journey:

> I have discovered from the pride
> Of temporal trophydoms, this theme,
> That silence is the ultimate guide.
> ('Elected Silence', ll.2-4)

The title of this poem, 'Elected Silence', was taken from the opening line of Gerald Manley Hopkins' 'The Habit of Perfection', written in 1866, the year Hopkins joined the Roman Catholic Church. Sassoon would not be received into this Church until 1957, which is a reminder of how long and painstaking his journey was.

He seems to have come to the conclusion that not only the gaining of personal experience was the wrong road to take, but now that he has taken it, it has become an obstacle for him. His worldly-wisdom has destroyed his ability to be amazed, to understand instinctively. Why this is so important to him is best explained by what he wrote in his biography of George Meredith, whose views on Nature he shared:

> the human race can rise to higher things by understanding its Mother Earth. Man must attain to the spiritual through the natural, not through the supernatural (*M*, 206).

In adulthood Sassoon had lost contact with nature. This is the theme of 'Farewell to Youth':

> spring
> Rests in the sunshine of the Square.
> Out there the leaves rejoice; they bring
> Some secret spell I may not share.

The poet is left out and unaffected by the "secret spell"; the reason for this is given in the closing lines, "Within my heart's mysterious walls / The dreamer that was youth lies dead". Using his by now familiar homely image of his heart as a room, Sassoon suggests that his inability to understand nature also makes it impossible for him to understand himself, and that locked up within his "heart's mysterious walls" his youthful spirit has been suffocated. This leaves the poet completely powerless; the road he has to take has forever been cut off by his mature experience. The longing for death, already a theme in *The Heart's Journey*, has now been explained, for the peace he is seeking is for him only attainable in death:

> I seek no mystery now beyond the hill
> And wait no change but to become more lonely,
> No freedom till the sleep that sets me free.
>
> ('War Experience', ll. 12-14)

Since it is part of his mature experience, Sassoon now also distances himself from his war-protest, "Not much remains, twelve winters later, of the hater / of purgatorial pains". In the wonderfully evocative last lines of this poem the poet seems to suggest that his actual war-experiences have become more and more unreal to him:

> And somewhat softly booms
> A Somme bombardment: almost unbelieved-in looms
> The day-break sentry staring over Kiel Trench crater.

Within the light/dark imagery of *Vigils* it is significant that it is twelve winters, not twelve summers later, and that it is the day-break sentry who is "almost unbelieved in".

As a pilgrim on a spiritual journey it is now the metaphysical experiences that have become much more of a reality to Sassoon. The "dreams of the pit" he had written about in his 1917 war poem, 'Does It Matter', were haunting him still, especially in the form of the ghosts of the friends that were killed:

> Again the dead, the dead again demanding
> To be, O now to be remembered strongly –
> The dead, reminding mindsight of their darkness –
> The dead who overhear us, listening longly.
> (*Vigils* 22, ll. 1-4)

At times the weary traveller tries to escape from their world of silence and darkness and force himself back into daily reality:

> Break silence. You have listened overlong
> To muttering mind-wrought voices. Call for lights.
> Prove these persistent haunting presences wrong
> Who mock and stultify your days and nights.
> (*Vigils* 17, ll. 1-4)

But for one who was as inclined to meditation as Sassoon was, there was no escaping from thinking about the past.

To avoid thoughts about the war, he goes back further in the past, to the days of his youth. This is the second reason why his early years become such an important theme in his later life and work: not only were these the years in which he was in close contact with nature, but they also allow him to ruminate without being haunted by his war memories. On a visit to Weirleigh, his childhood home, his 'mindsight' conjures up images of his past:

> My past has gone to bed. Upstairs in clockless rooms
> My past is fast asleep. But mindsight reillumes
> Here in my ruminant head the days where dust lies deep.
> Sleep-walkers empty-eyed come strangely down the stairs
> These are my dead selves, – once proud, once passionate with young prayers,
> Once vehement with vows.
>
> <div align="right">(<i>Vigils</i> 9, ll.1-6).</div>

The youthful prayers and vows were not realized in adulthood, and Sassoon admits that they were only dreams of his "Ignorant selves" (l.7). But for him 'ignorance' has lost its negative connotations: if he was ignorant before he discovered "worldhood's worth" (i.e. the war) then he would much rather be ignorant again. In the looks of the ghosts of his former selves he finds "Simplicities unlearned long since and left behind" (l.10), and as "unlearned" clearly indicates, he now considers that a great loss.

All that experience had given him were the disillusionment and the haunting memory of those killed in the war. Sassoon accepts that "On life's one forward track" ('In Sicily', l.2) what is done cannot be undone; he believes that he will only find lasting peace in death. But, as he explains in 'Unwisdom', in the naive and carefree dreams of his youth he can at least find a temporary escape:

> To see with different eyes
> From every day
> And find in dream disguise
> Worlds far away–
>
> To walk in childhood's land
> With trusting looks
> And oldly understand
> Youth's fairy-books

> Thus our unwisdom brings
> Release

For this reason his childhood becomes increasingly important to him, and his gradual idealization of his youth brings it ever nearer to the "Angel-infancy" of Henry Vaughan's 'The Retreat':

> Happy those early days! when I
> Shined in my Angel-infancy.
> Before I understood this place
> Appointed for my second race.

The Heart's Journey was published in the same year as *Memoirs of a Fox-Hunting Man*, and a year after the publication of *Vigils* in 1935, Sassoon began writing *The Old Century*, which again dealt with his childhood years and which he called "A happy dream, which relieved my troubled mind".[22] It was in his prose works that Sassoon tried to recapture the happiness and innocence of youth. Disappointed with life, he did not expect much from either the present or the future, and preferred to travel back in the mind to the past:

> life, encountered and unmasked in variant shapes,
> Dissolves in dust and cloud, and thwartingly escapes.
> But in remembered eyes of youth my dreams remain.
> They were my firstling friends. I have returned again.
> (*Vigils* 7, ll.11-14)

One is reminded of the unconsciously prophetic words Sassoon wrote nearly twenty years earlier in 'The Old Huntsman': "So I've loved / My life; and when the good years are gone down / Discover what I've lost".

VI

T.E. Lawrence thought the poems in *Vigils* exquisite, but also warned Sassoon not to pursue into the same direction: "I shouldn't like you to go on writing *Vigils*, world without end. They are seasonal fruits, but lovely. You can dare them because of your past fighting: and those of us who have deserved a rest will feel them and be grateful to you".[23] Whether Lawrence, one of Sassoon's closest friends, foresaw that it was indeed Sassoon's natural inclination to follow along the same path, will have to remain a matter of speculation. He was killed in a motor-cycle accident five months later. But it is tempting to explain the lack of cohesion in Sassoon's next volume, *Rhymed Ruminations* (1940), as a result of his attempts to force himself to change direction, a change of direction that went emotionally against the grain.

Whereas in *Vigils* title and contents were united in a mood of concentrated quietism, suggesting that the poems were predominantly written during the long nocturnal hours of contemplation that the poet spent in his room, in *Rhymed Ruminations* there is a sense of opening out, Heytesbury House and the surrounding countryside providing the setting for most of the poems. The fragile atmosphere that Sassoon managed to evoke in *Vigils* is not sustained in this volume. The alliterative title itself is a most unfortunate choice in that its misplaced jocularity makes it rather sound like one of Stephen Leacock's humorous books.[24] Its lighthearted tone in no way reflects the contents of the volume, but Sassoon probably chose it to show that he still had a sense of proportion and had no desire to be taken 'deadly serious' (in 'Thoughts in 1938' he refers to "my unambitious mid-maturity").

The opening lines of the first poem suggest a similar jocular mood: "I am that man who with a luminous look / Sits up at night to write a ruminant book", but the serious tenor of the rest of the poem makes clear that this cannot have been his intention. As with the satirical poems, which show him believing that his use of pompous language would achieve a humorous note, so here he apparently did not realize that his choice of words and rhyme created an unwanted, comic effect. All this leaves one with the distinct impression that Sassoon's poetic ear did not have perfect pitch and that his sense of register was at times seriously flawed. Edward Marsh responded to these lines by sending Sassoon a satirical reply, "I am that man who with a luminous nose / Sits up at night to write voluminous prose",[25] but even this far from subtle hint could not persuade Sassoon that a revision was called for.

The importance of the geographical setting is reflected in the titles of the poems ('Eulogy on My House', 'In Heytesbury Wood', 'On Edington Hill', 'A Local Train of Thought', 'Blunden's Beech').

Though the poet describes himself in the opening poem as a horseman: "that man who loves to ride alone / When landscapes wear his mind's autumnal tone", the way he perceives his surroundings is rather like that of Thomas Traherne's 'Walking': "To *walk* abroad is, not with Eyes / But Thoughts, the Fields to see and prize".

The thoughts in Sassoon's case are those in *Vigils*, but whereas that volume was mainly theoretical, in that he there first formulated his beliefs within the confines of his room, in *Rhymed Ruminations* he puts them to a practical test, applying them to the here and now of Heytesbury House and the surrounding countryside of the 1930s. It is here that he at times becomes truly prophetic, as when in 'Thoughts in 1932' – a poem that might equally well have been included in *The Road to Ruin* – he observes twenty-seven war-planes above Stonehenge and reflects that

> In years to come
> Poor panick-stricken hordes will hear that hum,
> And Fear will be synonymous with Flight.

In this poem the elements of time are united: the poet observes in the present (1932) the future (the planes) flying over the past (Stonehenge), and throughout this volume Sassoon attempts to take a historical overview of man and the human condition: his arrogance, cruelty and blindness, lack of humility and the essential insignificance of the individual in space and time, and this world is then juxtaposed with the timeless worlds of death and the dream.

The military manoeuvres that he witnesses on his rides through the Wiltshire countryside are a constant reminder of the threat of another world war. In 'On Edington Hill' and '878-1935' these preparations for a new war in a part of the country that once saw Alfred the Great defeat the Vikings convince him that human history is repetitive rather than progressive. It is a practical illustration of what he had written in *Vigils*:

> Enormous murmurings from the mind of man
> Accumulate as history; and from the void
> Obliquities of ignorance which began
> His growth, blind hordes have laboured and destroyed.
> ('Memorandum', ll. 5-8)

In rejecting the idea of human progress Sassoon follows the pessimistic view of Victorian poets such as Arnold, Hardy and Housman. But his humility takes him further: in "Tell me not here, it needs not saying" (*Last Poems*, XL), A.E. Housman had drawn attention to nature's indifference towards man:

> Possess, as I possessed a season,
> The countries I resign,
>
> ...
>
> For nature, heartless, witless nature,
> Will neither care nor know
> What stranger's feet may find the meadow
> And trespass there and go

Sassoon is struck by man's arrogance in simply claiming possession of nature:

> Possession thus we claim
> Of natural sights and sounds,
> Who purchase earth with pounds
> And take it all for granted.
> We nothings use a name,
> Nor ask whence acorns came
> Before the oak was planted.
> ('Property', ll. 8-14)

Seen in the light of time, it is his own brief existence that he is reminded of against the steady background of nature's continuous presence, and nature thus becomes a link with a future he will never know:

> Beech, cedar, lime, when I'm dead Me,
> You'll stand, lawn-shadowing, tree by tree;
> And in your greenery, while you last,
> I shall survive who shared your past.
> ('Outlived by Trees', ll. 5-8)

Though the humility is undoubtedly sincere, the poetical expression is awkward rather than meek: both in phrase ("dead Me") and form

Sassoon never comes even close to his main examples Herbert and Vaughan. In more light-hearted mood, he often lapses into the style of his satirical poems, his love of flowery adjectives resulting in the kind of over-written passages he had satirized in his Humbert Wolfe/Pynchbeck Lyre parodies: "That vista'd paradise which in his time had thriven / Those trees to which in cogitating strolls he'd given / Perennial forethought..." ('In Heytesbury Wood', ll. 9-11).

Ghosts are a recurrent feature in Sassoon's work. Elsewhere he described himself as "a believer in the power of spiritual presences" (*SJ*, 54), but the ghosts are now no longer the spirits of men who were killed in the war. In *Rhymed Ruminations* Sassoon gradually draws a subtle parallel between ghosts and the hidden inner-self. In 'While Reading a Ghost Story' the poet reflects on the mysteries of ancient buildings:

> Old houses have their secrets. Passions haunt them.
> When day's celestials go, abhorred ones taunt them.
> Inside our habitations darkness dwells.
> While dusk of dawn is on the unwatched stair
> And lofty windows whiten strangely, – there
> What presence thins – with what frustrated spells?

The ghost as a visitor from the world of the dead is free from the restraints of time. And as such for Sassoon the ghost, the old house, and the world of the dead have their parallels in Man's timeless soul, his body and the world of dreams.

In 'Old Music' he makes this parallel explicit, when he refers to his mind as "that shuttered room", but this inner world finds its fullest expression in 'Silly Sooth', which is the central poem of the volume (as is suggested by the parallel between the two alliterative titles, *Rhymed Ruminations* and 'Silly Sooth')

> Do not deny your dreams
> They are the absurd release
> From worldly wisdom themes
> To paradoxic peace.
>
> When sleep invites your mind
> To push the unhaspèd door,

> Be glad to leave behind
> The unrest of Evermore.
>
> There in that reasonless clime
> You are yourself; and thither
> You float, set free from Time
> And all its whence and whither.
>
> Farewell to hands and feet;
> Good-bye to mouth and eyes.
> Dreamer, go forth to greet
> What world within you lies.
> ('Silly Sooth', ll. 5-16)

At times he is unable to tell ghosts and dream-images apart; in 'Tragitones' he writes about the "stilled interior themes" that lure him away from reality: "These vistas where imagined presences / Lead me away from life, – loved ghosts or dreams?".

Sassoon's quest for a state of grace thus becomes a quest for a state of timelessness. He believes that as he grows older the loss of physical strength is compensated by an increase in his mental powers, and that it is especially his mind's eye that benefits in this respect:

> Losing youngness, the eye sees clearer
> (Inward eye, while our sight grows blurred.)
> ('Heart and Soul', ll. 2-3)

For the mind's eye and memory there is no difference between distance in time and distance in space. This is why in "A View of Old Exeter" he describes a painting depicting a scene from the 1850s as "A window on my wall", for he can now look back into time as easily as he can look out over Heytesbury Park. In 'Blunden's Beech' he recalls a favourite tree which he had named after his friend Edmund Blunden and where he sometimes used to rest, remembering lines by John Clare.[26] That the one is far away and the other is dead makes no difference: "The mind can make its legends live and sing"; it knows no boundaries of time and space.

The picture of the poet that emerges in *Rhymed Ruminations* is that of a man who is through with life and actively preparing for what is to come after:

> Heart, be brave as you go to your grave;
> Soul, be girt for the race unrun.
>> ('Heart and Soul', ll.10-11)

Sassoon's rejection of life is stated most clearly in the poems he wrote after the birth of his son in 1935. In 'Meeting and Parting' he addresses his child as "my self reborn", as if he relinquishes his own existence altogether on the birth of his 'successor'. That it is not just his own life but life in general that he finds undesirable is made plain in the closing lines:

> Alone I stand before my new-born son;
> Alone he lies before me, doomed to live.
> Beloved, when I am dying and all is done,
> Look on my face and say that you forgive.

The poet's preoccupation with his childhood is part of his preparation for the life beyond (though *The Old Century and Seven More Years* was published two years before, the poems in *Rhymed Ruminations* were written before, during and after the writing of this autobiography): the years of his 'angel-infancy' were the closest he had come yet to a timeless world. The importance of the peace of mind that he has gained (or rather, regained) on his 'pilgrimage' is that he hopes he will be able to relive his childhood memories now that he is once more in tune with his former self:

> Can I record tranquillity intense
> With harmony of heart, – experience
> Like a rich memory's mind-lit monochrome?
> Winged lovely moments, can I call you home?
>> ('November Dusk', ll. 5-8)

This desire to return to his childhood is partly induced by his awareness of the ever increasing war threat. In 'Doggerel About Old Days' he writes that "In 1909 the future was a thing desired", and this is not just a reference to his younger self's state of blissful ignorance, but a reminder of the collective ignorance of the Edwardians. For Sassoon ignorance was indeed bliss; it was as an innocent child that he had been closest to the state of grace he is now seeking and he is quite unapologetic about the escapist nature of much of his work. About *The Old Century and Seven More Years* he said that it was partly written "to afford people nostalgic escape in those years of imminent catastrophe" (*LC*, 14), and it remained his favourite book.

Sassoon's escapism was not that of one who could not face up to reality and turned away from it; he *had* faced up to it, but now as a spiritual pilgrim he was mainly concerned with the next phase that lay *beyond* this earthly reality: the survival of the soul. This is not to say that from that moment reality was completely ignored. The threat of war is a constant presence in *Rhymed Ruminations*, and the two penultimate poems, 'The English Spirit' and 'Silent Service', both written in May 1940, are patriotic calls-to-arms celebrating the indomitable English spirit. That he was now part of the Home Front he had so viciously attacked during the Great War was an irony that completely escaped him: it is a role reversal he never ruminates on. In an anonymous review in *The Listener* of January 1956, Herbert Read attacked Sassoon for writing during the Second World War "exactly like the people he satirized in the First World War". Read might have had an even better point if he had referred to the two patriotic war poems in *Rhymed Ruminations*, but instead he had quoted from what Sassoon had written when he heard that his friend Rex Whistler, an officer in the Welsh Guards, had been killed in action in France in July 1944.[27] In an emotional outburst, Sassoon had then written that it was imperative that the Allies defeat "these powers of darkness" and that "Germany must expiate the crimes committed by the Nazis".

On reading Read's article, Sassoon was livid and he threatened to take legal action, but the BBC avoided a public row by asking Read to write a letter of apology which appeased Sassoon, though Read remained unrepentant about his attack.[28] Sassoon never defended himself against the charge, probably because he genuinely felt that there was not a grain of truth in Read's accusation. He must have been completely sincere in his belief that the two World Wars were fundamentally different, without ever wondering if it were perhaps his own perceptions that had changed. In February 1967 he made a similar distinction on religious grounds between the senseless waste of the Great War and the sacrifices of the Second World War when he wrote to a correspondent that "The second war was, anyhow, a crusade against a Satanic organisation, wasn't it?"[29]

And yet he was very much aware of the changes that had taken place in his life. In 'Progressions' he traces the different stages in his life, from the "lovely child alone" to the "youth, impassioned by he knows not what", and then the defeat at the hands of worldy wisdom in maturity: "A man, confounded by the facts of life". In this last stage he describes himself as "A mind, renouncing hopes and finding lost loves holy". By abandoning all earthly hopes he in fact declares that he considers his existence a 'Hell on Earth', his only comforts being the happy memories of his childhood and the longing for the soul's ultimate release. Like Christian in Bunyan's *Pilgrim's Progress* he had left the world behind, passing through the Wicket Gate in search of spiritual fulfilment. *The Heart's Journey*, *Vigils*, and *Rhymed Ruminations* comprise the first half of Sassoon's pilgrimage; in these volumes his religious spirit is in search of an answer, without as yet finding one. In 1961 he wrote to Dame Felicitas Corrigan:

> Looking through this evening a MS. volume of the poems I wrote in the 1930s, it seemed that my intuitions were of more value than my thoughts and philosophizings. (By the way, on the title-page of *Vigils* I wrote 'My heart and my flesh cry out for the living God' – but I had to wait 25 years to find him!)[30]

Two years earlier he had written to her referring to *The Heart's Journey* and *Vigils* as "a case of undirected emotional aspirations, which ended in the spiritual desolation that preceded my conversion".[31]

His spiritual journey was to remain the subject of his poetry, while in his prose works he devoted himself to the evocation of his happy childhood years. It was in these prose works that he was to find his true literary voice.

- Part II -

BACKWARD STEPS

Some men a forward motion love,
But I by backward steps would move.

           – Henry Vaughan, 'The Retreat'

CHAPTER 6

MEMOIRS OF A FOX-HUNTING MAN

I

In his diary entry for 26 March 1921 Sassoon notes how he walked home that evening after dinner at the Reform Club

> feeling dangerously confident in myself and the masterpiece that I'll be writing five, ten, fifteen or twenty years hence. That masterpiece has become a perfectly definite object in my existence, but it is curious, and rather disquieting, that I always dream of it as a novel or a prose drama, rather than as a poem or series of poems (*D2*, 53).

The man who considered himself a poet long before he actually became one now believed himself capable of writing a prose masterpiece, although until that moment he had never even tried writing fictional prose.

At that stage he was thinking of a book the main theme of which would be homosexuality, "another *Madame Bovary* dealing with sexual inversion, a book that the world *must* recognize and learn to understand!". The insistence on being understood is reminiscent of the Prophet Sassoon, but the book was never written.[1] In 1920 E.M. Forster lent him *Maurice*, his unpublished homosexual novel, which Sassoon greatly admired. Forster offered to show him some short stories, "less reputable than what you have seen, also unlike it, but they do purport to be literature. I am glad I have got this stuff off my chest".[2] It seems likely that Forster and Sassoon had discussed their homosexuality and that both planned to 'get it off their chests' by writing about it. In that same letter Forster tells Sassoon that "I much hope you will finish what you have begun: it's among the few things I have cared for", but what this refers to remains a mystery.

143

A diary entry in September 1922 illustrates Sassoon's state of mind at the time:

> *I am clear about one thing*: my present life [...] has been a struggle to shake off the past (sexual fetichism, vague piano-playing, athleticism of golf, cricket and hunting etc.). I have been trying to catch up with the intellectualism of [W.J.] Turner, the Sitwells, and all the rest of my post-war friends. (Whether their brains are worth catching up, I don't yet know.) I have consciously repressed the past; trying to *discard* it (avoiding Weirleigh). In the same way I get real satisfaction from discarding old clothes, books which have ceased to possess any interest or significance, destroying my manuscript failures and so on.
>
> My whole life has become involved in an internal resolve to *prepare* my mind for a big effort of creation. I want to write a book called *The Man Who Loved the World*, in which I will embody my whole passionate emotionalism toward every experience which collides with my poetic sensitiveness. But at present I have not any idea of the architectural plan of this edifice. (*D2*, 236-37)

And so he continued to practise his prose writing in his diaries: "somehow I've got a feeling that I am getting my roots deeper in the soil, through these recordings" (*D3*, 65-6). In June 1921 he wrote a story, the writing of which he enjoyed, although the result could not please him. Two years later he showed it to E.M. Forster, together with his 1921-1922 journal. Forster thought the journals "great work", but he agreed that the story was a failure. Why it failed he could not really say,[3] but he suggested a different working method. "If it fails we must try something else, for certainly the stuff is inside you – indeed it is 'out' in your journal" (*D3*, 37).

This last remark about the qualities of his journal stuck in Sassoon's mind, and at some stage he must have combined it with some earlier advice from his literary mentor Edmund Gosse, who, in November 1918, had urged him to write a long poem: "He suggested that I might draw on my sporting experiences for typical country figures – the squire, the doctor, the parson, and so on" (*SJ*, 100). And when, in 1925, he found that an attempt to read the first part of

R.H. Mottram's war-trilogy *The Spanish Farm 1914-1918* (1925) only routed out "a muddle of morose memories from the lumber room of my own war experience" (*D3*, 220), this may well have suggested the juxtaposition of his own pre-war life and his war-experiences as a framework for his book. A few days later, at the Reform Club, he read J. R. Ackerley's recently published play *The Prisoners of War*, and he enthusiastically tells a friend about the new idea this has given him:

> I showed him the book, explaining that the hero is a tormented homosexual officer, which led me to dilate rather rashly on the subject of dealing with that theme in literature. 'Some day I shall write my autobiography,' I said, adding that I am accumulating material in my diaries (*D3*, 234).

The Prisoners of War was Ackerley's first play. Like Sassoon, he had been a second lieutenant in an infantry regiment and the first draft of the play was written while he was a POW in a neutral internment camp in Switzerland. Set in a POW-camp, it tells the story of a group of officers, one of whom, Jim Conrad, is secretly in love with a nineteen-year-old fellow inmate. Though its homosexual theme is never made explicit, it was easily recognizable: "I have heard you do not much like the fair sex," a merry Swiss widow asks Conrad. "The fair sex? Which sex is that?" he replies. In spite of excellent reviews the play had only a short run in the West End. It is likely that Sassoon went to see it, though he has left no record of it in his diary. But reading the play had made a deep impression on him: "I so seldom read anything even remotely connected with 'the subject nearest my heart' that almost any work of that kind causes a peculiar emotional disturbance in me" (*D3*, 235).

In June 1918 he had written to E.M. Forster that "A novel dealing with the bad side of the officer class in wartime would add something to the indictment against militarism",[4] but after reading Ackerley's play he thought it better to use his wartime experiences in a novel with a homosexual theme. Whether it was caution (Forster too decided never to publish *Maurice* during his lifetime) or some other reason is unclear, but at some stage he must have decided not to make homosexuality a theme in his book, but to restrict himself to his experiences as a sportsman and a soldier, for these form the basic ingredients of *Memoirs of a Fox-Hunting Man*, which he started writing the following year, in 1926.

II

In a retrospective piece, written in 1946, Sassoon says that he can claim to be "one of the earliest authors to demonstrate that it [the period the book covers, roughly 1896-1915] was good literary material, and that the remembering of its remoteness was enjoyable".[5] And his *Memoirs of a Fox-Hunting Man* certainly supports the idea of the Edwardian years as one long, pleasant summer afternoon, a bright and peaceful interlude between the stern Victorian Age and the bleak darkness that followed when the lamps went out all over Europe. But as J.B. Priestley rightly points out: "The Edwardian was never a golden age, but seen across the dark years afterwards it could easily be mistaken for one".[6]

And even then it was essential to belong to the privileged social classes. The Sassoon of the autobiographies and George Sherston, his *alter ego* in the *Sherston Trilogy*, are a far cry from the Labour Party supporter who eagerly awaited the Socialist Revolution. The young Sassoon was as callow and ignorant as the young George Sherston, but at no stage in any of the autobiographies does the mature and worldly-wise Sassoon show a more considered and thoughtful view of the social conditions of Edwardian England, though the injustices must have been pointed out to him often enough.

The fox-hunting theme also serves as a reminder of the class differences among Georgian writers: whereas Sassoon recounts his experiences as a hunting-man, some of his 'socially inferior' fellow-writers describe how they went to see a meet of the hounds and huntsman.[7]

Neither does Sassoon, the sensitive poet and lover of Nature ever question the value and morality of hunting, nor, perhaps even more significantly, does he feel the need to defend them. For his love of hunting must have frequently been attacked. His close friends Robert Graves and Edmund Blunden thoroughly disapproved of it. Another personal acquaintance, the poet W.H. Davies, made his opinion perfectly clear in his poem 'Sport' (1926):

> Hunters, hunters,
> Follow the Chase.
> I saw the fox's eyes,
> Not in his face
> But on it, big with fright –
> Haste, hunters, haste!

But Sassoon refuses to let similar thoughts disturb the peaceful pastoral world he has created. Describing how the hunters are digging out a fox that has gone to ground in a rabbit-hole, he does not deny any possible cruelty, but makes it clear that this is simply of no importance within the idyll: "However inhumane its purpose, it was a kindly country scene" (248).[8] This remark is a perfect illustration of the author's attitude. He is not interested in criticizing that lost world, instead he intends to portray it as a harmonious and intensely local world, where everyone knew his place and peace reigned supreme.

This approach exposes him to the charge of distorting the truth and being in general far too uncritical in his depiction of the Edwardian age, but though Sassoon's portrayal is undoubtedly romanticized to a considerable extent, he did put it to excellent literary use, for the perfect order and peacefulness of this little world form the ideal contrast to the complete chaos and violence of the Great War. In a letter to Robert Graves, written in March 1930, Sassoon said that "Sherston is only 1/5 of myself, but his narrative is carefully thought out and constructed".[9] The careful construction of the narrative in *Memoirs of a Fox-Hunting Man* has been frequently overlooked and misinterpreted. David Daiches describes the book as piece of straightforward realism:

> *Memoirs of a Fox-Hunting Man* is an impressive rendering of the tone and the rhythm of a kind of English life that has by now almost completely passed away – that of the cultivated squirearchy in the large country-house.[10]

While Paul Fussell regards it as an ironic illustration of how ill-prepared Edwardian England was for modern warfare:

> One large prevailing irony never overtly surfaces, but the whole course of events implies it. This is the fate of the cavalry in the

unanticipated war of static confrontation. The whole first part of *Memoirs of a Fox-Hunting Man* prepares us, as it prepares George, to expect from him a brilliant career in the cavalry, which was still in the days of his youth, virtually the equivalent of 'the Army'.[11]

Fussell's interpretation would have been a valid one had Denis Milden been the hero of the book, but George Sherston is portrayed as rather an awkward young man, and not as a man whose poise and good breeding would automatically lead one to believe that a brilliant cavalry career lay ahead of him. But Fussell is correct in drawing attention to Sassoon's "binary vision",[12] for, as in his war poetry, juxtaposition is one of the key devices in his prose writings.

III

Two of the main themes in the construction of *Memoirs of a Fox-Hunting Man* are 'order' and 'locality'. The small society in which the young orphan George Sherston grows up is like a miniature universe where all the planets revolve in their own fixed orbits. George's surrogate mother, Aunt Evelyn, has the great misfortune to live "fully two miles beyond the radius of Lady Dumborough's 'round of calls', and so "the aristocratic yellow-wheeled barouche never entered our unassuming white gate" (14). But Aunt Evelyn's own activities "extended no further then the eight or ten miles which she could cover in a four-wheeled dog-cart driven by Tom Dixon, the groom" (9). And for Tom Dixon, in many respects George's surrogate father, "the Kennels were the centre of the local universe" (15). In this little universe everybody is supposed to know his place. Aunt Evelyn adheres to a strict social code "which divided the world into people one could 'call on' and people who were 'socially impossible'" (11). George is soon made aware of this when he is "strictly forbidden to 'associate' with the village boys" (11). Tom Dixon may have his own silent wishes, but:

> The great thing about Dixon was that he knew exactly where to draw the line. Beyond the line, I have no doubt, lay his secret longing to have an occasional day with the Dumborough Hounds on one of his employer's horses (17).

1. Weirleigh, near Matfield in Kent, Sassoon's childhood home
2. Heytesbury House

3. Alfred Sassoon and his three sons, Siegfried, Michael and Hamo
4. Theresa Sassoon in the garden at Weirleigh

5. Sassoon in 1915 in officer's uniform wearing the 'Sam Browne' leather belt and the collar badges of the Royal Welch Fuseliers

6. Second Lieutenant
Robert Graves

7. Robert Nichols in
officer's uniform, 1915

8. W. H. R. Rivers in R.A.M.C. uniform

9. Craiglockhart War Hospital

10. G. F. Watts's 'Love and Death'

11. Sassoon and W. B. Yeats at
    Garsington, March 1922

12. Ralph Hodgson

13. Sassoon and his wife
Hester

14. Sassoon and his son
George at Heytesbury

15. Sassoon in old age

But he knows that this is socially impossible, and so he projects his ambitions on young Master George. It does not take George long to get used to the different positions within the social hierarchy. When Dixon accompanies him on his first day's fox-hunting he is not surprised to find that Dixon becomes quite dignified and aloof once they have reached the meet: "Of course I knew what it meant: I was now his 'young gentleman', and he was only the groom who had brought me to 'have a look at the hounds'" (37).

It is this perfect order and the hold on life it gave one that must have especially appealed to Sassoon at the time he was writing *Memoirs of a Fox-Hunting Man*. And in a passage like the following the voice of the mature George Sherston cannot be distinguished from that of Sassoon himself:

I wanted to be strongly connected with the hunting organism which at that time I thought of as the only one worth belonging to. And it was (though a limited one) a clearly defined world, which is an idea that most of us cling to. (261-62)

As will be seen later, the fixed 'order' in *Memoirs of a Fox-Hunting Man* is to be juxtaposed with the chaos that was brought about by the Great War. Locality is used for different purposes: *The Sherston Trilogy* can be seen as a kind of *Bildungsroman* which describes the gradual development of George Sherston's mind and character. By the time he started writing *Memoirs of a Fox-Hunting Man* Sassoon himself had severe reservations about the merits of gaining worldly-wisdom, and this is reflected in the construction of the book by the chapter divisions. The several stages in George's development keep pace with a gradual opening up of the world.

In the first chapter George tries to break out of Aunt Evelyn's ten mile zone, as when he and Dixon want to go to a meet that is outside her limits and they conspire to dupe her "by a system of mutual falsification of distances" (54). Chapter two begins when George returns home from Ballboro (a thinly disguised Marlborough) for the summer holidays (61). Chapter three takes place "in the summer after I left Cambridge" (93). George's world is then still a very small one, he knows "very little about London" and has "never been across the Channel", but he does meditate "on the coast-line of France and all the unvisualized singularity of that foreign land" (95). By chapter seven the established fox-hunter travels up to London regularly, but still "Europe was nothing but a name to me. I couldn't even bring myself to reading about it in the daily paper" (246). An important development in his career as a fox-hunter occurs when he follows his admired friend Denis Milden to the Packlestone Hunt in the Midlands – "a region which I couldn't even visualize" (277). Chapter eight is therefore suitably called 'Migration to the Midlands'. Chapter nine finds George a trooper in the Yeomanry, stationed near Canterbury. Life is still relatively pleasant there in his native county: "there was something almost idyllic about those early weeks of the War" (307), but the idyll is rudely destroyed when, on the last pages of the chapter, George receives news of the death of his hunting-friend Stephen Colwood, killed in action. This is immediately followed by the final chapter in the book, 'At The Front'. Thus the ten chapters that chronicle George Sherston's mental development also see him 'progress' from the centre of Aunt Evelyn's safe and comfortable little world to the front line of a gruesome World War.[13]

IV

In his autobiography, *The Gates of Memory*, Sassoon's personal friend and bibliographer Sir Geoffrey Keynes recalls that *Memoirs of a Fox-Hunting Man*

> was published anonymously because Sassoon, as a poet writing prose for the first time, had feared his unexpected venture might have been condemned on that account. When the book was instantly recognized as a work of art in its own right, the anonymity was quickly lifted.[14]

It is hard to imagine that there would have been any critic silly enough to have condemned the book on the grounds that 'it was written by a poet'. Sassoon was over-sensitive when it came to appearing in print, and his anonymous publication can be regarded as the prose equivalent of the privately published poetry editions: he wanted to test the waters before facing the general public under his own name. It shows a distinct lack of confidence and in this case especially he need not have been apprehensive. The book was an immediate success, both with the critics and the general public. It was awarded the 1928 James Tait Black Memorial Book Prize and the 1929 Hawthornden Prize for Imaginative Literature.

Though there may well be a suspicion of log-rolling in awarding the prize (the Hawthornden was very much a Georgian writer's prerogative, which did not have a little to do with the fact that J.C. Squire headed the jury), that does not alter the fact that as a prose debut *Memoirs of a Fox-Hunting Man* is indeed a masterpiece. Its outstanding qualities are its humour, the descriptive passages and the wistful and evocative nature of the prose. But the quality that may well have appealed most to the post-war reader was its 'Englishness'. This was the quality that T.E. Lawrence admired, not only in the book, but also in Sassoon himself. "If I was trying to export the ideal Englishman to an international exhibition, I think I'd like to choose S.S. for chief exhibit", he wrote to Edward Marsh.[15] Lawrence had admired Sassoon's war poetry because it had reflected his own attitude towards the war; reading *Memoirs of a Fox-Hunting Man* had given him "a shock of astonishment that he was so different and so good to know".[16]

What Lawrence probably meant was that this was his first encounter with Sassoon the Sportsman, for he cannot have been astonished by the innovative qualities of the book itself. *Memoirs of a Fox-Hunting Man* is firmly rooted in the Victorian novel-tradition: Aunt Evelyn's secluded little world is reminiscent of Mrs Gaskell's *Cranford*[17] and the Barsetshire of Anthony Trollope's series of novels. But the main influence, both in subject and approach, must have been the novels of R.S. Surtees.[18]

In all the hunting scenes the figures of John Jorrocks and Mr Sponge seem to be lurking in the background. George and his friend Stephen Colwood "adopted and matured a specialized jargon drawn almost exclusively from the characters in the novels of Surtees", and "Mr Jorrocks was an all pervading influence" (166-67). Staying with his friend Denis Milden at the Kennels gives George "an agreeable feeling of having got into a modernized Surtees novel" (282). V.S. Pritchett calls Surtees "an amateur who dealt almost entirely with background figures",[19] and in this respect also the world of *Memoirs of a Fox-Hunting Man* is certainly a Surteesian world. With the exception of George Sherston himself all the characters in the book are flat characters, and both their hunting adventures and names (Fred

Buzzaway, Captain Hinnycraft and Sir Jocelyn Porteus-Porteous) are in unmistakable Surtees-vein.

Sassoon's own style of humour, however, is quite different from the boisterousness of Surtees. It is far more gentle and self-mocking, as in the passage where George is not so much day-dreaming about winning the Colonel's Cup in his first ever horse race, but rather about *how* he will win the coveted trophy:

> Easy winning lacked intensity; I would have preferred something more spectacular and heroic. But this was difficult to manage; I couldn't win with my arm in a sling unless I started in that condition, which would be an anti-climax. (209)

The descriptive and evocative qualities of the prose cannot be discussed separately. When Sassoon wrote about George Meredith that

> He can make us remember what it felt like to be young, can recover for us the rapture and dizzying uncertainty of first love, can make us breathe the air of the early morning, and bring us back the forgotten strangeness of mountains looked on long ago (*M*, 240)

he might well have been describing his own prose. There is a poetic precision in the choice of words and the balancing of sounds, but Sassoon's most impressive achievement is the way he makes the past come to life. Undoubtedly his memories came to life in his own mind, but seemingly without effort he manages to achieve the same result in his prose. Chapter two opens with a beautifully evocative description of daybreak on the morning of the Flower Show cricket-match (63-5). The mood is at its most wistful when, in the same chapter, there is a constant shifting between the past of the cricket-match and the present, with the author cherishing his memories:

> The umpires are in their places. But it is in the sunshine of my own clarified retrospection that they are wearing their white coats. While I was describing them I had forgotten that they have both of them been dead for many years. Nevertheless, their voices are distinctly audible to me. (75-6)

At the climax of this passage past and present blend into one: "Thus the match proceeds until, twenty-five years ago, it is lunch time, and Rotherden has made seventy runs with three wickets down" (77-8).

This subtle use of the tenses is a literary device that suggests the influence of Walter Pater. Sassoon was a great admirer of Pater's prose,[20] and both in contents and composition Sassoon's prose works owe much to him. Sassoon's George Sherston is in many ways reminiscent of Pater's Marius the Epicurean; when it is said of Marius that

> he was ready now to concede [...] the first point of his new lesson, that the individual is to himself the measure of all things, and to rely on the exclusive certainty to himself of his own impressions[21]

the same thing holds true for both George and Sassoon himself. The way Sassoon's narrative shifts from a description of a hunting-man to one of nature and then moves on to a description of George's mental life is a pattern also found in *Marius*, and when George bursts in on a family prayer meeting at the Colwoods (183), the episode is oddly reminiscent of Marius overhearing a Cecilian family at prayer.[22]

In its descriptions of the countryside and its sense of 'man being one with nature' the book is reminiscent of George Meredith's work. In yet another evocative passage, Sassoon, who in his poetry complained so bitterly about his loss of understanding of nature, calls back to mind the members of the Ringwell Hunt, making clear that apart from the perfect order in the hunting world it was their being one with nature that is so very important to him:

> Memories within memories; those red and black and brown coated riders return to me now without beckoning, bringing along with them the wintry smelling freshness of the woods and fields. And how could I forget them, those evergreen country characters whom once I learnt to know by heart, and to whom I have long since waved my last farewell [...] the landscape belonged to them and they to the homely landscape. (216-17)

Phrases like "to whom I have long waved my last farewell" emphasise
that the world here recalled is a lost world, but this is not the only
way in which Sassoon makes this clear. Throughout the book there
are many signs and symbols that suggest that this is a doomed world.
On the title page Sassoon quotes a line from John of Gaunt's famous
speech in *Richard II*, "This happy breed of men, this little world", but
the preceding three lines in the play are nearly as relevant:

> This other Eden, demi-paradise,
> This fortress built by Nature for herself
> Against infection and the hand of war
> (Act II, i, 42-4)

These lines contain several of the key-words in Sassoon's vocabulary:
"Paradise" was his term for the destination of the pilgrimage he began
in *The Heart's Journey* (published two months before *Memoirs of a
Fox-Hunting Man*), "Nature" is one of his main themes and "the hand
of war" is a threatening presence throughout the book.

George is continually reminded of the Boer War, although he is
completely ignorant about any of the facts: "I never could make up
my mind what it was all about, that Boer War, and it seemed such a
long way off..."(65). But at home there is a picture of 'The Relief of
Ladysmith' in the pantry (65), and during the lunch-interval in the
cricket match George finds himself sitting next to a gentleman farmer
who has actually been to the war: "Taking a shy sip at my ginger-
beer, I think how extraordinary it is to be sitting next to a man who
has really been 'out in South Africa'" (80). On his walks through the
Weald George describes the hop-poles as "piled in pyramids like
soldiers' tents" (112), and there is a considerable dramatic irony in the
speech of the Master of the Hounds when he calls on the members of
the Hunt to "eliminate the most dangerous enemy of the hunting-man
– he meant barbed wire" (132).[23] The shop window of the London
tailor where George goes to collect his new hunting outfit is said to be
"fitted with a fine wire screening, on which the crowns and vultures
of several still undethroned European Majesties were painted" (145).
But the most intriguing and ominous symbol in the book is one of the
many photographic reproductions that decorate the walls in Aunt
Evelyn's house.

V

One of the dominating features of the downstairs drawing room is "The large photograph of Watts's picture, 'Love and Death'" (28). George is strangely attracted to it, "with its secret meaning which I could never quite formulate in a thought, though it often touched me with a vague emotion of pathos" (64). That George should find it difficult to grasp the meaning of 'Love and Death' seems in itself not too surprising: a guide to British nineteenth-century painting says that G. F. Watts "strove for recognition as a history painter, producing vast historical and mythological projects where his personal symbolism and allegory often confused his high-minded moral message".[24]

George Frederick Watts (1817-1904) was in his time a revered artist. Though nowadays he is mainly remembered for his fine portraits (and his brief marriage to Ellen Terry in 1864), his mythological and allegorical paintings were much admired during the 1880s and 1890s. Other works in this genre include 'Love and Life', 'Time, Death and Judgment', 'Physical Energy', 'Hope', 'Love Triumphant' and 'The Court of Death', which had inspired the young Sassoon to write one of his earliest poems in 1897. That Sassoon chose a picture by Watts as one of the key symbols in his book is not surprising: its symbolic value in the book is not dependent on the picture itself, but on its grand, allegorical title.

This is not to suggest that he used a title without knowing anything of either the painter or the picture. G. F. Watts was in a very literal sense a household name at Weirleigh (and his Aunt Rachel owned Watts's 'Orpheus and Eurydice'), and Sassoon made no secret of the importance Watts' work had for him:

> Towards the end of 1897 my mother took me to London to see the Watts Exhibition. She had known G. F. Watts quite well before she was married. His studio was next door to the house in Melbury Road which Grandpapa had built, and she had often told me how she used to go in and brighten him up, when he was feeling tired after painting all day.
>
>   Without being altogether aware of it, I had been strongly influenced by Watts's pictures. Large photographs of them were all over the house; there were several in the drawing-room, and

> I passed Mr. Watts himself (in his self-portrait) every time I
> went up or down the stairs. My brother Hamo was his godson. I
> wished it had been me, for Hamo took no interest in his
> godfather's pictures and even treated his second name as a joke,
> saying that he ought to have been Hamo What Sassoon. What I
> admired about Watts was his loftiness and grandeur. He painted
> the things that I wanted to write poems about. (*OC*, 160-61)

Though Sassoon does not mention 'Love and Death' in either his
autobiographies or his diaries, it is highly likely that it was one of the
"large photographs" at Weirleigh. The first stanza of 'Reward', an
unpublished war poem (dated 5 June 1918), contains what can only
be taken as a indirect reference to the painting:

> Months and weeks and days go past,
> And my soldiers fall at last.
> Months and weeks and days
> Their ways must be my ways.
> And evermore
> Love guards the door.[25]

Watts is said to have painted 'Love and Death' after he had been
commissioned to paint the portrait of a talented young aristocrat who
was suffering from an incurable disease. At each sitting Watts could
see how the young man gradually wasted away, and when he finally
died, Watts felt the need to express his emotions.

The painting inspired the Scottish poet William Bell Scott (1811-
90), a minor Pre-Raphaelite, to write the following sonnet:

> "Open the door! Thou canst not understand
> My mission, thou spoilt child of many a god,
> Thou who dost claim the heart for thy abode;
> Open the door, lest I put forth my hand
> And touch thee too, or give such dire command
> To thy vile brother Hatred, – now I hear
> The quills of thy unquiet wings with fear
> Quiver against thy flanks: no more withstand."

> "Oh Death, why comest thou so soon, so far?
> Why comest thou before the appointed hour?
> I shall not make way for a fate so dire."
> "Poor child, I pass despite thy bolt and bar,
> The torch lit here to grace the bridal bower,
> I make it mine to light the funeral pyre."

It is not known whether Sassoon knew this poem, but it seems a fair assumption to say that he did, not only because his mother brought him up on a steady diet of Pre-Raphaelite writings, but also because Death coming before "the appointed hour" is strongly reminiscent of Sassoon's war poem 'The Death-Bed' (1916). A memory of the week in July which he spent in the New Zealand Hospital in Amiens with trench fever, the poem describes the final moments of a young, mortally wounded soldier, who is already in a delirium when Death, "who'd stepped towards him, paused and stared". Like 'Love' in Scott's poem, the poet then tries to intervene:

> Speak to him; rouse him; you may save him yet.
> He's young; he hated War; how should he die
> When cruel old campaigners win safe through?

> But death replied: 'I choose him.' So he went.
> And there was silence in the summer night;
> Silence and safety; and the veils of sleep.
> Then, far away, the thudding of the guns.

In the concluding three lines the hospital ward in Amiens and the drawing room at Weirleigh seem to blend into one: for Sassoon wrote this poem in the safety of his mother's home in August 1916, and when he walked out into the garden, he could hear the sound of the distant guns on the other side of the Channel.

It would therefore seem that Watts' picture had been one of Sassoon's favourite symbols long before he used it in *Memoirs of a Fox-Hunting Man*. But whereas on the earlier occasions Sassoon had made use of the picture itself, he now referred solely to the title. Its symbolic meaning becomes clear in a crucial passage, which takes place on the day George decides to enlist without telling anyone:

> On that ominous July 31st I said long and secret good-byes to
> everything and everyone. Late in the sultry afternoon I said
> good-bye to the drawing room [...] I was alone in the twilight
> room, with the glowering red of sunset peering through the
> chinks and casting the shadows of leaves on a fiery patch of
> light which rested on the wall by the photograph of 'Love and
> Death'. So I looked my last and rode away to the War on my
> bicycle. (319)

This is the momentous occasion in George's life when, without as yet
realizing it, he says goodbye to the old world of the fox-hunting man,
the world he loved and knew, and leaves it all behind to enter a new,
as yet unknown world, that of the Infantry Officer. 'Love and Death'
symbolizes the two, as 'Love' and 'Death' respectively characterize the
fox-hunting world of his youth and the Western Front horrors of his
maturity.

VI

The world of George's youth had been a world in which one's position
in society was decided by one's social class. He had grown up in
complete ignorance of the Continent and the rest of the world, but in
the vague belief that the English were a superior race. But for George
this is only a stage in his life; in its most hardened form this attitude is
represented by George's hero, Denis Milden.

Milden is the real epitome of the fox-hunting world: a privileged
background and an Eton and Oxford education (265), followed by a
successful career as an amateur huntsman (241), and an equally
successful one as Master of Fox-Hounds. But he is also a
representative of Imperialist Britain in its most narrow-minded and
philistine aspects, which are revealed in a passage that shows the
subtlety of Sassoon's descriptive prose at its very best. Sitting in
Denis Milden's cottage after a good day's hunting George takes a
closer look at the living-room's interior:

> There were a few photographs, mostly in silver frames, of his
> contemporaries at Eton and Oxford, all in hunting or racing
> clothes; the walls were hung with monotonously executed

portraits of horses which he had owned, and there was one larger group of four hounds which had won a first prize at Peterborough Hound Show. There was also a coloured drawing of himself winning a University Steeplechase. A few standard sporting books (including Lindsay Gordon's poems and the leather-backed volumes of the *Foxhound Kennel Stud-Book*) filled a small bookcase [...] Finally (and there was only just enough room for it) an upright piano with a pianola apparatus attached to it, demonstrated that he was fond of a bit of music. A record of Dvorak's 'New World' Symphony appeared to be his only link with Europe. (265-66)

It is in passages such as these that George becomes as innocent an observer as Huckleberry Finn. For without realizing it, he describes the room of a huntsman-cum-philistine, whose privileged education is not reflected in academic achievements or memorabilia, but in photographs of schoolfriends with whom he went out hunting and a prize for winning the Oxford Steeplechase. That this education was wasted as far as developing a love for the arts is concerned is then illustrated in the subtle but mercilessly effective lines that follow. The paintings on the walls confirm the owner's limited interests: not only are the subjects restricted to horses and hounds, but the paintings also reveal a lack of taste and artistic discrimination, they are "monotonously executed". And so it is not surprising that the only bookcase in the room is "small" and filled with "a few standard sporting books", thus illustrative of not only his limited interests, but also a distinct lack of originality. All these hunting paraphernalia take up most of the space, and as a result there is "only just enough room" for the one thing not associated with hunting, the piano. It seems to have been squeezed in as an afterthought, for Milden is not the type to be deeply moved by music (as Sassoon himself was) but only "fond of a bit of music". He therefore has never felt the urge to learn to play the piano, but was content to install "a pianola apparatus", and have the *mechanical* playing (like the *monotonous* paintings) done for him. His only link with Europe is Dvorak's American symphony, which was composed in New York. When Milden later joins George it is revealed that though he has the advantage over George in that he has actually been abroad ("he had once been to Budapest to play in a polo tournament") this has not markedly widened his horizon, for their conversation over dinner is all about "how superior the English were to all foreigners" (266).

While still a member of the fox-hunting society, George is equally limited in his outlook and in the first part of the book the mature author gives many examples of his insensitive former self: that the local farmers might be less pleased with enthusiastic fox-hunters was a viewpoint that he at that time did not understand:

> The country was there to be ridden over [...] it had not occurred to me that a hole in a fence through which fifty horses have blundered is much the same as an open gate, so far as the exodus of a farmer's cattle is concerned. (129)

The appearance of rich self-made men among the hunters is not considered a welcome development; George looks down on Bill Jaggett with all the social 'not-one-of-us' arrogance he can muster: "He was a hulking, coarse-featured, would-be thruster; newly rich, ill-conditioned, and foul-mouthed" (150).[26] Towards the end of a day of stag-hunting it does not occur to George to feel pity for the poor deer they have been chasing (207), nor is he aware of the plight of the hop-pickers from London:

> Hop-picking was over early that year and the merry pickers had returned to the slums of London to the strains of the concertina and the accordeon. I was contemplating an expedition to the West End to order a short-skirted scarlet coat and two pairs of white breeches from Kipward & Son. (245)[27]

And so the first eight chapters of *Memoirs of a Fox-Hunting Man* continue to portray George as an ignorant and rather silly young man, who aspires to no more than to become a Denis Milden, and for whom the threat of socialists is much greater than the threat of a European war. Not that he knows much about either, but the socialists are closer to home and as such much more dangerous for the hunting world:

> There was, however, one discordant element in life which I vaguely referred to as "those damned socialists who want to stop us hunting". Curiously enough, I didn't connect socialists

with collieries, though there had been a long coal strike eighteen months before. Socialists, for me, began and ended in Hyde Park. (284-85)

VII

The last two chapters of the book mark George's gradual break with the past. The first stage does not yet constitute a complete severance of the links with his previous existence. Though he is now a soldier and no longer a man of leisure, this in itself does not mean that he has left the world of his youth behind. His friend and fellow-sportsman Stephen Colwood was in the army (as were his brothers) and George first joins the Yeomanry – just like the man he had met many years before at the Flower Show who had been in the Boer War (80). There are other instances in which his army life mirrors that of the fox-hunter: instead of visiting the tailor for a new hunting outfit (145) he now visits a tailor for a new uniform (325), and behind the lines in France he still indulges in an imitation hunt (358). His horses are requisitioned by the army, where George loses sight of them, but where the true huntsman catches up with them: "Denis [Milden] had disappeared into a cavalry regiment and was still in England" (319). When George first reports for duty in France he is still not entering a new world:

In a large dusky orderly room [...] the Colonel shook hands with me. I observed that he was wearing dark brown field-boots, small in the leg, and insinuating by every supple contour that they came from Craxwell. And since the world is a proverbially small place, there was, I hope, nothing incredible in the fact that the Colonel was a distant relative of Colonel Hesmon, and had heard all about how I won the Colonel's Cup. (344)

That George frequented the same London boot-makers and that his friend Colonel Hesmon is a relative of his Commanding Officer does not at all mean that the world in general is a small place, it is just that *their* world is a small place, and that as the upper layer of society, they will always meet each other in the senior positions; the play may be different, but the actors are still the same.

An ironic consequence of this state of affairs is that one is more likely to find former schoolmates fighting in opposing armies than to find them on either side of the officers-men divide: when George meets a fellow officer with whom he had been at 'Ballboro', and enquires after his "cousin Willie", he is told that "He's on the other side – in the artillery" (367).

It is this elitist world that is gradually eroded by the war: Stephen Colwood is killed in action (339), as is Dick Tiltwood (382); Dixon, still knowing his place, leaves the heroic deaths for the gentlemen and dies of pneumonia (374). But as George's understanding of what a good officer is supposed to be like increases, he begins to apply different standards. His Colonel still welcomes his subalterns according to the 'one-of-us' standard:

> I have always found that it was a distinct asset, when in close contact with officers of the Regular Army, to be able to converse convincingly about hunting. It gave one an almost unfair advantage in some ways.
>
> Mansfield (who had been received with reservations of cordiality), Dick (*persona grata* on account of his having been at Sandhurst) [...] and I (no comment required) were all posted to 'C' company. (344-45)

But George begins to realise that good breeding alone is not important: trying to become a good officer he has no reservations about admiring some of the new officers who have risen through the ranks:

> Durley was an inspiration towards selfless patience. He was an ideal platoon officer, and an example which I tried to imitate from that night onward. I need hardly say that he had never hunted. He could swim like a fish, but no social status was attached to that. (347-48)

In this context it is a significant detail that Durley is reading *The Cloister and the Hearth* "in an Everyman edition" (349).

It is George's open-mindedness that sets him apart from such die-hard Tories as Denis Milden and the Colonel. It allows him to see and appreciate the qualities in people from an inferior social background.

The war gradually brings out his best qualities: he has the modesty and self-knowledge that make him realise that he still has a lot to learn, and he possesses the flexibility to decide to imitate Durley, a socially inferior fellow officer. At the same time he begins to sense the social rigidity of the hunting world: unable to adapt to the changing conditions, the people at home are left behind, no longer able to keep pace with the changes that take place within George. On a visit home George decides that "England wasn't what it used to be" (377), but it is he himself who has changed the most.

If this is a positive effect of the war on George's mental growth, it also has a soul-destroying one: towards the end of the book Sassoon recalls George cleaning his puttees in a trench behind the support line. A shell passes overhead, in the direction of the enemy lines, and then explodes in a cloud of dark smoke:

> Perhaps the shell has killed someone. Whether it has or whether it hasn't, I continue to scrape my puttees, and the weasel goes about his business. The sun strikes the glinting wings of an aeroplane, fogging away westward. Somewhere on the slope behind me a partridge makes its unmilitary noise – down there where Dick was buried a few weeks ago. Dick's father was a very good man with a gun, so Dick used to say. (388)

The physical fatigue of trench life has caused a state of mental numbness and the awful business of survival has a dehumanizing effect on men: George is no longer capable of such human responses to the world around him as sympathy, pity, curiosity or grief. He does not care if the shell has caused human suffering and death, the lover of nature is no longer interested in the weasel that passes before his eyes, and when the partridge reminds him of Dick's burial and his thoughts drift off to what Dick told him about his father's partridge-shooting he stops dead in his thoughts: that way madness lies. Dick himself was killed by a sniper (382) – another "very good man with a gun" – and George does not wish to be reminded of his death. The aeroplane "fogging away westward" is another subtle reminder of death: in the trenches soldiers that had been killed were often referred to as having "gone west".[28]

VIII

The composition of *Memoirs of a Fox-Hunting Man*, carefully contrasting the hunting world and life in the trenches, suggests that originally Sassoon did not intend to write a sequel. A passage in Part Nine, 'In the Army', lends further support to the idea that it was not until the writing of *Memoirs of a Fox-Hunting Man* neared its completion that the thought of continuing his narrative in a second volume first occurred to him:

> All squalid, abject, and inglorious elements in war should be remembered. The intimate mental history of any man who went to the War would make unheroic reading. I have half a mind to write my own. (335)

Sassoon had obviously not reached a final decision when he completed his book. The ending of *Memoirs of a Fox-Hunting Man* in no way suggests that George's story is to be continued. In a clever and beautiful piece of writing, the two main settings are brought together in a final comparison: George has been on nightduty in the frontline trench:

> I stared at the tangles of wire and the leaning posts, and there seemed no sort of comfort left in life. My steel hat was heavy on my head while I thought how I'd been on leave last month. I remembered how I'd leant my elbows on Aunt Evelyn's front gate (it was my last evening); that twilight, with its thawing snow, made a comfortable picture now. John Homeward had come past with his van, plodding beside his weary horse. He had managed to make his journey, in spite of the state of the roads.... He had pulled up for a few minutes, and we'd talked about Dixon, who had been such an old friend of his. "Ay; Tom was a good chap; I've never known a better...." He had said good-bye and good-night and set his horse going again. As he turned the corner the past seemed to go with him....
> And there I was, with my knobkerrie in my hand, staring across at the enemy I'd never seen. Somewhere out of sight beyond the splintered tree-tops of Hidden Wood a bird had begun to sing. Without knowing why, I remembered that it was

Easter Sunday. Standing in that dismal ditch, I could find no consolation in the thought that Christ was risen. I sploshed back to the dug-out to call the others up for 'stand-to'. (394-95)

This passage operates on three levels. The first, and most obvious, is the old world-new world juxtaposition: the memory of the Kent landscape in the thawing snow is a "comfortable picture now", as he stares out over the desolate trench landscape. The carrier John Homeward managed to make his journey on his own, despite the poor conditions of the road. Lots of men and material were required (and even then it was at times impossible) to move a piece of artillery into position in the soggy ground behind the trenches. But the scene he remembers from home was at dusk, the day had ended, that world had gone, and when Homeward had turned the corner "the past had seemed to go with him".

At a second level this whole passage is an oblique reference to a poem that describes an end of an era and the promise of a new beginning, set in a dead winter landscape but with the hope of a rebirth, Thomas Hardy's 'The Darkling Thrush':

> I leant upon a coppice gate
>   When Frost was spectre-gray,
> And Winter's dregs made desolate
>   The weakening eye of day.
> The tangled bine-stems scored the sky
>   Like strings of broken lyres,
> And all mankind that haunted nigh
>   Had sought their household fires.

George had been leaning on Aunt Evelyn's gate and now he is standing on a firestep watching the sky; "the tangles of wire and the leaning posts" are the trench-landscape's equivalent of the "tangled bine-stems". Hardy had been alone, and George had been alone then as he is now, with all the men asleep in their dug-outs. In Hardy's poem the silence is broken by the thrush, that "Had chosen to fling his soul / Upon the growing gloom", and though the landscape around him is dead and gray, the voice of the thrush seems to sing of "Some blessed Hope, whereof he knew / And I was unaware". Hardy's poem was written on 31 December 1900, and the thrush, singing from

among the bare winter trees, is seen as the herald of a new century. When George Sherston hears the bird sing it is spring, but the landscape is dead, the bird is somewhere "out of sight beyond the splintered tree-tops"; spring in the trenches does not herald the earth's renewal, and neither is George able to find hope or consolation in the thought of Christ's Resurrection.

The Christian theme is the third and last level of this passage. The Anglican faith had been one of the solid cornerstones of the world of George's youth, with Aunt Evelyn and the Reverend Colwood as its main representatives. But in the trenches the Christian values disappear:

> the name of Christ was often on our lips, and Mansfield [...] was even heard to refer to our Saviour as "murry old Jesus!". These innocuous blasphemings of the holy name were a particular feature of the War, in which the principles of Christianity were either obliterated or falsified for the convenience of all who were engaged in it. (384)

In January 1917 Sassoon had been reading George Moore's biblical story *The Brook Kerith*. The book made a great impression on him, for as always when a book touched him deeply he quoted several passages verbatim in his diary.[29]

First published on 23 August 1916, *The Brook Kerith* is George Moore's remarkably eccentric biblical story. In his version, Jesus does not die on the cross, but is saved by Joseph of Arimathea who nurses him back to health but is then himself killed. Jesus returns to the strict religious community of the Essenes beside the Brook Kerith, of which he had been a member before he became the Messiah, and lives there quietly as a shepherd. He renounces his Messianic claim and all his teachings, but feels obliged to leave the community when he meets Paul, who is about to leave for Europe to spread the Christian gospel. In the closing pages of the book Jesus observes that Paul "is rapt [...] in the Jesus of his imagination" and he tells him that "now I knew thee to be preaching the resurrection of Jesus of Nazareth from the dead, thereby leading the people astray, I must return to Jerusalem to tell the priests that he whom they believed to be raised from the dead still lived in the flesh".[30] In the last part of Moore's novel an exhausted Paul arrives as a refugee at the Brook Kerith community of which Jesus is a member:

Sassoon's 1915-1918 diaries it can be easily ascertained that they provide the bulk of the material in the book. Parts of chapter four, describing the first day of the Battle of the Somme on 1 July 1916, are an almost literal transcript from the diaries.[1] This marked shift towards an almost purely autobiographical account again suggests that originally *Memoirs of a Fox-Hunting Man* was intended as a separate book and not as the opening volume of a trilogy. This is borne out by the difficulties Sassoon has in maintaining the credibility of the George Sherston persona, there being two main problem areas.

Brian Finney has summed up Sherston's development in *Memoirs of an Infantry Officer* as "his transformation from a self-destructive mock hero to the courageous if ineffectual author of the famous letter of protest against the war".[2] But at times Sassoon seems to have forgotten that George Sherston was only a "simplified version" of himself, and some slight inconsistencies creep into the narrative. Before the war George had only been interested in buying books without actually reading them: "I knew I ought to read *Paradise Lost* and *Pilgrim's Progress*. But there never seemed to be time for such edifications" (*MFH*, 144-45). It is therefore a bit surprising that the George Sherston of *Memoirs of an Infantry Officer* is quite knowledgeable on the subject of literature: he quotes from the *Rubaiyat of Omar Khayyàm* (172) and immediately recognizes quotations from Milton and Keats (173).[3]

But Sassoon encountered even more difficulties in leading his narrative up to his war protest. George Sherston has been denied a career as war poet, in which capacity Sassoon first aired his objections against the war. Since Sassoon does not introduce a new fictional element in George's career to make up for this, Sherston's decision to take a critical stand against the war comes somewhat unexpectedly. That it does not seem more illogical than it actually does, is due to Sassoon's whole treatment of his one-man action against the war. In the years that had passed since his protest, Sassoon had considerably distanced himself from the angry young man he then was; as he wrote in his poem 'War Experience' (published in *Vigils*, 1935, but obviously written around the time he completed *Memoirs of an Infantry Officer*): "Not much remains, twelve winters later, of the hater / Of purgatorial pains". As a result he is constantly playing down the importance of his war protest; in looking back he emphasizes the self-centred nature of his former self, portraying himself as an over-excited young subaltern who should not be taken too seriously:

> I can remember myself talking volubly to a laconic Stokes-gun officer, who had appeared from nowhere with his weapon and a couple of assistants. I felt that I must make one more onslaught before I turned my back on the War, and my only idea was to collect all available ammunition and then renew the attack while the Stokes-gun officer put up an enthusiastic barrage. It did not occur to me that anything else was happening on Allenby's Army Front except my own little show. My over-strained nerves had wrought me up to such a pitch of excitement that I was ready for any suicidal exploit. This convulsive energy might have been of some immediate value had there been any objective for it. But there was none. (236)

The distance between Sassoon and his former self is that between Sherston and the "laconic" Stokes-gun officer: both Sassoon and the officer do not quite see 'what the fuss is all about'. This distance is typical of Sassoon's attitude towards his war protest; though he never actually says so, his whole account of his protest clearly suggests that he no longer supports the actions of his former self; he is now in tacit agreement with the military authorities who did not take his 'Statement against the War' seriously. Sassoon looks back on his former self with all the patronizing sympathy of a father looking at his poor, deluded child:

> It seemed to me, in my confused and exhausted condition, that I was in a crisis in my military career; and, as usual, my main fear was that I should make a fool of myself. The idea of making a fool of oneself in that murderous mix-up now appears to me rather a ludicrous one; for I see myself merely as a blundering flustered little beetle; and if someone happens to put his foot on a beetle, it is unjust to accuse the unlucky insect of having made a fool of itself. (224-25)

The soldier cannot be said to have made a fool of himself amidst the chaos and unpredictability of the Western Front; the question that is left unanswered is whether that is supposed to mean that the young officer who, after careful deliberation in the safety of his home, decided on his individual action against the war *did* make a fool of himself.

II

Sassoon's were the last of what are now considered to be the three most important English war-memoirs to be published: Edmund Blunden's *Undertones of War* appeared in November 1928 and Robert Graves published *Goodbye To All That* exactly one year later. In tone, *Memoirs of an Infantry Officer* is somewhere half-way between the two. Sassoon's style is not as romantically poetic as Edmund Blunden's, who portrayed himself as the innocent observer, "a harmless young shepherd in a soldier's coat",[4] nor is it as horrifically realistic as Graves's (but then Sassoon had had his realistic period in his war-poetry). At times Sassoon even intervenes to tone down the book's realism, which detracts from the narrative's directness and tends to make the author sound somewhat prim, as when he carefully censors the expletive in a soldier's outburst: "I wish he'd arrange to go and fetch his (something) D.S.O. for himself!" (23). Describing a similar primness in his hero, on the other hand, works rather better, in that it affords him an opportunity for some mild, self-mocking humour; after dinner in Amiens with some fellow officers one of them

> remarked that he'd half a mind to go and look for a young lady to make his wife jealous. I said that there was always the cathedral to look at, and discovered that I'd quite unintentionally made a very good joke. (103)

The humour is purely self-mocking, for Sassoon is recording a personal experience. Significantly though, here too the tone has changed: in his diaries there is no reference to "a young lady", instead Sassoon uses the vocabulary of a stern Victorian moralist. Staying at the Hotel Belfort, Amiens in March 1917, he recorded in his diary: "tonight I've been guzzling at the Godbert restaurant with a captain of the Dublin Fusiliers, and a captain of the Cameronians, and three other Welsh [sic] Fusiliers [...] and the others have gone into the dark city to look for harlots; and I'm alone in my room" (*D1*, 146). At the time, Sassoon still preferred to think of himself as a Galahad, the Victorian ideal of the pure and healthy hero: in a prose passage, dated 27 February 1917, the poet-soldier writes about himself in the third person singular: "At any rate *his* body was strong and healthy; *he* wouldn't be 'fading away' to the Venereal Hospital like so many of the 'reinforcements', unlucky victims of a 'last night in town' before 'going out' (*D1*, 136).

Sassoon's decision to bowdlerize his war-memoirs was one of the topics of discussion in a brief but fascinating correspondence between him and Robert Graves in the early 1930s. By that time their friendship had all but ended and they no longer saw each other. The rot had set in after Graves's marriage with Nancy Nicholson in whose presence Sassoon had felt "nervous and uneasy". Matters did not improve when Graves took up with the highly intellectual Laura Riding, but Sassoon did not break off relations completely until 1928, after two incidents in which he felt Graves had not shown proper respect towards his old friends Edmund Gosse and Thomas Hardy.[5] When *Memoirs of a Fox-Hunting Man* was published later that year, Graves reviewed it unfavourably, accusing Sassoon among other things of having "side-stepped the moral question". In November 1929, less than a week before publication of *Goodbye to All That*, Graves' publisher Jonathan Cape wrote to him to say that he had been visited by an irate Sassoon, who objected strongly to two passages in the book. Without asking permission, Graves had included Sassoon's poem 'Letter to Robert Graves', which he had sent Graves in July 1918 but had never published himself. Also, Graves recounted a visit to Weirleigh in 1916 (without mentioning Sassoon by name), where he had witnessed Theresa Sassoon using spiritualist means to communicate with her dead son Hamo. At the time, Sassoon had told him that he thought his mother's behaviour pathetic and feared for her sanity. Now Sassoon threatened legal action and Cape, who did not want to postpone the publication date, felt compelled to black out these passages (in later editions they were deleted).

The correspondence between Graves and Sassoon took place in two brief periods: the first in February-March 1930, before publication of *Memoirs of an Infantry Officer*, the second from May to October 1933.[6] In the exchange of letters in 1930, Sassoon explains what had annoyed him about Graves' behaviour towards Gosse and

Hardy and why *Goodbye to All That* had upset him (he objects to Graves' journalistic – i.e. inaccurate and sensationalist – style, and points out several factual errors). In a curious postscript to his first letter Sassoon takes issue with Graves over his claim that officers visited brothels in Amiens while the battalion was billeted in Montagne.[7] Graves manages to prove his point, and then makes a crude jibe at his former friend: "It doesn't take long to fuck; but perhaps you don't know about that. T.E. [Lawrence] is similarly ignorant, I find". It was the sort of word Sassoon simply could not write: "*'It doesn't take long to *.'* Not a pretty remark, Robert. Yes, I know a little about the chronology, etc., of the act." The impression gained from this first exchange of letters is that Graves simply sticks to his guns, not concerned with the impression he makes on Sassoon. In contrast, Sassoon is not primarily focussed on the issues they discuss, but tentatively extending an olive branch, if only Graves would stop behaving so inconsiderately.

Their correspondence was resumed in 1933, and this time they also compare notes on their war-memoirs. Graves writes that "you [Sassoon] in *Goodbye* were written about with unmistakeable admiration, I in *Infantry Officer* was written about with unmistakeable malice". The first part of this statement is certainly true: Sassoon is mentioned quite often in *Goodbye*, and (unlike almost everybody else) nearly always favourably. Graves's second claim seems somewhat exaggerated, although it is true to say that his part in *Memoirs of an Infantry Officer* is not as favourable as Sassoon's in *Goodbye*. In *Memoirs of an Infantry Officer*, Graves appears as David Cromlech. There is no trace of malice when Sassoon writes about him that "At his best I'd always found him an ideal companion" (108), or that "although he was nine years younger than I was, I often found myself reversing our ages, since he knew so much more than I did about almost everything except fox-hunting" (149). But Sassoon has his reservations about Cromlech: he also says that "no one was worse than he was at hitting it off with officers who distrusted cleverness and disliked unreserved utterances" (108), and he also mentions "David's ingenuity at knocking highly-respected names and notions off their perches" (150). Certainly, these are not flattering remarks, but no reader of *Goodbye To All That* can deny certain provocative tendencies in the character of the man who, on the very first page of the book, claims that, as a baby, he apparently already had "a strong instinct against drawing-room activities" and calls the poet Swinburne "an inveterate pram-stopper and patter and kisser" as well as "a public menace".

The tone of these letters is mostly bad-tempered, Graves winning almost all the arguments, not so much because he is in the right, but because Sassoon is not a very skilful polemicist. "You are having a fine time off my loose bowling," he concludes wryly in one of his letters. Yet they also reveal how pleased Sassoon was with *Memoirs of a Fox-Hunting Man* ("one of the best-written and enjoyable books published since 1900"), and that Graves could be a harsh, but perceptive critic when it came to evaluating Sassoon's personality and work: he observes that the source of their literary differences lies in "the reverence that we are each prepared to pay to literary feudalism: you pay a lot, I pay none". He also accuses Sassoon of letting his loyalties towards the older generation prevail over his friendships with his contemporaries. But most of all the letters reveal what an ill-matched pair they were: complete opposites in almost every respect, they gradually had to come to terms with the realization that their brief careers as war poets had been the crossing point of two widely diverging paths. When the Graves/Sassoon correspondence ended in 1933 there was no further contact between them for over 20 years.

III

Sassoon's constant objections to what he considered to be Graves' hasty and careless style is an indication of how meticulous he had been in constructing his own books. Within the composition of *Memoirs of an Infantry Officer* it is easy to see that the controversial portrait of David Cromlech is not without its literary purpose: it is a vivid illustration of one of the underlying themes of the book, disorder. For unlike Tom Dixon in *Memoirs of a Fox-Hunting Man*, David Cromlech does not know where to draw the line:

> He [Cromlech] was with our Second Battalion for a few months
> before they transferred him to 'the First', and during that period
> the Colonel was heard to remark that young Cromlech threw
> his tongue a hell of a lot too much. (108)[8]

Fifteen years before it had been the war that had opened Sassoon's eyes to the lives of ordinary men and in the closing chapters of *Memoirs of a Fox-Hunting Man* George first began to see that there were admirable fellow-officers who did not hunt, and that in comparison with the other ranks the officer's position was a privileged one.

In *Memoirs of an Infantry Officer* this theme is further expanded: George observes how ineffectual officers were simply sent home, "But if a man became a dud in the ranks, he just remained where he was until he was killed or wounded" (44). As in his war poem 'Arms and the Man' (1916), he again mentions that officers could obtain artificial limbs free of cost (142), and just as Sassoon some fifteen years before him, George Sherston learns that "life, for the majority of the population, is an unlovely struggle against unfair odds, culminating in a cheap funeral" (209).

But if the war is an eye-opener for the naive George Sherston, as it was for the young Sassoon, for the mature author of the *Memoirs* war is synonymous with death, destruction and disorder. War is pictured as the creator of chaos, tearing down the fabric of society and bringing individual people together who would never have met under the strict 'social code' Aunt Evelyn adopted.[9] The heavy casualties among officers brought about the end of the old 'officer and gentleman' system, as represented by Holman: "a spick and span boy who had been to Sandhurst and hadn't yet discovered that it was unwise to look down on temporary officers who 'wouldn't have been wanted in the Regiment in peace time'" (109). When Sherston is transferred to No. 25 Stationary Hospital he again emphasizes the different backgrounds of the officers with whom he shares a tent: young Strangford, who is barely nineteen and whose father "kept a pack of harriers in County Down" is quite different from Parkins, who "was an obvious contrast to this modest youth. [.....he] was about thirty, and often reminded us that he had been to Cambridge" (170-71). Back in the front line, Sherston describes two newly arrived officers in his Company:

> Rees was a garrulous and excitable little Welshman; it would be flattery to call him anything except uncouth, and he made no pretensions to being 'a gentleman' [...] Shirley, on the other hand, had been educated at Winchester and the War had

interrupted his first year at Oxford. He was a delicately featured and fastidious young man, an only child, and heir to a comfortable estate in Flintshire. (210)

But the disorder does not only affect the officers' class-background: both officers and men get lost in the maze-like trench system, soldiers are sent up the line before they have been properly trained, and plans of attack are not sufficiently worked out. Visualizing the arrival in the trenches of such a 'green' battalion, George observes that

> I saw then, for the first time, how blindly War destroys its victims [...] I understood the doomed condition of these half-trained civilians [.....] Two days later the Welsh Division, of which they were a unit, was involved in a massacre and confusion. Our own occupation of Quadrangle Trench was only a prelude to that pandemonium which converted the green thickets of Mametz Wood to a desolation of skeleton trees and blackening bodies. (96-97)

The destructive and chaotic effects of the war are of course the greater on the naive mind of the young George Sherston, whose only means of comparison is the comfortable and safe world he left behind in England. There everything was part of a whole, the fox-hunters belonged to the landscape and the landscape to the fox-hunters; in the trenches that has all changed, War is a threat to Nature and they seem incompatible: "A young yellow-hammer was fluttering about in the trench, and I wondered how it got there: it seemed out of place, perching on a body which lay trussed in a waterproof sheet" (66-7). And the destructive influence of War is not restricted to the battlefields only.

The England George finds on his visits home has totally changed: his old friend Captain Huxtable is working his farm with only two elderly men and a boy (49), the cricket field lies derelict because there are not enough men left to form the teams (134) and few people come out to the hunts that are organized: "The game was being kept alive for the sake of the boys at the Front" (140). Slowly it begins to dawn on George: "I felt that People weren't the same as they used to be, or else I had changed. Was it because I had experienced something that they couldn't share or imagine?" (130). George had been elated at going out in the great big world, and the prospect of gaining experience had been as inviting as the words "DRINK ME" on the label of the little bottle Alice finds in the house of the White Rabbit: "'I know *something* interesting is sure to happen,' she said to herself,...'I do hope it will make me grow large again, for really I'm quite tired of being such a tiny little thing!'".[10] And at first George is indeed "elated at having outgrown the parish boundaries of Butley [his native village]" (137). But just like Alice, who finds it "very uncomfortable" when she grows too big for the Rabbit's house, George gradually discovers the consequences of his new life. His war experience has removed him very far from his childhood world, and he has lost contact with the people he knew there, and even with his former self. The war has changed his outlook, and the world that he had loved for nearly thirty years has suddenly become quite small, insignificant and even slightly ridiculous: "Meeting a tractor-engine had been quite an event in my childhood", George recalls (100). When George, on leave from the dangers of the Front, climbs the cedar tree in the garden to cut some dead wood, Aunt Evelyn begs him to be careful "adding that it would be no joke to tumble out of such a big tree" (133). That same evening she tells him to be careful about extinguishing the oil lamp: "Oil lamps were far from safe – downright dangerous, in fact!" (135). To George, as an experienced soldier, the people he knew and respected now all seem so ignorant, ineffectual and even ridiculous; about his old friend Colonel Hesmon he is told that "the old boy was known to have practised revolver-shooting in his garden, addressing insults to individual tree trunks and thus ventilating his opinion of Germany as a whole" (141).

George cannot begin to explain the horrors of the war to these people; a wide, unbridgeable gap has opened up between them. His knowledge and first-hand experience of the war make it impossible for him to either share or understand the undisturbed ignorance of the Home Front. Only a few years ago he had been equally unknowing: "At the age of twenty-two I believed myself to be unextinguishable" (*MFH*, 99), but now he knows that "a soldier signed away his independence; we were at the front to fight, not to think. But it became a bit awkward when one couldn't even look a week ahead" (203).

IV

Sudden death is the constant threat overhanging the soldier's existence. *Memoirs of an Infantry Officer* is in effect a continuation of the closing chapters of *Memoirs of a Fox-Hunting Man*, and the reproduction of G. F. Watts' 'Love and Death' can still be said to be its central symbol. For 'Death' is indeed the key word to this second volume. The book seems to be Sassoon's own 'Menin Gate', in which he has recorded the many "intolerably nameless names", the "unheroic Dead who fed the guns".[11] George Sherston's narrative is partly a long casualty list to which new names are continually being added. The deaths of Dixon and Stephen Colwood, important figures in George's past life, were already recorded in *Memoirs of a Fox-Hunting Man*. At the Army School George meets Allgood, whom he knew from his public school-days: "A couple of months afterwards I saw his name in one of the long lists of killed" (19-20). Back in the line, he finds himself near "the dressing station where Dick Tiltwood had died a couple of months ago" (299). George is awarded an MC for bringing the body of Corporal O'Brien, killed on patrol, back to the trench (38). His replacement is nineteen-year-old Lance-Corporal Kendle, who is killed by a sniper in the Battle of the Somme (90), and even when George is back home on leave he is reminded of the wastage of war: "Two of our nearest neighbours had lost their sons" (134). Letters from the front give him the latest depressing news:

> Poor Edwards was killed leading his Coy. Also Perrin [...] Asbestos Bill died of wounds. Fernby, who was O.C. Bombers, very badly hit and not expected to live [...] Miles and Danby both killed (138-39).

One death that is not recorded in Sherston's narrative occurred when his regiment was held in reserve at Basseux in April 1917: "The Battle of Arras began at 5.30 next morning" (205). Later that same day, 9 April 1917, second-lieutenant Edward Thomas was killed in battle by a shell blast.

Within the chaos and disorder of war, death is the great leveller: the "uncouth" Rees and "fastidious" Shirley "were killed before the autumn" (210), and while George is back in England recovering from a shoulder wound, the news of the deaths of Ormand and Dunning, two of the longest serving officers, reaches him: "Dunning had been the first to leave the trench; had shouted 'Cheerio' and had been killed at once" (270). By this time George has become "definitely critical and enquiring about the war" (249), and the last part of the book relates how, disillusioned with the war and estranged from the people at home, he embarks on his individual action against the war. He composes a statement "of wilful defiance of military authority" (308), and then waits at home to see what the outcome of his action will be. The main themes of the book come together in a scene which is the equivalent of the 'drawing room scene' in *Memoirs of a Fox-Hunting Man* – when George says his last farewell before cycling off to war (*MFH*, 319) – and like that scene, it takes place on a sultry afternoon. After a walk, George sits down in Butley Churchyard to think things over:

> Gazing at my immediate surroundings, I felt that 'joining the great majority' was a homely – almost comforting – idea. Here death differed from extinction in modern warfare. I ascertained from the nearest headstone that Thomas Welfare, of this Parish, had died on October 20th, 1843, aged 72. 'Respected by all who knew him'. Also Sarah, wife of the above. 'Not changed but glorified'. Such facts were resignedly acceptable. They were in harmony with the simple annals of this quiet corner of Kent. One could speculate serenely upon the homespun mortality of such worthies, whose lives had 'taken place' with the orderly and inevitable progression of a Sunday service. They made the past seem pleasantly prosy in contrast with the monstrous emergencies of today. (303)

This prose-elegy in a country churchyard juxtaposes the perfect order and harmony of rustic life with the chaos and wastage of war; the normal pattern of life, with the old dying and the young taking their places, has been completely upset: now the older generation lives on in this safe and quiet corner of Kent, while the young men from the village are killed off in the trenches of France and Flanders. But George is also particularly sensitive to such phrases as 'Respected by all' and 'Not changed but glorified', for his biggest worry at this moment is how people will interpret his personal stand against the war. He is afraid that friends like old Captain Huxtable will see it as

an act of cowardice, because to him "a Conscientious Objector was
the antithesis of an officer and a gentleman" (311). Aunt Evelyn does
not do George's strained nerves any good when, just before he gets in
the taxi to report back to Base, she remembers to hand him "the
bundle of white pigeon's feathers which she had collected from the
lawn, knowing how I always liked some for pipe-cleaners" (314). The
symbolism cannot have escaped him.[12]

As it is, David Cromlech/Robert Graves and a Medical Board save
him from a court martial[13] and he is content to be sent up to Slateford
War Hospital: "I gazed up at the blue sky, grateful because, at that
moment, it seemed as though I had finished with the War" (334).
Sherston is quite relieved to have reached the end of his protest action
– "I was aware that an enormous load had been lifted from my mind"
(331) – and he is not at all bothered by the way his heroic stand has
fizzled out. The futility of his action had already been foreshadowed
in his symbolic act of defiance while he had been awaiting the
authorities' reaction to his statement:

> Wandering along the sand dunes I felt outlawed, bitter, and
> baited. I wanted something to smash and trample on, and in a
> paroxysm of exasperation I performed the time-honoured
> gesture of shaking my clenched fist at the sky. Feeling no better
> for that, I ripped the M.C. ribbon off my tunic and threw it into
> the mouth of the Mersey. Weighted with insignificance though
> this action was, it would have felt more conclusive had the
> ribbon been heavier. As it was, the poor little thing fell weakly
> onto the water and floated away as though aware of its own
> futility. One of my point-to-point cups would have served my
> purpose more satisfyingly, and they'd meant much the same to
> me as my Military Cross. (326)

This is again a fine example of Sassoon's ingenious writing at one of
the dramatic highlights of his narrative. At surface level, the passage
describes a symbolic action, but at a deeper level it denotes much
more than simply an impotent act of defiance. George wants to
damage or obstruct the military machine; "the mouth of the Mersey"
becomes the symbol of a mighty war-god, which remains unperturbed
by Sherston's vain sacrifice: the M.C. ribbon, symbol of his protest, is
carried along by the current, as Sherston (and Sassoon) were

eventually to be carried along by the military machine. The whole action thus comes to stand for George's ultimate defeat, and this is then cleverly contrasted with his point-to-point cup, a symbol of a personal victory, but also of the world he has left behind.

V

Unlike *Memoirs of a Fox-Hunting Man*, the construction of *Memoirs of an Infantry Officer* does not hinge on a basic juxtaposition. The narrative simply follows the chronological line of Sassoon's own war experiences, but the book does show certain similarities with its predecessor, and certain features of the writing are even improved on. The death and destruction of the war add a poignant edge to the still essentially mild humour: "It was beginning to look as if I had enlisted for a lifetime (though the word was one which had seen better days)" (143). Sassoon's fondness for alliteration, a device that so often mars his poetry, is here applied with great care and to good effect: "The war had become undisguisedly mechanical and inhuman. What in earlier days had been drafts of volunteers were now droves of victims" (147). There is even another oblique reference to the work of G. F. Watts: when Sherston leads a fatigue party, it seems to him as if his struggling men are acting out one of Watts's allegorical paintings: "I can believe that my party, staggering and floundering under its loads, would have made an impressive picture of 'Despair'" (221).

Towards the end of *Memoirs of a Fox-Hunting Man* Denis Milden, George's hero, disappears into a cavalry regiment. Had Sassoon decided for a more fictionalized approach, Milden might well have been reintroduced in the story. As it is, Milden is completely lost sight of, but Sassoon retains George's hero-worship and his desire to look up to someone (another unmistakeably autobiographical element). In *Memoirs of an Infantry Officer*, Milden is 'replaced' by the much-feared Colonel Kinjack, who is as aloof and superior as Milden, and George is equally delighted to earn his approval: "I felt a wild exultation. Behind me were the horror and the darkness. Kinjack had thanked me" (39). But as Sassoon had written to Robert Graves, the composition of *Memoirs of a Fox-Hunting Man* had been thought out and constructed"; the mainly autobiographical account of *Memoirs of an Infantry Officer* did not allow a role for Colonel Kinjack that was comparable to that of Milden.

VI

Memoirs of an Infantry Officer is clearly not a novel; in the course of his narrative Sassoon is even hampered by his earlier decision to make Sherston an only partly autobiographical persona and has some difficulty explaining the origins of George's war protest. Just like its predecessor, the second volume of Sassoon's memoirs was an immediate popular success on publication: during the next four years it was issued in eight different editions. Even critics who think little of Sassoon's other writings have been kind to this book. Craig Raine calls it his "one real masterpiece", claiming that whereas "in his other prose works there is a struggle between his originality and his models, in which the stereotypes win", in *Memoirs of an Infantry Officer* "the uniqueness of the events deprived Sassoon of possible models".[14] Apart from the fact that Raine clearly underestimates *Memoirs of a Fox-Hunting Man*,[15] the "uniqueness of the events" can only point to Sassoon's war protest. Many of the other events are staple ingredients of Great War literature: the fighting soldiers' dislike of staff officers, the differences in treatment between officers and other ranks and the ignorance of the Home Front are also expressed by Blunden and Graves and in such classic war novels as A.P. Herbert's *The Secret Battle* (1919), R.H. Mottram's *Spanish Farm Trilogy* (1927) and Richard Aldington's *Death of a Hero* (1929).

Whether the *Memoirs* is fiction or non-fiction is a question that keeps the critics divided. On the one hand there is Paul Fussell, who claims that "the *Memoirs* is in every way fictional and that it would be impossible to specify how it differs from any other novel written in the first person and based on the author's own experiences";[16] on the other hand, Jon Silkin clearly takes it as a straight autobiographical account, at times not even allowing for the fact that George Sherston and Siegfried Sassoon are not completely identical.[17] A recent commentator has placed the *Memoirs* in the no man's land between novel and memoir:

The blurring between fiction and memoir occurs famously with Siegfried Sassoon, who writes the 'memoirs' of George

Sherston and also his own. Sherston is clearly not Sassoon, but the overlap is considerable and both sets of memoirs can be seen as versions of one body of material.[18]

But the matter can be complicated even further. The first eight chapters of *Memoirs of a Fox-Hunting Man* are mainly concerned with an account of the world and the people of George's youth and as such they are proper subject of a memoir. However, in the concluding chapters, where George has enlisted and has his first front-line experiences, there are the first signs of George outgrowing his past. There is a gradual shift of focus in the narrative to George's personal development, a process that becomes even more pronounced in *Memoirs of an Infantry Officer*, where George's war protest is the real climax of the book. So irrespective of the question whether Sherston is Sassoon or not, there is a good case to be made for the claim that the book should have been called *Autobiography of an Infantry Officer*. It is at the point where the memoir becomes an autobiography that George Sherston and Siegfried Sassoon almost become one and the same person. This yet again suggests that Sassoon decided on a sequel at a later stage: what prevents Sherston from becoming a pseudonym for Sassoon are the differences between the writer and the persona Sassoon first imposed on Sherston in *Memoirs of a Fox-Hunting Man*: no mother, no brothers and no literary career. That Sassoon increasingly saw Sherston as his *alter ego* is made clear in his correspondence with Robert Graves, when they discuss how Graves persuaded Sassoon to give up his war protest in 1917. In a letter dated 7 February 1930 (seven months before the publication of *Memoirs of an Infantry Officer*) Sassoon objected to the way Graves described this episode in *Goodbye to All That*:[19]

For instance your account of July 1917 was surely an opportunity for impartial exactitude. If such a story was to be divulged by you, nothing should have been omitted. Yet you omitted the crucial fact, that I only consented to take the Medical Board (after refusing the first one) because you swore on the Bible that nothing would induce the authorities to court-martial me.[20]

Sassoon's own meticulous account in *Memoirs of an Infantry Officer* (330-31) is therefore at least partly an attempt to set the record straight. This in turn also means that at that point the *Memoirs* is no longer the autobiography of George Sherston, but of Sassoon himself. Intriguing though this matter is, it is of no particular relevance in assessing the literary qualities of *Memoirs of an Infantry Officer*. As the record of one man's personal war-experiences, it has taken its rightful place among the great British war memoirs. But whereas with the ending of *Memoirs of a Fox-Hunting Man* Sassoon could have conveniently concluded Sherston's story, the more open ending of *Memoirs of an Infantry Officer* more or less forced him to continue his narrative.

CHAPTER 8

SHERSTON'S PROGRESS

I

When Sassoon wrote in his letter to Robert Graves of March 1930 that the narrative of George Sherston had been "carefully thought out and constructed", he was only referring to the first two volumes of the trilogy. Not only did another six years elapse before *Sherston's Progress* completed George Sherston's story, but the book lacks both the intensity of narrative and the cohesive structure of the two preceding volumes.[1] In both *Memoirs of a Fox-Hunting Man* and *Memoirs of an Infantry Officer* George's story is set against a background that gives extra depth to his narrative, and by sharply contrasting the hunting world and the Western Front, Sassoon cleverly illustrated the sudden jolt in his hero's mental development.[2] But in *Sherston's Progress*, the setting has no special function; neither is there a conscious attempt to link the book with the preceding two in any other way than by George Sherston's continuing narrative.

Sassoon must have had great difficulties in devising an overall structure for the book, and the reader's conclusion can only be that he did not succeed in finding one. The gradual shift from a slightly fictionalized memoir in *Memoirs of a Fox-Hunting Man* to an almost straight autobiographical account in *Memoirs of an Infantry Officer* had left him little or no leeway in his narrative, and *Sherston's Progress* suffers greatly under these restrictions. In every respect this final volume is the odd-one-out within the trilogy: the title does not link it with the *Memoirs*, unlike the first two books – which were both divided into ten chapters – *Sherston's Progress* is divided into four parts, and it is much shorter than the others. The publisher made a brave attempt to hide this fact by reducing the number of lines per page from 31 to 25 and printing the titles of the four parts on separate pages, each followed by a blank page. *Sherston's Progress* runs to 280 pages, the first two volumes to 395 and 334 pages. In the first one-volume edition of the *George Sherston Memoirs*, published by Faber in 1937, the number of pages for each of the books is 339, 283 and 175 respectively.

Sherston's Progress starts off well enough: the first part, simply called 'Rivers', is a tribute to his doctor at Craiglockhart, W.H.R. Rivers. By using his friend's real name, Sassoon is all but giving up the pretence of a fictional narrative. The hero-worship that was a characteristic Sassoon shared with his fictionalized *persona*, culminates in the figure of Rivers. This hero-worship could have been one of the unifying themes in the trilogy, but it fails to be so, partly because Colonel Kinjack's role in *Memoirs of an Infantry Officer* is too insignificant in comparison with that of Denis Milden in *Memoirs of a Fox-Hunting Man* and Rivers in *Sherston's Progress*, but also because Sassoon's love and admiration for Rivers are unrestricted: Rivers is not portrayed as a man who was great in George's idolatrous eyes, but as a man whose greatness the reader is expected to freely acknowledge.

II

William Halse Rivers Rivers (the rationale behind his second and third Christian names remains a mystery) was born in Luton on 12 March 1864 and brought up in Maidstone, Kent, in the same part of the country where Sassoon was to spend his youth. Rivers' youth and schooldays were happy, hampered only by the fact that he had a bad stammer. His uncle had published a study on stuttering and stammering in 1854 and later set up an institute for speech therapy near Hastings in Sussex. After his early death in 1869 his work was continued by Rivers' father. Among the patients he received at home was the Oxford don and author of the two *Alice* books Charles Lutwidge Dodgson. During these visits Dodgson seems to have remained true to his dictum "I am fond of children (except boys)", for Rivers' younger sister Katharine later recalled that her brothers were "rather upset" by Dodgson's obvious preference for the company of her sister and herself. Rivers benefited little from his father's treatment and continued to speak with a slight stammer throughout his life.

In 1886 Rivers received his Bachelor of Medicine degree at the University of London and in 1893 he was appointed Lecturer in Psychological and Experimental Psychology at Cambridge. He once said of himself that the desire for change and novelty was one of the strongest elements in his mental make-up, and throughout his life his interests remained varied. Five years later, in 1898, he joined an anthropological expedition to the Torres Straits (a group of small islands north of Australia) and later he also did field work in Egypt and India. In 1903 he started a neurological experiment with his friend and colleague Henry Head, which lasted until December 1907. In order to study nerve regeneration Rivers cut some of the nerves in Head's arm and they carefully recorded the sensory changes during the healing process. Sassoon met Head through Rivers, and they remained close friends after Rivers' death.

When the war broke out Rivers was attending a science conference in Australia. On his return in 1915 he joined the staff of a military hospital in Lancashire as a civilian physician. He was commissioned a Captain in the Royal Army Medical Corps in 1916, and transferred in October of that year to Craiglockhart War Hospital. Towards the end of 1917 he left Craiglockhart, and accepted an appointment as psychologist to the Royal Flying Corps, with the Central Hospital, Hampstead, as his new basis.

Rivers bitterly resented the fact that the military authorities were slow to recognize war neurosis as a serious illness, and that when they finally did accept its existence, they did so for the wrong reason: the behavioural breakdown was attributed to organic injury resulting from high-explosive blast, which made it morally acceptable. Hence "the unfortunate and misleading term 'shell-shock' which the general public have now come to use for the nervous disturbances of warfare".[3] Rivers, on the other hand, believed that the neuroses were caused by the severe and constant mental strains and stresses that the front-line soldier had to contend with. He also made a distinction between the neuroses of private soldiers and of officers, claiming that neuroses among soldiers – who were trained to obey – resulted in physical or sensory disorders which rendered them unfit for further active service, whereas among officers – who were trained to take responsibility – they took the form of mental disorders such as nightmares, hysteria and obsessions. By the end of the war, Rivers was acknowledged as one of the foremost experts on the subject of war neuroses.

As a R.A.M.C. officer it was Rivers' task to prepare his patients for a return to the front. Sassoon's case was extraordinary in that he was not a genuine shell-shock victim, but Rivers still regarded it as his duty to persuade Sassoon to go back. At first he was convinced of the rightness of his stance, but ironically enough, his meetings and conversations with Sassoon (with whom he held an hour's consultation three times a week) were partly responsible for the fact that Rivers eventually gave up his unconditional war support in favour of a preference for a negotiated victory. Sassoon had encouraged him to read Henri Barbusse's anti-war novel *Under Fire* and the *Cambridge Magazine* in which many of his own war poems first appeared.

In Rivers' book *Conflict and Dream* (1923) Sassoon makes a brief appearance as Patient B, though Rivers discusses his case mainly to point out his own moral conflict in trying to persuade Sassoon to give up his protest:

> As a scientific student whose only object should be the attainment of what I supposed to be the truth, it was definitely unpleasant to me to suspect that the opinions which I was uttering might be influenced by the needs of my position, and I was fully aware of an element of constraint in my relations with B on this account. So long as I was in uniform I was not a free agent.[4]

After the war, Rivers returned to Cambridge, concentrating on his work on psychology, psychiatry, sociology and ethnology. He wrote extensively on the theories of Freud and Jung (which he supported – with some reservations), analyzing some of his own dreams in *Conflict and Dream*. He never actively encouraged Sassoon's Labour Party support, but at the time of his death (and much to the disapproval of his Cambridge colleagues) he was himself an official candidate for the Labour Party in the 1922 General Election (in 1920 he had declined an invitation to stand). Through Sassoon, Rivers was also introduced to literary circles: Robert Graves first met him when he delivered Sassoon at Craiglockhart, and was enormously impressed, dedicating his *On English Poetry* (1922) to him (and T.E. Lawrence), and Sassoon also introduced him to H.G. Wells and Arnold Bennett, who became a regular visitor.[5]

Rivers never married, but there is no evidence to suggest he was homosexual. He paid regular visits to his brother and two sisters in Kent (which partly accounts for his frequent visits to Weirleigh). He died unexpectedly on 4 June 1922.

III

George Sherston's surrender to Rivers in *Sherston's Progress* is as complete as Sassoon's had been: already in the very first pages Sherston/Sassoon seems to dismiss his war protest as an emotional and thoughtless action:

> As an R.A.M.C. officer, he [Rivers] was bound to oppose my 'pacifist tendency', but his arguments were always indirect. Sometimes he gently indicated inconsistencies in my impulsively expressed opinions, but he never contradicted me. Of course the weak point about my 'protest' had been that it was evoked by personal feeling. It was an emotional idea based on my war experience and stimulated by the acquisition of points of view which I accepted uncritically. (21)

The reader may well wonder if the way Sherston accepts Rivers' opinions is in any way less uncritical, but it is with this acceptance that the spiritual development of the Sportsman/Soldier George Sherston effectively comes to an end:

> My talks with Rivers had increased my awareness of the limitations of my pre-war life. He had shown that he believed me to be capable of achieving something useful. He had set me on the right road and made me feel that if the war were to end tomorrow I should be starting on a new life's journey in which point-to-point races and cricket matches were no longer to be supremely important and a strenuous effort must be made to take some small share in the real work of the world. (72-3)

It is at this point that Sassoon's narrative collapses as a result of the irreconcilable differences between the limitations of the Sherston persona and the autobiographical facts that are here referred to. Sassoon never gave Sherston the literary career that had helped him to bridge the Hunting Man-Infantry Officer gap, nor did he allow George to develop an interest in socialist politics as a result of his war protest. So the 'new life' that George could build up as a civilian remains totally obscure: within the restrictions he has placed on the Sherston persona this narrational avenue is effectively blocked.

Sassoon must have gradually begun to realize that he had painted himself into a corner, which made the writing of *Sherston's Progress* a laborious task. His grip on the narrative slackens as he more and more begins to comment on his own writing: at the beginning of Part I, chapter II he claims that:

> While composing these apparently interminable memoirs there have been moments when my main problem was what to select from the 'long littleness' – or large untidiness – of life. (33)[6]

Sassoon may well have been a bit misleading here: it is not so much that he had to consider what he *would* put in, as that he had to think what he *could* put in. A few lines down he admits that "while writing about Slateford I suffer from a shortage of anything to say" (33). This is hardly surprising: apart from his encounter with Rivers, the main events during his stay at Craiglockhart in 1917 had been the visits from his London friends, but these he cannot mention because George has no London friends; and the first meeting and ensuing friendship with Wilfred Owen, which he cannot describe because George is not a famous war poet. At times Sassoon cannot resist an oblique reference to one of his London friends, but the only effect this has on his narrative is that he tends to lose his grip on George even further, since these mysterious friends suggest a life for George outside Sassoon's *Memoirs* which the reader until then would never have even suspected: George's constant companion is a little talisman: "It was a lump of fire-opal clasped on a fine golden chain. Someone whose friendship I valued highly had given it to me when I went to France ..." (53). The friend in question was Lady Ottoline Morrell, who also came to visit Sassoon at Craiglockhart, but within the Sherston narrative she had to remain anonymous (and, strictly speaking, she should not have been mentioned at all).

And so Sassoon had to restrict himself to an account of the changes in his state of mind while at Craiglockhart. But that did not provide him with a lot of material either; he had been so willing to see the error of his ways that the confrontations between Rivers and Sherston were a rather one-sided affair: the few occasions that George does speak up in his own defence, Rivers does not even deign to reply:

> In the silence that ensued I was aware that I had said something particularly fatuous, and hurriedly remarked that the people in Germany must be getting jolly short of food. I was really very ignorant, picking up my ideas as I went along. (22)

Again the reader is fully justified in thinking that at this moment Sherston is picking up his ideas from Rivers, but Sassoon had no irony in mind here. Under Rivers' influence, he had distanced himself from his war protest, as is made plain in his encounter with Doctor Macamble. Macamble is a leading pacifist who has heard about Sherston's action and comes to see him at Slateford to propose a continuation of his protest:

> Doctor Macamble advised me to abscond from Slateford. I had only to take a train to London, and once I was there he would arrange for me to be examined by an 'eminent alienist' who would infallibly certify that I was completely normal and entirely responsible for my actions. (41)

The suggestion seems reasonable: in *Memoirs of an Infantry Officer* (331) Sherston was persuaded to face the Medical Board because Cromlech told him that he would never be court martialled but simply locked up in a lunatic asylum. Macamble offered Sherston the chance to fight that decision on medical grounds. But Sherston's critical stance is a thing of the past, his loyalties lie elsewhere now: "all I thought was, 'Good Lord, he's trying to persuade me to do the dirty on Rivers!'" (42). Sassoon is not interested in saddling Sherston with a moral conflict of divided loyalties between Rivers on the one hand, and the pacifists who backed his protest on the other. And so he obscures the reasonableness of Macamble's proposal by ridiculing the man himself:

> After listening to him for about an hour and a half I could be certain of one thing only – that he believed himself to be rather a great man. And like so many of us who maintain that belief, he had so far found very few people to agree with him in his optimistic self-estimate. I suspect that he looked on me as a potential disciple; anyhow he urgently desired to shepherd me along the path to a salvation which was, unquestionably, the exact antithesis to army life. (40)

Again there is an unintentional irony here: George is not as independent-minded as this passage wants to suggest, but is in fact following a different Messiah,[7] one who has convinced the man who a month earlier had challenged the military authorities of the fact that his salvation cannot lie at the end of a path that takes him away from the army.

Time and time again Sherston refuses to face up to the moral dilemmas. As soon as the question arises he allows his thoughts to drift off. One afternoon, sitting in his room cleaning his golf clubs, George realizes that if he is no longer a 'man with a message' he is staying at Slateford under false pretences and ought to return to the front:

> Against this I argued that, having pledged myself to an uncompromising attitude, I ought to remain consistent to the abstract idea that the war was wrong. Intellectual sobriety was demanded of me. But the trouble was that I wasn't an 'intellectual' at all; I was only trying to become one. I was also, it seemed, trying to become a good golfer. Rivers had never played golf in his life, though he approved of it as a healthy recreation. (51-2)

The thoughts of the mature Sassoon intrude on those of the young Sherston when he observes that he was only trying to become an intellectual: that was the gradual discovery Sassoon had made in the early 1920s. But eventually Sherston does decide that he has to return to the front, and with this decision Part I effectively comes to an end, though the final paragraph contains an impassioned plea for more understanding of shell-shock victims and a diatribe against the Churches that "sanctioned and glorified" the explosives that had destroyed these brave and noble men (89).

Part II is mainly set in Ireland and though entertaining, it is repetitive and of no real importance for the story. Michael Thorpe has observed that "its presence is responsible for the diminished intensity of the final volume of the trilogy",[8] and this is unmistakably the case. Sassoon copied George's itinerary before he is posted to Ireland from his diaries without sufficient editing, for again there is a mention of London friends and theatre visits that fit uneasily into George's narrative (100). The episode in Ireland is in essence no more than a comic interlude, a return to the Surteesian hunting scenes of *Memoirs of a Fox-Hunting Man*, and Sassoon does not attempt to suggest that George's attitude to this world has significantly changed. He still enjoys a good ride and refrains from critical comments and/or observations.

Part III consists of four months of Sherston's diaries, February-June 1918 (when Sassoon's was with the 25th Battalion RWF first in Palestine and then transferred back to France), which in its way does nothing to unify the narrative and lends further support to the idea that Sassoon had lost interest in the trilogy (the *Diaries 1915-1918* confirm that there are only minor changes and omissions). One of these omissions was necessitated by the fact that Sassoon had been carefully selecting the best material from his war diaries for *Memoirs of a Fox-Hunting Man* (which yet again suggests that originally he never intended to write a trilogy). The extract from a soldier's letter quoted in the book, "*Everywhere we go seems such a long way*" (*MFH*, 351), has in fact been taken from his 1918 diary (*DI*, 250).

In the course of Part IV Sassoon observes that "our inconsistencies are often what make us most interesting, and it is possible that, in my zeal to construct these memoirs carefully, I have eliminated too many of my own self-contradictions" (242). This is as close as Sassoon gets to admitting that he had run out of possibilities with the Sherston persona.[9] This lack of interest is also suggested by other inconsistencies in the Sherston persona, as when he is suddenly shown to be quite keen on novels (he reads Lamb, Scott, Tolstoy, Hardy and Duhamel) and modern poetry: "after tea the mail came in; a good one for me as it contained de la Mare's new book of poems"

(212). Sherston's enthusiasm about *Motley and Other Poems* (1918) is completely out of character, as is his delight at finding that Velmore (V.S. de Sola Pinto), his new second-in-command, is equally literary-minded: the junior officers "exchange embarrassed glances" and leave as soon as possible as Velmore and Sherston start reading J. E. Flecker's *The Golden Journey to Samarkand* aloud to each other (230-31). In spite of these inconsistencies, Part IV, the final section of the book, is a marked improvement on the preceding two parts. The narrative relates Sherston's last months at the Western Front, how he was shot in the head by one of his own men on sentry duty when returning from a patrol in no man's land,[10] and ends with Rivers visiting him in an English hospital. The return of Rivers neatly rounds off the structure of *Sherston's Progress*, though it cannot compensate for the weaknesses of Parts II and III.

On his patrol in no man's land Sherston actually reaches the German trenches, and for a moment it seems as if his soldiering career reaches some sort of a climax, in that it is the first time he actually sees the enemy:

> I was at last more or less in contact with the enemies of England. I had come from Edinburgh via Limerick and Jerusalem, drawing full pay for seven months, and I could now say that I had seen some of the people I was fighting against. (254)

There is a certain ambiguity in this passage: on the one hand Sherston says that he is "at last" in contact with the enemy, which would suggest that it is the very first time, but the following sentence makes plain that he is only referring to his post-Slateford period. Sassoon must have felt that he had *almost* found the theme that could unify the trilogy: it would have been appropriate to end the story of the fox-hunter who became a soldier, a rebel, and then a soldier again, with his first real encounter with the enemy. But unfortunately it was *not* the first time Sherston saw real-live Germans: in *Memoirs of an Infantry Officer* Sassoon had given the autobiographical account of his one-man attack on an enemy trench, when "quite unexpectedly, I found myself looking down into a well-conducted trench with a great many Germans in it" (*MIO*, 91), and he had thus deprived himself of the chance to use this as a unifying theme.

Sherston's second meeting with the enemy, then, is handled with an irony that is reminiscent of a similar scene in *Memoirs of a Fox-Hunting Man*. The enemy George creeps up on proves to be something of an anticlimax: "what I saw was four harmless young Germans who were staring up at a distant aeroplane" (254). This is not unlike George the young fox-hunter's first encounter with a fox in Park Wood: "Something rustled the dead leaves; not more than ten yards from where we stood, a small russet animal stole out on to the path and stopped for a photographic instant to take a look at us" (*MFH*, 58). George's reaction then had been to shout out "Don't do that; they'll catch him!", in response to Denis Milden's hunting call. His reaction now is equally inglorious: on being spotted by a young German he beats a fast retreat (255). Similarly, where in *Memoirs of a Fox-Hunting Man* Sassoon carefully avoids involving Sherston in the bloodier episodes of hunting, he is here equally keen to stress the harmlessness of Sherston's aggressive actions: when George later returns with a Corporal, throwing a few Mills bombs, he notes that "I don't for a moment suppose that we hit anybody, but the deed was done" (263-64).

Earlier Sassoon had pointed out that in the memoirs "it is my own story that I am trying to tell, and as such it must be received; those who expect a universalization of the Great War must look for it elsewhere" (*MIO*, 17). The blood-and-guts phase of the war poetry lay a long way behind him; there he *had* tried to universalize the war, in the memoirs the anger is replaced by a detached mildness. A year before his death, Sassoon wrote that as far as his writings on the war were concerned, he believed that it was the *Memoirs* that would prove to be of lasting value:

> I am a firm believer in the Memoirs, and am still inclined to think that the war poems (the significant and successful ones) will end up as mere appendices to the matured humanity of the Memoirs (*LC*, 14).

IV

When Sassoon started writing *Memoirs of a Fox-Hunting Man* in 1926 it was a first attempt to write prose; its success gave him the confidence he so badly needed after the disappointing results of his poetic ventures *Picture Show* and *Satirical Poems*. Ten years later, when he completed *Sherston's Progress*, Sassoon's circumstances had altered completely: financially secure, he was living in the peace and quiet of Heytesbury House. In *Sherston's Progress* the former war rebel and socialist explains this withdrawal:

> A ruminator really needs two lives; one for experiencing and another for thinking it over. Knowing that I *need* two lives and am only allowed one, I do my best to *lead* two lives; with the inevitable consequence that I am told by the world's busybodies that I am 'turning my back on the contemporary situation' (104).

The Sherston *persona* has by now lost its *raison d'être*, and Sassoon carelessly shifts from 'I' to 'Sherston'. In the concluding lines of the *Sherston Trilogy* the voice is Sassoon's:

> It has been a long journey from that moment to this, when I write the last words of my book. And my last words shall be these – that it is only from the inmost silences of the heart that we know the world for what it is, and ourselves for what the world has made us. (280)

This is no longer the voice of the author of the first two volumes of the trilogy, rather it is the poet of *The Heart's Journey* and *Vigils*, the weary pilgrim in search of peace and inner stability. By virtue of its title *Sherston's Progress* is obviously linked with Bunyan's *Pilgrim's Progress*,[11] a connection which is further underlined by the quotation from *Pilgrim's Progress* Sassoon uses as the epigraph to his book. The line he quotes is one spoken by Faithful: "I told him I was a Pilgrim, going to the Celestial City".[12] The Great War which Sassoon had survived was a fitting equivalent of the City of Destruction that Christian left behind, but at the end of John Bunyan's book Christian has completed his journey and entered the Celestial City. Siegfried Sassoon realized that he still had a long way to go, especially since in the course of writing *Sherston's Progress* he must have come to the conclusion that if he wanted to investigate his past, he would have to start all over again.

And so *Sherston' Progress* ends the trilogy with Sherston in hospital and with the reappearance of Dr Rivers. In these last pages, the religious element that the book's title and epigraph had introduced at the outset, is personified in the benign figure of Dr Rivers. Moments earlier Sherston has been worrying himself close to despair:

I was nearly thirty-two and nothing that I'd done seemed to have been any good. There was some consolation in the feeling that one wasn't as old as one's age, but when I tried to think about the future I found that I couldn't see it. There was no future except 'the rest of the war', and I didn't want that. (278)

Then the door opens and Rivers, the man Sherston had called his 'father-confessor', enters to drive away all the terrible thoughts that have been tormenting him:

And then, unexpected and unannounced, Rivers came in and closed the door behind him. Quiet and alert, purposeful and unhesitating, he seemed to empty the room of everything that had needed exorcising. (279)

The hero-worship of the earlier volumes has become part of the religious pilgrimage Sassoon had embarked on in his poetry. Rivers is welcomed as his personal Saviour, and he willingly surrenders his self to the trusted doctor.

In March 1917 Sassoon had noted in his diary that "*Religious feeling* is a snare set by one's emotional weakness" (*D1*, 142), and George Sherston on that bleak Easter Sunday of the last page of *Memoirs of a Fox-Hunting Man* had been unable to find "consolation in the thought that Christ had risen" (*MFH*, 395). But the religious vocabulary in *Sherston's Progress* and the priest-like figure of Dr Rivers clearly point in which direction Sassoon and his *alter ego* Sherston were heading.

One is reminded of a last instance of unintentional irony, when in *Memoirs of a Fox-Hunting Man* Sassoon adds an aside on Colonel Winchell's Adjutant: "The Adjutant, by the way, became a Roman Catholic priest after the War, and it doesn't surprise me that he felt the need for a change of mental atmosphere" (*MFH*, 365).

CHAPTER 9

THE PAST REVISITED:
THE AUTOBIOGRAPHIES

I

"Far off in earliest remembered childhood I can overhear myself repeating the words 'Watercress Well'. I am kneeling by an old stone well-head: my mother is standing beside me and we are looking in the water". This is the first of the two evocative memories that Sassoon recounts in the Prelude which opens *The Old Century and Seven More Years* (1938).[1] In the second he again hears his own voice: "This time it asks a question. 'What will the seeds be like when they come up?' I am standing beside my mother, who is making a water-colour sketch of a man sowing". These two earliest memories symbolize the purpose of the book, in which the author means "to tell whither the water journeyed from its source, and how the seed came up". This seems to suggest that Sassoon seriously intended to reinvestigate his youth in an attempt to come to a better understanding of his own personality, without making the mistakes he confessed to towards the end of the Sherston-trilogy, when he wrote that over-simplification had made self-analysis impossible. But if ever this was his intention, he does not carry it through. As in the *Memoirs of a Fox-Hunting Man*, Sassoon shies away from an objective investigation of the late-Victorian and Edwardian Age and his own youth. Towards the end of the book he admits that he does not want to recall the sad and unhappy events of his youth: "All human beings desire to be glad. I prefer to remember my own gladness and good luck, and to forget, whenever I can, these moods and minor events which made me low-spirited and unresponsive" (245). In later years Sassoon emphasized these escapist purposes, claiming that he wrote *The Old Century* (in the winters of 1936 and 1937) "to afford people nostalgic escape in those years of imminent catastrophe" (*LC*, 14). It seems likely, however, that this decision was made in the course of writing the book, for the early chapters of *The Old Century* strongly suggest that originally Sassoon *did* intend to write an autobiography in which he would faithfully analyze his early years and background.

But it was not purely Sassoon's escapist desires that made him change course half-way through *The Old Century*:

> having concentrated on one set of dichotomies within his personality in the Sherston memoirs, Sassoon found that he couldn't repeat himself. So the new dichotomies which he displays for the first time in the three volumes of straight autobiography once again present a partial picture of the complex totality.[2]

In *The Old Century* Sassoon sets out to provide many of the elements in his life that were left out of the Sherston memoirs. In the first five chapters he focuses on people: his parents, his brothers, the Thornycroft relatives, and his Aunt Rachel (his father's younger sister).[3] In chapters VI to IX he concentrates on his younger self: how his brothers were technically-minded and he was quite content to remain alone, how recurring ill-health regularly kept him a convalescent at home, and how this drew him to his mother. The artistic background and interests that Sherston never had are widely discussed: these are numerous references to painters, musicians, writers, his reading habits and his early efforts at writing poetry.[4] But then in chapter X these activities are put in a different perspective. Writing about his younger self, the adventure novels he read, the many dreams he dreamt about all he wanted to be and do, he is delighted by the general feeling of expectancy and optimism:

> Merely to think of it makes me feel quite young again, and for a moment I am disknowledged of this time-trod world to which I was then awakening, ignorant of myself and light as the air. (165)

Sassoon then continues to indulge in these distorted, nostalgic reminiscences, at times interrupting his narrative to explain that he is aware of the distortion, but that his account is not the deadly serious high-brow stuff intellectuals might write:

> While attempting to compose an outline of my own mental history, I have sometimes been interrupted by a nudging suspicion that I am not recording the past as it really was ... And I feel the unbending visages of the realists reproving me for failing to imitate their awful and astringent example. (245)

This is the voice of the Georgian writer, attempting to please a wide audience and critical of the intellectuals (i.e. Modernists), whose high demands on what good art is supposed to be, take away all the pleasure and enjoyment, both for the writer and his readers. But Sassoon conveniently forgets that in the Prelude to his book he did claim that the aim of the book was to investigate "whither the water journeyed" and "how the seed came up", and that he said nothing about intending to take a nostalgic look back at the late-Victorian and Edwardian years. The truth is, that by leaving out all his sporting activities, the picture he presented of his younger self was again incomplete. Also, his homosexuality, although it had consistently featured as a major theme in his plans for a prose book in the early 1920s, was never discussed in either the Sherston memoirs or the autobiographies. And so, in the course of writing *The Old Century*, Sassoon decided to follow his inclinations, and for a second time gave up his idea of an autobiographical self-analysis.

II

Whereas the works of R.S. Surtees were a dominant influence on the mood and setting of *Memoirs of a Fox-Hunting Man*, it is in Walter Pater's footsteps that Sassoon is following in *The Old Century*. In *The Weald of Youth* he recalled how, as a boy, Pater's *Imaginary Portraits* (1887), with "their atmosphere of life treated as 'an act of recollection', subdued to the stately movement and lulling cadences of his style" (*WY*, 33), had captivated him: "I became such a devotee of Pater that for the time being I could read no-one else" (*WY*, 33). Though he is not among the authors mentioned by name in *The Old Century*, both subject and style are a constant reminder of his work.

In August 1878 Pater's most autobiographical piece, 'The Child in the House', was first published in *Macmillan's Magazine.*[5] It is this story that must have been at the back of Sassoon's mind when he conceived *The Old Century*, for in theme and atmosphere both writings show many similarities. Pater's 'The Child in the House' is the story of Florian Deleal, who, on one of his afternoon walks, meets an old man who by chance mentions the place where Florian had spent his earliest years. That night he dreams about his childhood home, and

> it happened that this accident of his dream was just the thing needed for the beginning of a certain design he then had in view, the noting, namely, of some things in the story of his spirit – in that process of brain-building by which we are, each one of us, what we are. (173)

This is exactly what Sassoon set out to do in the Prelude of *The Old Century*. Also, Florian's early years were spent in a homely atmosphere that was remarkably similar to Theresa Sassoon's Weirleigh, and both homes were in the same part of the country:

> With Florian, then, the sense of home became singularly intense, his good fortune being that the special character of his home was in itself so home-like. As after many wanderings I have come to fancy that some parts of Surrey and Kent are, for Englishmen, the true landscape, true home-counties. (179)

For Pater, the childhood home is of particular importance, because it

> gradually becomes a kind of material shrine or sanctuary of sentiment; a system of visible symbolism interweaves itself through all our thoughts and passions; and irresistibly, little shapes, voices, accidents – the angle at which the sun in the morning fell on the pillow – become part of the great chain wherewith we are bound. (178)

The importance of Weirleigh in *The Old Century* is more than obvious: the book consists of two parts ('The Old Century' and 'Seven More Years' – Sassoon originally intended to call the second part

'Educational Experiences) and the first part is almost exclusively set at Weirleigh. The significance of little shapes, voices and accidents is immediately illustrated in the two childhood memories of the Prelude, where in both instances it is his own voice that Sassoon hears.

Though Pater's story stresses the importance of the family home and how the people living in it bring it to life, it ends by reminding the reader that a house dies as soon as its occupants leave. When the family move out and Florian returns to fetch a pet bird, the sight of the empty house leaves a lasting impression:

> as he passed in search of it from room to room, lying so pale, with a look of meekness in their denudation, and at last through that little, stripped white room, the aspect of the place touched him like the face of one dead". (196)

This was not an experience Sassoon wanted to share: he did not take the risk of making a sentimental journey to Weirleigh, but he did revisit the Edingthorpe Rectory, the house where the family spent their 1897 summer holiday. He later referred to this chapter in *The Old Century* as "one of the best things I ever wrote" (*LC*, 14), and it indeed displays the evocative power of Sassoon's writing.[6]

The summer of August 1937 must have been an extraordinary one: when Sassoon revisited the Norfolk village he was struck by the peace and quiet of that summer afternoon; it was as if time was suspended and the past within easy reach

> It happened that I met no one at all this time; going into the past, forty years afterwards, seemed almost as easy as thinking oneself back there. I had only to sit, with one finger on the steering-wheel, and stare around me. Everything was very quiet, as though it were keeping quite still so that I could have a good look at it. (132)

The man who went in search of his past to the Somerset village of East Coker that same month had a similar experience; he too was struck by the feeling that for the moment time had stopped:

> the deep lane insists on the direction
> Into the village, in the electric heat

Hypnotised. In a warm haze the sultry light
Is absorbed, not refracted, by grey stone.
The dahlias sleep in the empty silence.[7]

In that quiet, hot summer weather T. S. Eliot and Siegfried Sassoon both experienced a moment of timelessness on their journey back in time: Eliot returning to his seventeenth-century English ancestors, Sassoon to his former ten-year-old self:

how easily it showed me myself as I then was – a boy in a brown jersey and corduroy shorts bleached by many washings, sitting in the long grass with his knees up to his chin, reading *The Invisible Man*. (140)

At this extraordinary moment the mature Sassoon becomes "the invisible man", standing next to his younger self:

He doesn't look up or move as I stand beside him – that H.G. Wells-absorbed boy with reddish-brown hair. He knows nothing of the delusions and discontents which he must muddle his way out of before he can be looked back on, almost as though he were someone in another life. (140)

Pater always avoided the disappointments of maturity: Marius and Florian are only described as young men, and the promising, sensitive young men in the *Imaginary Portraits* all die an early death. The first of these *Imaginary Portraits*, 'A Prince of Court Painters', is based on the life of Antoine Watteau, the successful early eighteenth-century French painter of fashionable society. Pater describes him as a keen observer who sees through the superficiality of this glamorous world: "For him, to understand must be to despise".[8] In Sassoon's case it was rather that to understand must be to become disillusioned, but like Pater, he had no desire to dwell on this: in *The Old Century* there are no further references to the trials and tribulations that were to follow.

Of Pater's style it has been said that "although generated by temporality and flux, [his] art perversely aspires, syntactically, to the atmosphere of a painting or a tapestry: static, pictorial, nonlinear".[9] At times Sassoon and Pater are almost indistinguishable:

(I)

> The perfume of the little flowers of the lime-tree fell through
> the air upon them like rain; while time seemed to move ever
> more slowly to the murmur of the bees in it, till it almost stood
> still on June afternoons. How insignificant, at the moment,
> seem the influences of the sensible things which are tossed and
> fall and lie about us, so, or so, in the environment of early
> childhood.

(II)

> Meanwhile the warm air was aromatic with the musky smells
> of the autumn garden; trails of gossamer wavered silkily across
> vistas of sunshine, and everything seemed imbued with
> reluctance to do more than doze on into an idle afternoon.

The mood and style of these passages are very similar. But the
difference in style becomes apparent when the following lines are
quoted: in the first passage, which is from Pater's 'The Child in the
House' (177), the flow of the sentence comes to a halt when Pater's
search for the right word and exact phrase for the formulation of a
timeless truth leads to numerous clauses, sub-clauses and excessive
punctuation:

> How indelibly, as we afterwards discover, they affect us; with
> what capricious attractions and associations they figure
> themselves on the white paper, the smooth wax, of our
> ingenious souls, as 'with lead in the rock forever', giving form
> and feature, and as it were assigned house-room in our
> memory, to early experiences of feeling and thought, which
> abide with us ever afterwards, thus, and not otherwise.

In the second passage, on the other hand, Sassoon maintains the flow
of the sentence. He creates his effect with words rather than with
syntax, and instead of his narrative ending in a generalization, the
introduction of the personal pronoun leads to a personal observation:

> These old friends of ours hadn't changed very much since my
> childhood, I thought. I had looked up at them for the first time
> as I played on this sloping path, where I sniffed the scent of

June from the tree-peonies which hung large white heads after a
shower of rain. (302)

Sassoon is a follower of Pater in his celebration of the innocence and
impressionability of childhood, in his sensitive and carefully observed
descriptions of nature and in his disillusionment with the world as he
grew older,[10] but they differ in that Sassoon's prose always remained
easily accessible – both in style and content – and in that Pater always
used a *persona* or a generalization for his personal observations,
whereas for Sassoon the first-person narrative was the natural mode.

III

By Sassoon's own admission, *The Old Century* is not a rigorous self-
analysis, but neither is it the happy escapist book he claims it to be. In
the first ten chapters of the book, his looking back is nearly always
tinged with a slight sadness and melancholy, which is best described
as 'a sense of loss'. Compared to the childhood memories of Sassoon's
contemporary Gwen Raverat,[11] as recorded in *Period Piece* (1952),
The Old Century could not possibly be called a 'happy' book. Raverat
describes her carefree Cambridge childhood with delightful humour
and without any regrets that it belongs to the past and will never come
back. When Sassoon looks back on his childhood in the Kentish
Weald the mood is closer to A.E. Housman's:

> That is the land of lost content,
> I see it shining plain,
> The happy highways where I went
> And cannot come again.
>
> (*A Shropshire Lad*, XL)

There is always a regret that the past is now forever out of reach.
Raverat's description of her endearingly ridiculous relatives may well
cause bursts of laughter, but in Sassoon's book, where a mood of
carefree happiness is absent, the humour at best evokes only a smile,
and in most instances only a sad smile. This is best illustrated in one
of the most poignant passages, when he remembers a visit from his
father, who was then separated from his wife and only occasionally
coming over to spend an afternoon with his three sons:

> She [Theresa Sassoon] used to shut herself up in the drawing-room when my father came, but one autumn afternoon we were out in the garden and he was giving us a ride in the gardener's handcart. We were all three shouting and thoroughly enjoying ourselves when we came round the corner of some rhododendrons and met my mother, whose self-repression had perhaps relaxed and had released her in the forlorn hope of some reconciliation. Anyhow, there she stood and we all went past her in sudden silence. I have never forgotten the look on her face. It was the first time I had seen life being brutal to someone I loved. But I was helpless, for my father's face had gone blank and obstinate, and the situation, like the handcart, was in his hands. (28-9)

The witticism in the last line is a rather feeble attempt to relieve the tension of this poignant scene, but the best it can hope for is a rather wry smile.

There are too many similar episodes in the first part of *The Old Century* for it ever to become a happy book. Chapter II is devoted to the deaths of grandmother Thornycroft and Sassoon's father, and the departure of Mrs Mitchell, the children's nurse: Sassoon's timeless past is in fact full of changes. The impression he gives of himself as a child is that of a quiet, over-sensitive boy, who already at an early age had a wistful understanding of the meaning of the word 'never': when his father dies he feels desolate "because of so much happiness which could never happen now that he was dead" (50). When Mrs Mitchell is about to leave the family because the children are getting too old, Siegfried is not looking forward to this new chapter in his life:

> We shall never go blackberrying with her again, I thought; and I saw the past as something cosy and familiar [...] The future was like an empty room in which we had to start all over again after a thorough spring-cleaning of our prolonged childhood. (49-50)

Immediately after her departure the sense of loss is still very strong: "Gazing rather wistfully at the Ariston organ and its pile of cardboard tunes on the shelf in the corner, I suddenly realized that she would

never grind its handle again. Our nursery jollifications were all over"
(53). Although Sassoon had written in his 1930s poem 'Doggerel
About Old Days' that "In 1909 the future was a thing desired", this is
not the impression he gives in his recollections of his former self; for
the young Siegfried each change meant an ending rather than a new
beginning.

That the past would be a source of comfort for the war-weary
Sassoon is perfectly understandable, but what *The Old Century* seems
to reveal is that for him there had been a 'happy past' at every stage of
his life. He always seems to have had an almost masochistic
awareness of a past that had been better but that would never return.
As a child he was deeply affected by his parents' separation, and
standing in the spare bedroom the eleven-year old boy is reminded of
happier days by a long frame of photographs hanging over the
mantelpiece: "All the photographs were of my mother's friends as
they used to be before she 'began to see so little of them'. There was a
sort of 'happy past' feeling about them" (116). Ten years later similar
thoughts occur to him when he is in his mother's studio:

if only the Studio could write reminiscences of its grown-up
childhood how interesting they would be! My mother seldom
spoke of those times, but the Studio had seen the happiness that
came before those sad times which had so impressed
themselves on my mind; and I would have liked to hear more
about my father as he was at his best. (293-94)

The young boy is longing for happy times that occurred before he
actually was born!

IV

In *The Golden Sovereign* the poet and novelist Richard Church (1893-
1972), Sassoon's near-contemporary and like him the author of an
autobiographical trilogy, recalls how at the age of seventeen he came
under the spell of Thomas Hardy: "And Hardy's sombre genius,
saturated in nostalgia for an ever-vanishing past, flowed into my
character, through channels already prepared by my childhood
experiences". He then goes on to say that the two writers of his

generation "who are equally, if not more indebted to the same monitor are Siegfried Sassoon and Cecil Day-Lewis".[12]

Sassoon was in his late twenties when he started reading Hardy: "Since the war began I had taken to reading Hardy and he was now my main admiration among living writers" (*SJ*, 13). That he developed his preference for Hardy's work during the war years illustrates its importance for the growth of Sassoon's mental independence: his mother did not approve of Hardy at all, referring to him as "an unpleasant writer" (*D1*, 171). Like Richard Church, Sassoon was deeply affected by what he called the "grim, wise fatalism" of Hardy's writing (*D1*, 171); and especially in the at times bleak mood of the first half of *The Old Century*, Hardy's influence is unmistakable.

When Sassoon writes about his "queer craving to revisit the past and give the modern world the slip" (140), it seems likely that his own war-memories and the threat of a new global war were not the only reasons for his desire to escape from 'the modern world'. The particular circumstances in the modern world were not all-important; what his self-portrait in *The Old Century* seems to suggest is that from his earliest youth he had wanted to escape from reality. He mistrusted change, and the reality of the present is that it is ever changing. But in his memory the past was fixed and unchanging.

The book ends on Sassoon's twenty-first birthday, the day he reaches maturity (in years if not in spirit), and when he goes to his mother's studio he finds a butterfly fluttering against the window. He manages to catch it and then discovers "that one of the loftiest ambitions of my childhood had been belatedly realized. I had caught a Camberwell Beauty" (291). As a child he had spent many an afternoon catching butterflies, but now that he has finally managed to get this rare specimen it makes him realize that he has changed: "there it was - casually caught, and now ironically reminding me that it was no longer the apex of my ambitions" (291-92). Time travels on, and his childhood now lay behind him.

Ten years before, in the winter of 1897, his mother had organized some tableaux vivants. In one of them, 'The Artist's Dream', a painter dreamed of the masterpiece he would one day create. When the curtain rose and his mother threw gold dust from behind the stage

A girl with an aureole of fair hair and angel's wings was standing with my younger brother, a beautiful dark child also in white. He looked as if he really was an angel, and her face seemed timeless in a serenity that could never be altered. Gazing at those seraphic forms in the snowstorm of slowly descending motes of gold, I could feel that I had never seen anything more lovely. I did not know how sadly true to time and life it was – that entrancing illusion of perpetual innocence. (83-4)

The serenity "seemed" timeless and the scene of perpetual innocence was only an "illusion", an illusion that was painfully 'unlearned' in later life: the girl's name is forgotten and his younger brother was killed in the Great War. It seems as if the author of *The Old Century and Seven More Years*, who repeatedly writes about his "desire not to remember unpleasant things very clearly" (260), tried to transform his childhood into an equally entrancing, timeless illusion, an illusion he vigorously wanted to believe in and one he was careful never to destroy, but that does not mean to say that it is a happy book. The writing of it may have given Sassoon much happiness, the reliving of some of the episodes may have given him great contentment, but for the reader *The Old Century* is essentially a wistful book, a book about lost happiness rather than just happiness.

V

There is a two-year gap between *The Old Century* and *The Weald of Youth*,[13] which begins in May 1909. Michael Thorpe suggests that

This work might aptly be sub-titled 'The Growing Pains of a Poet' [....] It continues the story of a lucky life, a life which has known no tragedy, struggle, or deep misfortune throughout its first twenty-eight years.[14]

Though I would agree with the first part of this statement (as in *Memoirs of a Fox-Hunting Man*, Wordsworth's *The Prelude* seems still to have been at the back of Sassoon's mind), I do not think it would be correct to claim that Sassoon had known no deep misfortune or tragedy. Certainly his life was a privileged one from a material point of view, but one cannot simply ignore the effects that the separation of his parents, the unhappiness of his mother, and the death of his father had on the sensitive boy of *The Old Century*. The image of a peaceful, happy youth which Sassoon wanted to create in his autobiographies is by his own admission a deceptive one: it is an illusion he wanted to believe in, but a careful reading will at times reveal glimpses of a reality that was decidedly less rosy.

The Weald of Youth, then, is mainly concerned with the initial stages of Sassoon's career as a poet, though there are occasional lapses into "open-air memories" (i.e. point-to-point races), which, according to the author, "make easier and more enjoyable recording than my activities as a man of letters" (146). It is, therefore, doubtful whether the title of the book is ideally suited to its contents. Sassoon took it from one of his own poems, 'Heart and Soul', published in his 1939 volume *Rhymed Ruminations*, two lines of which he quotes as the epigraph to the book:

> Looked on, the darkening weald grows dearer.
> Weald of Youth, a remembered word.

This would suggest that the book's setting is on the whole not different from that of *The Old Century*. But in actual fact it covers the years 1909-1914, from Sassoon's twenty-third up to his twenty-eighth year, the period of his life in which he moved to London and was first introduced to the literary world.

In *The Old Century* Sassoon recalled how, during his years at Cambridge, he first became aware of "the sense of time slipping away from me, of not making serious use of my opportunities" (*OC*, 265-66). One might expect that such an awareness would have induced some activity, but the young Sassoon of *The Weald of Youth* is characterized by a total lack of initiative. It has been argued that in this second volume

> the author's self is less interesting than in *The Old Century*, since he shows no significant development [.....] But since [it] is not so narrowly the focus of interest as in the previous book, his slow development is not fatal to the book as a whole.[15]

I do not think that it is the development of the self that accounts for the quality of *The Old Century* (there was no significant development in that volume either), rather I think that Sassoon is at his best in the evocation of his childhood years: the quality of Sassoon's writing is equal to the interest he takes in its subject, and for him his childhood was by far the most interesting period of his life.

A new feature of this second autobiography is the brief sketches of literary figures Sassoon encountered in London. With his mother he is invited to an afternoon party at the Gosse's (a party in honour of the now all-but-forgotten Dutch novelist Maarten Maartens, who wrote most of his works in English).[16] Here he meets Edward Marsh, who persuades him to move to London and finds him rooms at Gray's Inn, and there are brief encounters with Rupert Brooke, W.H. Davies and George Moore.

As with the other autobiographies, what *The Weald of Youth* shows above all is how firmly Sassoon was rooted in the nineteenth century. *The Old Century and Seven More Years* ends with Sassoon donning Tennyson's cloak and hat in his Uncle Hamo's studio (*OC*, 299), *Siegfried's Journey* contains a generous tribute to Thomas Hardy, and in *The Weald of Youth* it is Sir Edmund Gosse who is fondly remembered. In chapter III Sassoon recalls the parties and balls he attended at the country houses of his youth, before "mechanized trafficry" changed the Kent countryside (41). It was a world that did not survive the Great War, and he ends this section by saying "how more than once I have thought that it was well for my old friends that they went when they did" (43). As Sassoon increasingly began to identify with this nineteenth-century world in his prose writings, it underlined his sense of alienation from the world he lived in.

Perhaps the most interesting and significant character in the book is the old family friend, 'Wirgie' (Helen Wirgman). After thinking about her one night Sassoon recorded in his 1922 diary that "she belongs to the unobservant period of my life [...] I saw her quite often in May and June 1914 when I was at Gray's Inn and rather friendless" (*D2*, 237). In *The Weald of Youth* he describes her as "Lonely and sociable, complex and single-hearted, she came and went among her submissive friends, lighting up their lives by the imaginative vitality of her spirit" (107). Sassoon shows the immaturity of his lonely, inexperienced self by juxtaposing it with the lonely, experienced Wirgie, a juxtaposition that evolves around what was already one of the main themes in *The Old Century*: change.

Sassoon says of himself that he "had lived [his] way to almost twenty-eight in what now appears to have been an unquestioning confidence that the world had arrived at a meridian of unchangeableness" (274). Experience had since taught him otherwise, and it is the mature, sensitive author of the autobiographies who fully understands what might have gone through Wirgie's mind when she visited his rooms at Gray's Inn:

> she may have had a prevision of what must have happened to her with many of her young friends, whom time had carried into highways of experience where their intuitive association with her was remembered only in a passing pang of self-reproach for having lost sight of her. The confiding and receptive young creatures came and went; and she enjoyed her intimacy with them while it lasted. She could have told them how life imposes its laws of change and recurrence; but it should not have been understood, though I dimly guessed what it meant to be old and poor and lonely. (242-43)

This passage is given an added poignancy by a diary entry for September 1922, in which Sassoon recorded one of his dreams: "Last night I invoked the white hair and faded finery of Helen Wirgman, who has slipped out of my existence owing to age and ill-health and reclusiveness and poverty" (*D2*, 237).

There is one interesting exception to Sassoon's general rule of being kind to those he remembers: towards the end of the book one can detect a veiled criticism of Edward Marsh. That Sassoon distanced himself from Marsh in the 1920s was clear from his blunt refusal to contribute to *Georgian Poetry 1920-1922*, but in *The Weald of Youth* he suggests that already before the war he objected to Marsh's life-style. On a visit to the Russian Ballet he meets Marsh in the company of two Bloomsbury snobs (258), and later that night, when Sassoon is home in bed he lies there thinking "how the party was in full swing by now, and Eddie Marsh was certain to be there" (260). In a letter to Dame Felicitas Corrigan in 1965 he wrote that

> dear old Eddie was hollow inside – a prime case of what Belloc wrote in *Portrait of a Child* about people who discard sacredness. He did many good services to the arts, but was

inwardly frivolous, and ended in despair – all his social world having collapsed.[17]

That he was critical of Marsh as early as the spring of 1914 is not supported by any other evidence (this was before the war and his contributions to *Georgian Poetry II* and *III*), which means that there is always a possibility that Sassoon projected some of his post-war feelings on to his pre-war self. This critical attitude fits somewhat uneasily into the general picture of a naive and indolent young man.

Though Sassoon's descriptions of his former self are often self-mocking, there is never any outright criticism; he may not really understand the naive and passive young man who cycles off to war, but he never condemns him: "I find it difficult to imagine and share the emptiness and immaturity of mind, so clueless, so inconsequent, so unforeseeing" (273). For Sassoon, the difference between youth and maturity was that between simplicity and sophistication, and, as in poetical principles, he preferred simplicity:

> Remembering myself as I then was, I am inclined to moralize on the contrast between simplicity and sophistication. For it is a somewhat solemn warning, when we contemplate the safeguarding ignorance of our immaturity. Solemn, because to have learnt a little more usually meant becoming more unwise in a worse way, since not all the wisdom in the world can defend us when we are abandoning the integrity of our acceptive innocence. (263)

In *Memoirs of a Fox-Hunting Man*, George Sherston says his goodbye to his past in the drawing room (*MFH*, 319). *The Weald of Youth* ends with a similar farewell, only this time Sassoon, always eager not to repeat himself, takes a parting look at the landscape. He writes of himself that he went to war because he was "blankly resigned to the impossibility of bicycling away from this tidal wave which was overtaking all that I had hitherto considered secure" (274-75), and then takes his last look at the world he knew so well: "The Weald had been the world of my youngness, and while I gazed across it now I felt prepared to do what I could to defend it" (278).

Sassoon regarded this as a crucial moment in his life; it was the moment he stood at the crossroads and decided to set out on the road to worldly-experience, a decision he came to regret so very bitterly, and at this moment he not only said a final goodbye to the world of his youth, but also to the person he had been and would never be again. "Never such innocence again", as Philip Larkin wrote in the last line of his poem 'MCMXIV'.

VI

As the second volume of an unofficial trilogy *The Weald of Youth* is less impressive than its predecessor. In his first trilogy, *Memoirs of an Infantry Officer*, though very different from *Memoirs of a Fox-Hunting Man*, had maintained its hold on the reader: the evocation of the childhood world was replaced with the raw, but at least as fascinating, descriptions of the Western Front. *The Weald of Youth* introduces no new gripping element: where *The Old Century* was an autobiography with the added ingredient of the magic of childhood, a subject that well-suited Sassoon's prose writing skills (a quality he shared with Walter de la Mare), *The Weald of Youth* is an autobiography with no distinguishing features. The magic of the first book is here replaced by the recollections of meetings with contemporary writers, and though in itself not uninteresting, Sassoon does not manage to make these descriptions in any way unique, especially since in recalling these people he does not indulge in the kind of mud-slinging, back-stabbing and character assassination that usually makes the reading of autobiographies and memoirs such an enjoyable pastime.

This is not to say that *The Weald of Youth* shows a reversal of the change that I have indicated in the Sherston trilogy, for there is no shift from an autobiography to a memoir. If anything Sassoon is more honest than in *The Old Century* where half-way through he refused to recall further unpleasant events, thus in effect falsifying his account. Though he admits that he finds the recording of his outdoor activities more enjoyable than the chronicling of his literary career (146), he generally sticks to the task, and in chapter X, which deals with his fox-hunting in Warwickshire – and is as such the pendant of the 'Migration to the Midlands' chapter in *Memoirs of a Fox-Hunting Man* – he notes how he gradually began to feel the need to be alone, since hunting-society provided all that was needed for physical fitness, but little or nothing to stimulate mental activity (168).

That he refuses to condemn his younger self for wasting some of
the wonderful opportunities his friendship with Edmund Gosse and
Edward Marsh gave him, that he does not really regret his past
ignorance and passivity, as in the meeting with the self-assured and
enterprising Rupert Brooke, are opinions he is perfectly entitled to.
The important point is that he has made no attempts to conceal these
imperfections from either the reader or himself. One significant
episode is not recounted, however. Sassoon does not tell the story of
his letter to Edward Carpenter and their ensuing meeting in the
summer of 1911: his homosexuality was not to be discussed in any of
the works published during his lifetime.

In spite of this omission, *The Weald of Youth* is still a largely
sincere attempt to portray the young Sassoon. On the last page he
recalls himself cycling off to the war, leaving behind his youth and
the landscape he grew up in: "The Weald had been the world of my
youngness" (278). In leaving these behind, Sassoon lost the two
themes that had inspired his autobiographical interest; the third
volume was to suffer accordingly.

VII

Siegfried's Journey[18] is the last of Sassoon's autobiographies and
covers the period August 1916-August 1920. The title is reminiscent
of *Sherston's Progress* and the similarity does not stop there: both
books are the last volume of a trilogy (and arguably the weakest parts
of it), and the titles of the books present the author in his by now
familiar vision of himself: a solitary pilgrim travelling along "life's
one forward track". Sassoon did not enjoy writing the book. In a letter
to Sydney Cockerell, written just before he finished it, he said that he
was "terribly stale on the book".

In Michael Thorpe's opinion, this is partly due to the period in
which it was written: "the extreme depression into which he was
plunged by the Second World War made it a labour for him to write at
all".[19] But I would suggest that it is largely due to the period that the
book covers. As with *Sherston's Progress*, in which there are clear
signs that the author lost interest, Sassoon felt less strongly about his
post-war, or rather his post-war protest existence. What meant most to
him was his childhood and the pre-war world he grew up in; his

writing is at its best when he is dealing with this period. His mature self was a less inspiring subject: the writing lacks spirit and, though both *Sherston's Progress* and *Siegfried's Journey* contain interesting and well-written passages, the books as a whole are not satisfactory.

Siegfried's Journey is crowded with the names of writers and artists of the period, over 200 in as many pages.[20] Sometimes they are only mentioned in passing, but some of the best passages in the book are to be found in its brief portraits, especially those of Wilfred Owen, Thomas Hardy and Wilfred Blunt. Thorpe thinks that "One of the most attractive aspects of the previous volumes had been the manner in which he [Sassoon] has paid his debts of friendship".[21]

This is indeed one of the most sympathetic characteristics of Sassoon as an autobiographer, and *Siegfried's Journey* is in this respect no exception. But it is typical of Sassoon that the people who were less congenial to him are either dealt with kindly, though in a way that clearly suggests that this is only the tip of the iceberg, or not dealt with at all. An example of the first instance is the way he describes his fellow Georgian poet John Drinkwater. After recalling a meeting with him at Eddie Marsh's, where Drinkwater kept them up late reading out his latest poems, Sassoon writes that

> He was anxious to be friendly, but somehow an acquaintance never matured. Now I come to think of it, at our subsequent meetings I almost always heard him read his works aloud. This prejudiced me against him, owing to my preference for bards who hide their lights under bushels. Drinkwater never did that, though he was much liked by those who knew him intimately. (99)

Drinkwater had indeed done his best to establish friendly relations with Sassoon. His 1919 volume *Loyalties* contained a poem 'To Siegfried Sassoon', in which he heralded the war poetry of Sassoon, Graves and Nichols as the coming of a new poetic age:

> And I knew that the difficult moods had come again with fire
> To touch the brain of men who were boys to my passing youth,
> And I was glad, for the true song is the poet's desire,
> Though he hear it afar on the dawn when he passes the eye of
>   noon,

And I was glad for the springing of seed from from the shares of
truth.

        ...

And so the young man gives to the younger the salutation of song,
For lonely is companionship of the prides that sing.

This rather overwrought effort did not have the desired effect.[22]
Sassoon never liked John Drinkwater, abhorring his style of self-
promotion. For Sassoon professional modesty was very important in a
writer: "I seldom write my name in visitors' books, warned by the
Drinkwaterish habit of my advertising contemporaries" (*D3*, 201).
But Drinkwater had died in 1937, and in remembering him in
Siegfried's Journey, Sassoon is careful not to speak ill of the dead.
That explains the diplomatic language in this passage, which on
closer scrutiny fails to convince: for if he says that he *now* comes to
think about it, this contradicts the past tense in "prejudiced". And that
"he was much liked by those who knew him intimately" means that he
was liked by his friends, which is stating the patently obvious. The
truth of the matter is that Sassoon loathed Drinkwater, whom he
referred to in his diary as "That supremely pompous literary humbug"
(*D2*, 160).[23]

An example of Sassoon consciously erasing somebody from his
memoirs occurs at the beginning of Chapter XV, where he writes how
in the summer of 1919

> the first number of a Miscellany called *The Owl* made its first
> appearance. Originated and financed by William Nicholson, it
> was a thin folio containing prose, verse, and drawings finely
> reproduced in colour. (147)

But as Sassoon knew only too well *The Owl* was in fact "originated"
by William Nicholson and his son-in-law, who was also the editor of
the magazine. The son-in-law was Robert Graves and he is not once
mentioned in *Siegfried's Journey*, although Graves and Sassoon had
been close friends at the time.[24] Similarly, though Robert Ross is
regularly mentioned, and Sassoon describes his face at their last
meeting as "grey with exhaustion and ill-health" (83), he never hints
at the reason for Ross' untimely death: there are no references to
either Lord Alfred Douglas or T.W.H. Crosland. As had been the case

in *The Weald of Youth*, Sassoon had obviously decided that there was to be no suggestion of homosexuality in the pages of *Siegfried's Journey*, for his own friend at the time, the artist Gabriel Atkin, is never referred to either. This clearly illustrates the problem with Sassoon as a reliable autobiographer: he is usually honest in everything he writes about, but he does not usually write about everything.

Another case in point is Sassoon's description of Garsington Manor during the war years. Lady Ottoline Morrell and her husband, the Liberal MP Philip Morrell, had moved into Garsington Manor, their country house near Oxford, in May 1915, and the house soon became a meeting-point for young intellectuals, politicians, writers, artists, and musicians. Philip Morrell was an active member of the No-Conscription Fellowship (NCF),[25] and in 1916 a group of conscientious objectors (COs) came to work on the farm.[26] Lady Ottoline had wanted to meet Sassoon ever since first reading his 'To Victory' in *The Times* in January 1916, and when Sassoon was convalescing in Oxford in August that year, Robert Ross took him to meet her. In *Siegfried's Journey* he describes their first meeting, suggesting that she was interested in him as a soldier-poet: "Lady Ottoline's elevated notion of me as a romantic young poet needed a lot of living up to" (20). The 'living up' he had to do in their intimate discussions:

> our exchanges of thought moved on a plane of lofty but vaguely-formulated ideas. She was in some ways an idealist, essentially generous but deficient in constructive comprehension of the problems which she contemplated with such intensity. At that period her idealism was still in the full flush of its immaturity. She had yet to learn that the writers and artists she befriended were capable of proving ungrateful. (23)

The somewhat intellectually superior tone with which Sassoon here takes the measure of Lady Ottoline is put in perspective by Lady Ottoline's impression of Sassoon:

> I found him very sympathetic and wonderfully intimate to me and I was very moved at knowing anyone whose thoughts were so akin to my own, simple, yet imaginative, and he had

spiritual insight, combined with gay humour. For however greatly I enjoyed the companionship of our intellectual friends, they were none of them – with the exception perhaps of Lytton [Strachey] – intimate to me, nor moved me. None of them had ever entered into that chamber of my being whence springs the fountain of romance, where a strange and magical coloured light plays upon the intruder.[27]

Garsington in the war years must have been a fascinating place to be, but Sassoon's description of life at Garsington is disappointingly brief, though at the time he was one of the regular guests. This is probably due to the fact that although Lady Ottoline remained a good and supportive friend, he was suspicious of the Liberal/intellectual climate at Garsington. His only reference to the COs is to say that "my being in uniform created a barrier between us" (22) and he never mentions Virginia Woolf, Lytton Strachey, D.H. Lawrence, Clive Bell or Aldous Huxley.

Garsington was also closely linked with his war protest (Lady Ottoline herself had actually assisted him in the preparation of his protest action), but already in *Memoirs of an Infantry Officer* it was clear that Sassoon had emotionally distanced himself from his revolt. At Garsington he had met the intellectuals who had supported him in his action, but who were not interested in him as a poet and sportsman. As in the case of Robert Graves and John Drinkwater, Sassoon's policy in dealing with these people is one of reticence. Also, Sassoon heartily disapproved of the 'treacherous' way certain writers repaid Lady Ottoline's kindness: D.H. Lawrence portrayed her as Hermione Roddice in *Women in Love* (1916) and Aldous Huxley ridiculed Garsington and all its inhabitants in *Crome Yellow* (1920).[28] Sassoon, who must have witnessed many an incident and who held outspoken opinions (some of which have fortunately now been published in his *Diaries*), remains the gentleman he was, careful not to give offence. His attitude in *Siegfried's Journey* is best summed up in the words of Sebastian, the hero of Vita Sackville-West's *The Edwardians*: "'Since one cannot have truth,' cried Sebastian, struggling into his evening shirt, 'let us at least have good manners'".[29]

VIII

In Chapter V of *Siegfried's Journey* Sassoon gives a fresh account of his war protest, relating that part of the story that was not told in *Memoirs of an Infantry Officer*. Here he tells of the roles that were played by the Morrells, Bertrand Russell and John Middleton Murry, but, as with most of the writing in *Siegfried's Journey*, it is largely a dry and unadorned factual account. There then follows one of the most moving episodes in the book. He recalls a night in June 1917, when he was in his club in St. James's Street, shortly after composing the text of his war protest, but still before its publication. He remembers how he stood in front of the window looking down in the street full of soldiers, and suddenly wondered if there was any point in making his protest:

> And somehow the workings of my mind brought me a comprehensive memory of war experience in its intense and essential humanity. It seemed that my companions of the Somme and Arras battles were around me; helmeted faces returned and receded in vision; joking voices were overheard in fragments of dug-out and billet talk. These were the dead, to whom life had been desirable, and whose sacrifice must be justified, unless the War were to go down in history as yet another Moloch of murdered youth. (53)

Suddenly the old power and conviction return to the narrative. This passage illustrates Sassoon's ambiguous position in relation to his war protest. It is important to realize that although Sassoon had distanced himself from his former self, the powerful emotions that had first given rise to his action were still latently present within him. This explains why Sassoon never condemned the anger in his own war poetry, nor ever explicitly stated that he regretted making his war protest: his feelings had not altered, it is just that he had distanced himself from them.

It is therefore interesting that in this passage he seems to suggest that he was driven to his action by the memories and dreams of the men that had been killed as much as by a sense of responsibility for those still alive that he had left behind in France. As his poetry shows, the dreams about the war in which his former comrades appeared never left him; his socialist ideals, on the other hand, were now totally alien to him. Thinking and writing about the war must have brought back many painful memories, and Sassoon was understandably reluctant to relive them: his account of his protest action ends abruptly shortly afterwards

> My experiences during the next three weeks, which ended in my being sent to the shell-shock hospital, have already been related in *Memoirs of an Infantry Officer*. I am thankful not to be obliged to drag my mind through the details again. (55)

That this resulted in a fragmented and disjointed narrative is something that obviously did not bother him. Perhaps it was more important to him that by not discussing the events of the following three weeks he also avoided having to mention the major part that was played by Robert Graves.

IX

About himself Sassoon says that he is "by nature a recorder" (138), and most of *Siegfried's Journey* is certainly written by a recorder: the author has distanced himself from what he recounts, and as a consequence his narrative is on the whole rather bloodless. The book lacks passion, conviction and intensity. As usual in his autobiographies, he has omitted all 'affairs of the heart', he never mentions any quarrels, and just as in *Sherston's Progress* he had already distanced himself from his war protest, so he is now similarly dismissive about his political activities: he casually refers to his Labour sympathies as having been "superficially adopted" (135).

On the last page of the book Sassoon describes how he stood on Trafalgar Square one Saturday afternoon, shortly after returning from his American lecture-tour: "Lulled by the splash of the water, he asked himself what it was that he had returned to" (224). This seems to be the main problem: more even than in *Sherston's Progress*, *Siegfried's Journey* lacks a destination, a theme or event that gives direction to the narrative and enables the author to construct his story. For a long time there was no such event or purpose in Sassoon's post-war life, and so he wandered along rather aimlessly until the 1927 inheritance enabled him to retire to a country house in Wiltshire. From that moment on his travelling was done from his chair in the library of Heytesbury House: a journey in the past in his autobiographies and a journey in the mind in his poetry. But in the period *Siegfried's Journey* covers, the years 1916-1920, he was at a loss what to do, and the book is therefore not so much concerned with the tracing of his spiritual development (for the simple reason that there was none to speak of) as with the people he knew and met during these years. *Siegfried's Journey* is therefore a volume of memoirs rather than an autobiography, and though well-written and of historical interest for its chapters on Thomas Hardy and Wilfred Owen, its value as a work of literary art is negligible.

In moods of despair, when we look out at this world-menace of 'poverty and population', and at the hostility of totalitarian governments to the privacy and dignity of the individual, we may wonder if the human race has had its day, and is now rushing to the brink [...] Such cynical, fatalistic thoughts are too general to interest us for long. The particular event, here and now, offers more drama, though miniature. That is because it is personal, part of the individual's homecoming. What then is this controlling passion, that takes command as soon as consciousness dawns in the child's mind, and remains insistent throughout life, undeflected by the multitude of other desires and impulses that drag us aside on our journey?

– Richard Church, from *The Voyage Home* (1964)

CHAPTER 10

GOD'S TREASURE

I

After the completion of the last volume of his autobiographies, Sassoon did not immediately return to his poetry. Instead, he started work on *Meredith*, a biography of one of the favourite authors of his youth, George Meredith. In August 1947 he wrote to Max Beerbohm

> Well, Max, I have completed my biography of Meredith, a task which I undertook with much anxiety and effected with enormous drudgery last winter [...] Meredithians will find my comments elementary. But Trevelyan countenanced the proceedings with preliminary encouragement and I have illustrated adequately with copious quotations from contemporary critics. (*LMB*, 97)

Sassoon dedicated the book to G.M. Trevelyan (1876-1962), the eminent historian, who had been a personal friend of Meredith. In 1906 Trevelyan published his *The Poetry and Philosophy of George Meredith* and he contributed the explanatory notes to the 1912 edition of Meredith's *Poetical Works*, published by Constable, who also published *Meredith*. Sassoon's apparent need to make up for his own lack of critical competence by extensively quoting recognized critics suggests that *Meredith* is to a large extent an appreciative, rather than a critical work. Though the book is not a hagiography, Sassoon makes no attempt to concentrate or expound on Meredith's weaknesses. For the purposes of this study, however, the most interesting features of the book are the author's relation to his subject and the occasional glimpses of his own taste and personality.

One of the most endearing qualities of Sassoon as a biographer is that – as the letter to Max Beerbohm has already indicated – he is all too well aware of his own critical shortcomings, and so there are several instances where the author refrains from discussing a particular work, explaining that he does not feel qualified to do so. Of 'The Day of the Daughters of Hades' Sassoon says that Meredith himself, as well as "two of his most eminent admirers and expositors, Quiller-Couch and G.M. Trevelyan", considered it one of his finest achievements. He then continues

> This makes me wonder whether, after all, I am an appropriate person to write about him. For I have always preferred brevity to amplitude in poetry. If a poem must be long, I want it to be in the form of a dramatic monologue – subjective utterance rather than impersonal narrative. This one aimed at sustained lyrical and descriptive excitement; the subject demanded it. But I find the mental effort required too exacting. (209)[1]

And so he goes on to a discussion of the sonnets in the same volume.

But his doubts about whether he was the right person to write about Meredith cannot have been many, for there are numerous passages that betray the strong affinity he felt for his subject. Meredith had been his favourite author in youth because of his love of nature and his celebration of the outdoor life, but in the course of his book Sassoon makes clear that there were many other qualities that he felt they shared: he loves the moments when Meredith is at peace with his surroundings "because I am myself an inveterate quietist and self-corrector of inherent excitability" (239). He refers to him as a "spiritual pilgrim" (293), and when he tries to explain the captivating qualities of Meredith's first major novel, *Richard Feverel* (1859), he could well have been writing about his own favourite books, *Memoirs of a Fox-Hunting Man* and *The Old Century*:

> Meredith was using material from his most impressionable period with a sense of delight in producing his effects for the first time. Much of it came from his heart, and from his memories of the countryside (36)

This is the innocent happiness of youth again, but Sassoon also felt close to his subject for more personal reasons. Like Meredith's first marriage with the daughter of Thomas Love Peacock, Sassoon's own marriage was not a success:

The birth of their son George in 1935 was a happy event for the Sassoons and might have been expected to help in ensuring that the marriage would prove permanently happy; but it was unfortunately a factor in producing division and estrangement, each of the parents trying to outdo the other in winning the boy's affection. In addition, a too-possessive wife came to irritate a rather neurotic poet and creative writer who needed much solitude and tactful, not fussy, affection.[2]

Edith Olivier, who lived not far from Heytesbury House, remembered that in the early 1940s George was a difficult child and that his mother could not always handle him. This got on Sassoon's nerves, but when asked to intervene he always sided with his son, which, understandably, angered his wife. In the mid-1940s they separated and Hester moved to the Isle of Mull. Sassoon remained at Heytesbury House, looking forward to the periods that George, his "ideal companion", came to stay with him. This set-up explains the impassioned description of the relationship between Meredith and his son Arthur, after the separation of the parents:

> For in those years Arthur was his sustaining happiness [...]
> With deep and undeviating devotion he made Arthur the
> purpose of his existence and his money-earning endeavours,
> concentrating on him the parental love which is fathomless and
> immeasurable in terms of emotion, being decreed by Nature.
> (58)

Sassoon's isolation increased even further when George turned out to be as 'mechanically-minded' as Sassoon's brothers had been.

One of the few new friends who to visit him in the late 1940s was J. A. Ackerley, whose *The Prisoner of War* had made such a deep impression on Sassoon in 1925. Both men were lonely, Sassoon longing for the visits of his son, Ackerley largely depending on the company of his Alsatian Queenie.[3] They first came to stay with Sassoon at Heytesbury House in the summer of 1949, and Ackerley's diary gives a telling description of their host:

> Siegfried sweet, kind, loquacious, absent-minded, lonely,
> dreadfully self-centred and self-absorbed. I like him very much,
> there is something very touching about his aged, beautiful worn
> face, the light in the eyes dimmed from constant looking
> inwards. He scarcely ever meets one's eye – he never has, I
> think, – but talks, talks away from one, from side to side, or
> into his lap or over one's head, always about himself, his life,
> his past fame, his present neglect, his unhappy marriage, his
> passionate love for his son. It is all intensely subjective (he
> hardly ever asks about oneself – a flash or two of effortful
> interest, but always reminding him about himself) and
> threnodic, it is a man who has spent years and years of
> loneliness talking his thoughts at last aloud to an ear.[4]

Sassoon struck him as a sad figure, though his impressions are
slightly coloured by the fact that Sassoon reminded him so much of
his own position. But the picture he paints, that of a man who has
survived himself and is not in tune with the present, is in keeping with
the voice which speaks from the pages of *Meredith*.

For what *Meredith* shows above all, is how much Sassoon
sympathizes with the spirit of the nineteenth-century: towards the end
of the book he unequivocally states his dissatisfaction with the
present age, in which the Victorian belief in human progress had been
disproved when man's scientific discoveries were used to destroy
young lives in the Great War. When he discusses Meredith's belief
that "Age can only justify its existence by service to Youth", he
interrupts his narrative with a diatribe against the contemporary
situation:

> Tragic words for the generations, old and young, of to-day,
> who have wrought and inherited ruin and ruin redoubled, in a
> world where belief in human progress has been replaced by
> stoical despair and the foundering of all philosophies which
> sustained the spiritual fortitude of homo sapiens, for whom
> omnipotent Science has provided knowledge which he cannot
> be trusted to use without destroying himself. (254)

Sassoon here touches on the subject that took him beyond Meredith.
His own religious feelings and his increasing need for spiritual

sustenance found no complete response in Meredith, who, like him, did believe that "the human race can rise to higher things by understanding its Mother Earth", but unlike him left it at that: "Man must attain to the spiritual through the natural, not through the supernatural" (206). Like Wordsworth, that other favourite poet of Sassoon's youth, Meredith was content, in George Herbert's words, to "rest in nature, not the God of nature".[5] He did not believe in an afterlife, and found the concept of immortality inconceivable:

> Which personality is it which endures? I was one man in youth, and another in middle age. I have never felt the unity of personality running through my life. I have been six different men: six at least. (206)

For Sassoon this matter was equally inconceivable, but unlike Meredith, who apparently simply dismissed it from his thoughts, his spiritual pilgrimage now entered a phase in which religious questions increasingly dominated his life and work.

II

Sassoon was sixty-one when *Meredith* was published. Two years later, in November 1949, he made a half-hearted attempt to start a new autobiography, but he gave up after a hundred pages. The probable reason for the failure of this attempt is given on the very first page, where he explains that he feels completely alienated from his former self: "the distance between us has widened in more than years [...] It seems that I, his successor, have outlived our former intimacy".[6] He told his son that writing another autobiography would mean "simply copying out his diaries".[7] When he asked Rupert Hart-Davis to become his literary executor he gave him no directions as to what to do with the diaries: "I can't bother with all that posthumous stuff. I leave it to you" (*D2*, 10).

Sassoon made no further attempts at writing prose; it had been in the prose stage of his pilgrimage that he had concentrated on his past, trying to once again get in tune with his pre-war self. Now that this had been achieved, he entered the last stage of his pilgrimage: he had made his peace with the past, he was now to make his peace with the present and future.[8]

The poems that Sassoon began to write in the late 1940s are almost without exception short and concise, to the extent that they come close to T.E. Hulme's 'hard and dry' dictum. The dominant theme of the poems is that of a religious quest: the poet is in search of a spiritual dimension, a higher power, a Creator or God. In a diary-entry (no date given, but probably 1948 or 1949) he wonders about this preoccupation:

> Why all these enquiries about the Creator? Wouldn't it be more profitable – and entertaining to public readers – to write something nearer everyday reality? There is always satire, of course, which I can do with gusto when stirred up. But I have outlived all impulse to wax indignant with the world – the state of it has gone beyond satire. My existence consists in facing the circumstance of growing old and teaching myself to submit to it philosophically and learn what I can from the process. This results in eliminating most human activities as no longer worth taking seriously. One watches with some interest; but wonders how they manage to go on believing in the urgent occupations. *And very few things seem worth writing about. Only one, really*...the situation of a thoughtful human being against the background of nature and the universe. And the achievement of faith in spiritual guidance from beyond the apparitional existence of the flesh. (131-32)

One last time Sassoon was faced with the Georgian dilemma: whether to attempt to please a wide readership and pursue the popular successes that his prose works had brought him, or to follow his own inclinations and continue his spiritual journey. As the diary-entry quoted above shows, it was not a question he had any difficulties in answering. The three slim volumes of poetry that he published between 1950 and 1956 were once again all privately printed in small editions. The first, *Common Chords* (1950), consisted of 18 poems and was published in an edition of 107 copies; it was followed a year later by *Emblems of Experience* (20 poems, 75 copies) and in 1954 by *The Tasking* (24 poems, 100 copies). In 1956 the three volumes were combined in a single volume under the title *Sequences*, and published by Faber in an edition of 3000 copies.

The two opening poems of *Common Chords* immediately establish the direction in which the poet/pilgrim is travelling. 'Release' seems a farewell to the poet/prophet who saw it as his task to keep a critical eye on the world of Man; the nearness of Nature evokes a purely instinctive and spontaneous response, blotting out anything else:

> One winter's end I much bemused my head
> In tasked attempts to drive it up to date
> With what the undelighting moderns said
>   Forecasting human fate.
>
> And then, with nothing unforeseen to say
> And no belief or unbelief to bring,
> Came, in its old unintellectual way,
>   The first real day of spring.

This is one of the moments where the peaceful mood of Sassoon's spiritual pilgrimage is interrupted by rumblings of a polemical crusade against the 'intellectual moderns'. Describing the arrival of spring as "unintellectual" may be intended as a means of establishing a contrast between the man-made world and Nature, but it is typical of Sassoon that he singles out the 'intellectual moderns', holding them solely responsible for the decline of the civilized world. The division he thus creates between the world of man and that of Nature then also becomes a division between the urban-oriented, intellectual poetry of the Modernists and the Nature-loving, non-intellectual Georgians.

In 'Release' Sassoon is still very close to Meredith, in that the poem seems to echo Meredith's belief that man can only attain spiritual release through an understanding of Nature. This release is illustrated in 'An Example'; in his search for inner peace the poet has come to the silence of a forest:

> I stood below a beech
> And said to stillness, teach
> Tranquillity. I told
> Dumb patient earth to hold
> My unquiet mind from speech

His attention is then drawn by a cole tit in the tree, and, mesmerized by the busy little bird, he forgets everything

> The moments passed; and I
> No self-concernment knew
> But one small purposed thing
> Which from my presence flew
> On deft unstartled wing...
> And I was tranquil too.

On the last page of *Memoirs of a Fox-Hunting Man* Sassoon's *alter ego* George Sherston had been unable to find hope or release in a bird's song. 'An Example' indicates the progress he had made since. The poem reminds one of Keats' 'Ode to a Nightingale':

> That I might drink, and leave the world unseen,
> And with thee fade away into the forest dim:
> Fade away, dissolve, and quite forget
> What thou among the leaves hast never known,
> The weariness, the fever, and the fret
> Here, where men sit and hear each other groan

But the mood in Sassoon's poem is even more optimistic. When the nightingale flies away the speaker in Keats's 'Ode' is left in a state of bewilderment, wondering if the intensity of his experience was real or imagined, but Sassoon is left fulfilled since Nature *has* taught him tranquillity.

In 'The Unproven' Sassoon brings in the religious element. Again referring to the world of man, he juxtaposes it with Heaven:

> Looking at Life, some unbelieved-in angels
>   Asked one another when
> Science would overhear them and encourage
>   Their ministries to men.

Meredith did write about the mysterious powers of Nature, but he was never much concerned with Christianity; the poem thus marks the point where Sassoon is about to diverge from both Meredith and

Hardy, two of the writers whom he up to then had been very close to spiritually.

Thomas Hardy is the subject of 'At Max Gate', a poem which in effect echoes Yeats's 'Long-Legged Fly'. From the outset, Sassoon had emphasized that his pilgrimage was to be undertaken in solitude and silence; in *The Heart's Journey* XI he had written

> *Alone...* The word is life endured and known.
> It is the stillness where our spirits walk
> And all but inmost faith is overthrown.

In 'At Max Gate' Sassoon sets out to explain that a great mind like Thomas Hardy's also "moved upon silence". In the opening octave of this 12-line poem Hardy is presented as the friendly host

> Old Mr. Hardy, upright in his chair,
> Courteous to visiting acquaintance chatted
> With unaloof alertness while he patted
> The sheep dog whose society he preferred.

This picture of a genial old man is then juxtaposed in the quatrain with the visionary poet and novelist

> Head propped on hand, he sat with me alone,
> Silent, the log fire flickering on his face.
> Here was the seer whose words the world had known.
> Someone had taken Mr. Hardy's place.

The operative words in these passages are "chatted" and "silent": it is only in "stillness" that the great mind manifests itself.

Though the poems in *Common Chords* clearly show Sassoon's need for spiritual sustenance, they at the same time reveal that he had no definite ideas about what particular form that religious need would take. Hardy's influence is also noticeable in 'An Asking', where the poet addresses a higher power not as God but as 'Primordial Cause'; this is reminiscent of Hardy's 'Immanent Will', the moving force behind the scenes in *The Dynasts*.[9] Sassoon himself described these poems as "part of my human cry for salvation and my reaction against

the modern denials of religious faith" (140-41); in his 1953 diary he
added that

> If asked what they amount to, I would say that they are merely
> an exhibition of the spiritual and intellectual shortcomings of a
> man trying to find things out for himself – *attempting to*
> *formulate his private religion* step by step, in hopes that it may
> be of some slight service to a period which appears to have
> rejected religious beliefs in favour of psychology and scientific
> research. (154)

Sassoon almost seems to make a claim for the social usefulness of his
poetry, in that it provides the reader with a spiritual haven in a secular
world, but since he wrote this in 1953, three years before the
publication of *Sequences*, its service would have been very slight
indeed: the combined editions of *Common Chords* and *Emblems of*
Experience amounted to no more than 182 copies.

Most of the other poems in *Common Chords* are also on the theme
of a cold, calculating contemporary world, run by statesmen and
scientists, which has no time for the decent human values that religion
had once instilled in society:

> Most minds decide to-day
> That mercy doesn't pay.
> ('An Absentee')

> Elsewhere. The undestructible exists
> Beyond found formulas of scientists.
> Our spiritual situation stood the same
> In other epochs when
> To thwart all ministries of mercy came
> The arrogant inventiveness of men.
> ('Elsewhere')

In contrast with this human coldness of the outside world, the poet
finds examples of the values he believes in, in the unquestioning faith
between master and dog: "My trust in him; in me his trust" ('Man and
Dog') and the self-denying love of his mother: "you have not sought /
Rewards that can be bought" ('To My Mother').[10] But Sassoon no

longer feels that he can change the world he lives in, nor does he desire to be a powerless prophet, worried by a merciless world that does not heed his warnings. And so he has partly turned to the spiritual to escape from these concerns, as he explains in 'In Time of Destruction':

> Stillness, man's final friend,
> Absolve this turmoiled thought
> Of ills I cannot mend
> That so my brain be brought
> An unimpassioned pride
> Where perfidies prevail,
> And – old beliefs belied –
> Philosophy to fail.

Sassoon's religious quest thus also becomes a search for the power to accept defeat and his own essential insignificance. The titles of the last two poems of the volume, 'Resurrection' and 'Redemption', suggest that he increasingly expected to find this power in the Christian religion. In 'Resurrection' he wonders *what*, come the hour of judgement ("And I that instant stood / Absolved of unfulfilment and essential fault"), would remain of his self "To stand with those white presences delivered through death?". In *Emblems of Experience* this fascination with his own insignificance was to lead to a renewed interest in Man, though not with his contemporaries, but with bygone generations.

Emblems of Experience, published one year after *Common Chords*, shows no major thematic changes; Sassoon continues to follow the path he had chosen in *Common Chords*, though by now some of the ideas that were still vague in the earlier volume have crystalized into more definite views. The imagery and ideas in *Emblems of Experience* are firmly rooted in the Christian tradition, and the God he addresses is the Christian God. In July 1953 Sassoon finished reading H.G. Wells' *Food of Gods* (1904), and in his diary he reflected on Wells' socialist utopianism and his obsession with changing the world:

> Thirty years ago and after, even I dreamed my dreams of a quickly improved world – dreams backed by almost complete

ignorance of human history and conditions and the terrible forces of Nature. What does one *believe* in now? Only in the human decency and goodness which one has met within one's own tiny experience and environment. One's awareness of Evil has been much increased. One's sense of significance as a single human being has shrivelled almost to nothing. I see myself as a fly buzzing against the window pane of 'reality' beyond which there is the world of the spiritual and the supernatural, the Universe and all the rest of it! No use attempting to understand what it is all about (147).

The picture that emerges in *Emblems of Experience* is also that of an evil, God-forsaken world, and the ease with which Sassoon dismisses Wells' attempts at improving mankind as futile and the result of basic misconception make plain that he believes saving the world to be beyond man's power. In 'The Need' he asks his God to reveal himself and through the chosen few who are willing to listen:

> Speak, through the few,
> Your light of life to nourish us anew.
> Speak, for our world possessed
> By demon influences of evil and unrest.
> Act, as of old,
> That we some dawnlit destiny may behold
> From this doom-darkened place.
> O move in mercy among us. Grant accepted grace.

Who "the few" are, remains unclear. Sassoon later described this phase as "an attempt to formulate a personal religion", in which case "the few" would definitely include himself and at best perhaps also those in his own environment who had shown him "human decency and goodness". Of these, many have already died, and in 'Solitudes at Sixty' Sassoon describes his increasing isolation in old age, though a vivid memory enables him to summon up former friends in his thoughts

> Beloved or valued ghosts, these reappear
> At my peculiar prompting. Known by heart,
> Finite impersonations, learnt by ear,
> Their voices talk in character and depart.

The sustaining power of memory is also the subject of 'Ultimate Values', a poem in which Sassoon, after one of the best opening lines he ever wrote, seems to say that his belief in older "wisdoms" is at least partly the result of a selective memory that may distort the past to strengthen its consoling power.[11]

> The hour grows late, and I outlive my friends,
> Remaining, since I must, with memoried mind
> That for consolement deepeningly depends
> On hoarded time, enriched and redesigned.
> So is it with us all. And thus we find
> Endeared survivals that our thought defends.

As someone who was so out of touch with the world around him, it is understandable that Sassoon felt a strong desire to find things or people he could identify with. In 'A Fallodon Memory' Sassoon recalls the former Liberal Foreign Secretary, Edward Grey, Viscount Fallodon.[12] He remembers seeing him at Fallodon, his Northumberland home, standing tall and still, "In the twilight of his wood". But the poem is not just a recollection, its real purpose becomes clear in the closing lines, where Sassoon describes Grey as

> human-simple yet profound,
> And strength of spirit no calamity could change.
> To whom, designed for countrified contentments, came
> Honours unsought and unrewarding foreign fame:
> And, at the last, that darkened world wherein he moved
> In memoried deprivation of life once learnt and loved.

Sassoon, the Edwardian country gentleman and celebrated war-poet, here remembers another Edwardian country gentleman who gained fame without seeking it, and the qualities he ascribes to Grey are equally applicable to the poet. Now himself an old man, Sassoon remembers the elder Grey lost in his memories, though in his case the "darkenend world" was caused by his deteriorating eyesight that put an end to his political career, whereas Sassoon's dark world is one deprived of spiritual light.

Sassoon found a similar kindred spirit in the writings of Alcuin, the eighth-century Saxon theologian and scholar. In 'Awareness of

Alcuin' he recounts how, through reading Alcuin's verse, he recognizes a man whose spiritual quest was identical to his own:

> Alcuin, from temporalities at rest,
> Sought grace within him, given from afar;
> Noting how sunsets worked around the west;
> Watching, at spring's approach, that beckoning star;
> And hearing, while one thrush sang through the rain,
> Youth, which his soul in Paradise might regain.

Alcuin's "beckoning star" has its equivalent in Sassoon's 'Befriending Star'; in the poem of that title he begs the star to become a heavenly sign by which he can be guided:

> Withdraw, while watched by me, your magnitude – your dire
> Unmeaningness for man. Heart-simplified, appear
> Not in ferocity of elemental fire,
> But, for my lowly faith, a sign by which to steer.

His "lowly faith" is a reminder of the poet's human insignificance. In *Rhymed Ruminations* Sassoon had included a poem, 'In Heytesbury Wood', on the previous owner of his manor, evoking "the old lord" on a solitary walk through his wood. Now he pictures himself in a similar situation; in 'A Proprietor' he muses on life's transience and man's ignorance in claiming possession of a wood that through the centuries has seen many owners, now all forgotten:

> Wondering what manner of men
> Will walk there in the problem'd future when
> Those trees he planted are long fallen or felled,
> He twirls a white wild violet in his fingers
> As others may when he's no more beheld,
> Nor memory of him lingers.

There are several other poems in *Emblems of Experience* in which Sassoon focuses on Man's insignificance, presenting the human race as if it were a relay race in which Nature and material objects are handed down from generation to generation. In 'Old Fashioned

Weather' he ruminates on the fact that, through the ages, the weather has always been a constant quantity:

> Weather's the same for all. Though Science tells
> The world to-day what Newton never guessed,
> He woke to sunshine sparkling on crisp snow;
> Heard, clear across the pastures, midnight bells,
> And thought, as I do now, with quiet zest,
> Of New Year's Eve a century ago.

In 'Cleaning the Candelabrum' he muses about the people before him who have cleaned the brass candelabrum which "has illuminated, one might say / Much vista'd history, many vanished lives...". Identifying with these forgotten generations, he is in fact stripping himself of all individual aspects, reducing himself to one anonymous part of the human chain that links past generations with future ones.[13]

George Meredith had found the concept of immortality inconceivable because he could not understand which part of his personality, which he felt had seen many changes in the course of his life, would survive. Sassoon had wrestled unsuccessfully with this problem in 'Resurrection', one of the last poems in *Common Chords*, but in 'The Messenger' he expresses the solution he has found: mind and body are the constituent parts of man that give him his individual qualities, the soul is the "messenger" from God, a third part with no individual characteristics, but sent by God as the link between man and heaven. His 1954 diary provides a further explanation of this concept:

> I assume 'my soul' to be a visitant from the spiritual Whole which merely frequents my physical existence. When my body dies, I announce, this guest of mine will be resumed into the whole – not as *my* consciousness. This idea, I suppose, will be condemned as a loose-minded notion. But it is my way of disclaiming any expectation of 'survival', while believing in the reality of spiritual influence on my carnal condition. I see myself as 'primitive man', on whom have been bestowed some tentative conceptions of spiritual immanence. But he does not even claim that 'the soul' belongs to him. It belongs elsewhere,

and he has only received hints and intimations of its workings
in his animal nature. (163)[14]

Sassoon's unscholarly mind had come up with a hotch-potch of ideas
which, especially in its phrasing, is not so much loose-minded as
confusing. The uncertainties about the nature of the supreme power
present in *Common Chords* seemed to have been resolved in *Emblems
of Experience*, where the vocabulary was purely Christian, as were the
underlying ideas of God, heaven and the soul. But now Sassoon has
devised a philosophy which is largely Platonic, with an ideal spiritual
Overworld to which the soul of man returns after his death, though he
continues to use a Christian terminology.

In *The Tasking*, the last of the three volumes he published during
the early 1950s, this Christian/Platonic spiritual realm is still very
much present. In the title poem he explains that seeking communion
with this spiritual world is the task he has set himself:

> To find rewards of mind with inward ear
> Through silent hours of seeking;
> To put world sounds behind and hope to hear
> Instructed spirit speaking:
> Sometimes to catch a clue from selfhood's essence
> And ever that revealment to be asking;
> This – and through darkness to divine God's presence –
> I take to be my tasking.

Though this spirit moves within him, it is not part of his personality:
"I am but the brain that dreamed and died" ('The Humbled Heart'). In
his diary he wondered if this task was compatible with his duties as a
writer:

> The Wiltshire minor prophet is composing his ultimate
> banalities about the back of beyond, his predicament is the
> universe, and his expectations of there being no such thing as
> the music of the spheres. And not even doing it with the object
> of being listened to by an applausive audience. No; he is doing
> it for his own 'self-realization'. And doing it under some inward
> compulsion which inhibits him from writing on secular subjects

with lively inventiveness and enjoyment, as he would prefer to do. Who *wants* this stuff? (164)

One could quibble over Sassoon's claim that he would prefer to write about secular subjects with "lively inventiveness", fictional inventiveness never having been one of his strongest points, but there is no doubt that he always regarded the Georgian concern with the writer's duties towards his readership as a valid point. Still, Sassoon felt he had to proceed in the direction he had chosen:

> There is nothing left for me (as for all grown old) but to make my peace with life, and to try to express the process. It is a private pilgrimage, authentically experienced. *The Tasking* is an accurate title for my volume. Some inward compulsion has made me do it, and has prevented me from attempting pleasanter and less anchoritic themes. An old man asking himself whether he believes in God, and unable to believe much in the spectacle of himself. 'What a pity he can't write some more about fox-hunting,' the Public will say. (165)

The need to make his peace with life is a reminder of the enormous emotional damage that the war had caused. Six months earlier, in October 1953, he had revealed in his diary that his one earthly concern was the well-being of his son George and that neither his own existence nor his literary reputation were of any value to him:

> I don't think I should care whether my literary works were remembered or forgotten. More than ever it seems that creative human existence as a whole is what matters to the future. (How obvious!) That the spirit of God (or good) should pervade and prevail. My own existence seems so insignificant. And my ageing body craves eternal rest – as it craves each night for dreamless sleep (which it never gets). (148)

The "dreams from the pit" were haunting him still. The "goodness", whether of a divine nature or not, that he desires to believe in, has by now become purely spiritual. Much as he loved the countryside, he has now left behind Meredith's understanding of Nature, realizing that nature can also manifest itself in a more hostile way. In 'The Trial' he describes himself as "Zealous to walk the way of Henry Vaughan / Who glimpsed divinity in speechless things".[15] As yet Sassoon has not reached that stage; he can neither deny not explain the brutal forces of God's creation

> Question the tropical jungle, through what guise
> He manifests therein His ministrant law,
> And how he justifies fang, swamp, and claw.[16]

But Sassoon shows himself to be a true believer: reality shall not persuade him he is wrong, and he is determined not to doubt his inner convictions, rather regarding it as a test of his faith:

> Nature and knowledge daunt me with dire denial
> The inward witness and the innocent dream.
> On such rough road must faith endure its trial,
> Upheld by resolution to redeem
> The soul, that world within an ignorant shape
> One with the solar system and the ape.

This faith was strengthened by the change in the creative process he had observed; in December 1953 he wrote:

> Such verse as I've written in the last five years or more really has been a dedication of the spirit to its task. The lines describe the process by which I now produce my best verse – the complete absence of emotional excitement or preliminary mental chemistry, just listening for the message to come through, unstimulated by any other mental experience. (149)

His own poetry has thus become his only tangible proof of the existence of the spirit world:

> "How did I do it?" I ask, when contemplating one of my lucky performances in verse. It wasn't my ordinary self who sat there in a state of intense mental concentration, and who overheard something which he couldn't have achieved by conscious thinking. (150)

Sassoon believes himself no longer to be a conscious artist, rather he has become the medium through which the unknown spirit communicates: "Someone else invades me for an hour or two / Clocked occluded self wrote never lines like these" ('The Visitant').

In his desire to write both concisely and imaginatively, Sassoon sometimes burdened his poetry with ugly phrases and compounds: his fondness for alliteration led him to use "clocked occluded", though it seems rather a laborious way of referring to his mortal self, nor does the phrase sound particularly euphonious.

Similarly, in his *Pynchbeck Lyre* satires he had made fun of Humbert Wolfe's habit of changing nouns into verbs ('June Un-juned'), apparently not realizing that it was in fact also a feature of his own serious poetry. In 'The Worst of It' he comes up with an almost exact imitation of Wolfe's 'June Un-juned', when he refers to contemporary man "Unfuturing his future". Still these excesses do not occur with the same frequency as in the *Satirical Poems*: one beneficial result of the more concise style of the religious poems is that it keeps Sassoon's word-music within bounds.

Sassoon's new-found perception of himself as an instrument rather than an independent, creative writer makes him regard his own world as a microcosm, a true reflection of the Universe, that thus loses some of its mystery.

This revelation is the subject of 'Retreat from Eternity':

> Just now I stared out on a star-strange night
> With man's habitual wonder at the sight,
> And the old, lonely question – stellar space
> Coincident wherefore with one human face?
> Then, while the firelight flickered, musing here,
> I saw, in mimic constellation shown,
> Reflected sparkles on the chandelier,
> And was no more benumbed by the unknown.

He expresses his newly acquired metaphysical awareness in some striking lines, which give his poetry a Vaughan-like quality:

> I know a night of stars within me;
> Through eyes of dream I have perceived

> Blest apparitions who would win me
> Home to what innocence believed.
>   ('Human Bondage', ll. 1-4)

Sassoon believed the end of his pilgrimage to be in sight, and in two related pieces, he juxtaposes life in the contemporary world with his own hermit-like existence. In 'The Worst of It' he claims that man has brought disaster on himself ("self-assigned to suicide"): the pursuit of scientific knowledge has destroyed man's existence and condemned it to "doom's dismay". Sassoon borrowed the title of his poem from Browning, whose 'The Worst of It' – from *Dramatis Personae* (1864) – is the address of a husband to the unfaithful wife he had thought incapable of sin: "Should you forfeit heaven for a snapt gold ring". Sassoon believed the contemporary world to be in a similar state: mankind had sacrificed spiritual bliss for short-term material gains. In the poem's companion piece, 'The Best of It', he contrasts this with his own existence: he has made his peace with life: surrendered to its current and accepted his past existence and present old age: "Passion outlived. Regret there need be none". In 'The Chord', the last poem of this volume (and of his *Collected Poems*), Sassoon expresses his gratitude for the peace he has found. Using a musical metaphor, he beautifully conveys the sense of fulfilment that he had acquired at what he thought was the end of his spiritual pilgrimage:

> On stillness came a chord,
> While I, the instrument,
> Knew long-withheld reward:
> Gradual the glory went;
> Vibrating, on and on,
> Toward harmony unheard,
> Till dark where sanctus shone;
> Lost, once a living word.
>
> But in me yet abode
> The given grace though gone;
> The love, the lifted load,
> The answered orison.

III

Sassoon was mistaken when he thought he had reached the end of his spiritual pilgrimage. The years following the private publication of *The Tasking* in 1954 were a bleak period in which he wrote no further poetry. What happened next he recounted in a letter to Felicitas Corrigan, dated 30 October 1959:

> Three years ago I was in a complete black-out: impossible to realize or comprehend now. In January '57, the Mother Superior at the Assumption Convent in Kensington Square wrote to me, after reading my volume *Sequences*, in which my spiritual predicament was apparent & somehow I was helped to realize that deliverance had arrived.
>
> She has been the greatest benefactor of my life, and has never made a glimmer of a mistake in her guidance & influence [.....] I tell you all this because it is by far 'the most important' thing that has ever happened to me, & has completely transformed my life, & made my old age blest & endurable. 'How came it? – ask your angel – ask that vigilant voice.' (Mine talks to me quite a lot – one of my childish indulgences!). (175)

In August 1960 he wrote her again, looking back on his religious search ("groping" would have been Sassoon's word) from his new vantage-point. It is as if he has climbed the height and has now a clear overview of the maze he spent such a long time seeking his way out of. The distance he has put between his former and his present self is reminiscent of the author of *Memoirs of an Infantry Officer*, who looked back on the misguided war-rebel with a mixture of sympathy and incredulity at his former self's limitless ignorance:

> I was a complete ignoramus about religion. It amazes me to look back on it. I never said a prayer. Never consulted any religious book, or *thought* about doctrine. Just went blindly on, clinging to the *idea* of God, unable to believe that salvation applied to *me*, though firmly convinced of the existence of a spiritual world & heaven above. Again & again in these past years, I have asked myself how I endured it, so unendurable it

seems in retrospect. *Was* it some kind of dark night of probation? The instant release in 1957 suggests it. Reading Newman, I wonder what effect it would have made if someone had given it to me 10 years ago. Everything I needed is there, waiting for me! All clear as daylight. And as simple as falling off a log – just unconditional surrender! But I have always been queerly lacking in method in everything I have tried to do – no conscious method in verse-writing – or even in cricket and golf – or teaching myself to play the piano. Just muddling on by instinct. I can see now that I was standing at an immaterial doorway, wearing my knuckles out in vain. And M.M. [Mother Margaret Mary, the Mother Superior at the Assumption Convent in Kensington Square] just came along and opened the door, through God's mysterious providence. It *had* to happen, didn't it? & happened in my ultimate *need*. All my life I have instinctively reacted against worldliness, only conforming to it with – as dear Robbie Ross once said – 'the expression of an offended deer-hound'. (167-68)

Sassoon's conversion to the Roman Catholic faith on 14 August 1957 added yet another name to an already considerable list of British writers who had become converts: Coventry Patmore (1864); Alice Meynell (1868); Frederick Rolfe, 'Baron Corvo' (1887); Ernest Dowson (c.1891-2); Ford Madox Ford (1892); Aubrey Beardsley (1897); R.H. Benson (1903); Ronald Firbank (1907); Maurice Baring (1909); David Jones (1921); G.K. Chesterton (1922); Graham Greene (1926); Alfred Noyes (1927); Evelyn Waugh (1930); Roy Campbell (1935); Muriel Spark (1954) and Edith Sitwell (1955). In psychological terms, Sassoon's conversion can be seen as the culmination of his desire for guidance, and in that respect, though somewhat paradoxically, it could be said that the Mother Church was the last in the long row of 'father-figures': Tom Dixon (the Richardson of *Memoirs of a Fox-Hunting Man*), Norman Loder (on whom Denis Milden was based), Sir Edmund Gosse, Robert Ross, W.H.R. Rivers, and Henry Head.[17] He had found a new home, and through the sense of security that gave him, he attained what he had been searching for ever since the war; that what George Herbert in 'The Pulley' had called "God's treasure": Rest.

The Sassoon that emerged after the conversion was strengthened and more vigorous. The publication of *Sequences* in 1956 had been a painful experience; the critical reception had not been favourable: "The reviews of *Sequences* were heart-breaking, after sixteen years of patient silence and preparation. Blunden alone has asserted that I am essentially a religious poet" (*LC*, 15). He had come to see his later poetry as a faithful report of a human struggle, the record of a crisis that might offer succour to others going through a similar experience. On 31 December 1952 he wrote a poem he called 'Apologia', in which he conveyed the purpose of his poetry, at the same time disclaiming any innovative or original qualities in his work.

> My words – that non-surprising choice –
> My thoughts – not found evocative –
> My untransparent tone of voice –
>   Forgive.
>
> Word, thought, and voice but testify
> What time has urged me to believe:
> This, in a world gone much awry,
>   Receive.
>
> From one whose solitudes would share
> Such good as mind and heart can make
> With others. Homespun it is there
>   To take.

The poem was never published, but the sentiments it expresses suggest that the reviewer who referred to Sassoon's later poetry as "*human* achievements" rather than "poetic achievements" certainly made a valid point. Sassoon, however, was not impressed:

> The 'critical world' doesn't seem to have any bearing on what I really am. The main trouble is, that all poetry now *has* to be intellectual, and they are utterly incapable of understanding my essential simplicity and naturalness. Meanwhile my poems are read & loved by innumerable non-professional people with literary taste and judgement, so all is well. I am fully aware of my limitations as a thinker and a verse practitioner, but I had to

be myself, and by 1920 I was too old to indulge in technical experiments. The strange thing about it is that my poems should have been liked by other good poets – Hardy, de la Mare, Belloc, Masefield, Blunden, for leading instance – (Edith Sitwell too, though *she* has cooled off, owing to me being regarded as old-fashioned!). (208-09)

Sassoon is right that his poetry being old-fashioned rather than modern need not in itself signify an inferior literary quality, a point sufficiently proven by such poets as Walter de la Mare and Edmund Blunden, both admirers of his work. Less convincing is his claim that by 1920 he was "too old to indulge in technical experiment". His pre-1920 poetry can hardly be said to be characterized by an experimental quality either, and had he been so inclined, the creative crisis he experienced immediately after the war would have afforded him ample scope for an experimental period in which to discover a new poetic voice. The truth is that as a writer he never set out to break new ground in verse form or technique; being a man of conservative tastes, he always felt perfectly at home with the traditional forms, an attitude that only hardened as he started writing his religious poetry.

IV

Sassoon wrote little, and published even less poetry after his conversion. During the last ten years of his life he wrote only some fifteen poems, almost all devout pieces in which he expresses his gratitude for the spiritual home he had found. By far the most interesting is 'Lenten Illuminations', which, according to Sassoon, "epitomized the seven months of 'all things made new' before I was received" (178). In the poem the recent convert visits a church one afternoon before Easter:

> Not properly Catholic, some might say, to like it best
> When no one's in the cool white church that few frequent
> These sober-skied vocational afternoons in Lent.
>
> (ll. 1-3)[18]

The poet then looks back on his former self, wondering how it was that as a regular church visitor he had always felt attracted to the outward trappings of religious faith, without ever becoming a true believer:

> What were you up to – going into churches all those years
> Of faith unfaithful?...Kneeling respectfully when others knelt,
> But never a moment while reflective there alone.
> The aids were manifest; but only for your eyes and ears,
> In anthems, organ music, shaft-aspiring stone,
> And jewelled windows into which your mind might melt.
>
> (ll. 19-24)

He then recalls how in "watches of the night" he "implored illumination" which never came. For this he blames his lack of humility: his requests went unheeded because he never surrendered to his Lord in prayer: "But never being bowed / Obedient – never conceived an aureoled instance, an assuring spark" (ll. 45-6). Release had come when he had followed his soul, rather than his misguided mind:

> There had been many byways for the frustrate brain,
> All leading to illusions lost and shrines forsaken...
> One road before us now – one guidance for our gain –
> One morning light – whatever the world's weather – wherein
> wide-eyed to waken.

The joy at his new-found faith is expressed in terms that recall the morning-minded young poet of his youth. In its best passages, 'Lenten Illuminations' records this momentous occasion in the poet's life in euphonious and easy flowing lines. But there are also less successful moments, when the syntax falters and the words, weighed down with meaning, sound heavy and obscure:

> This day twelve months ago – it was Ash Wednesday – one
> Mid-day between us two toward urgent hope fulfilled
> Strove with submission. Arduous – forbidding – then to meet
> Inflexible Authority. While the work was willed,
> The riven response from others to the task undone
> Daunted a mind confused with ferment, incomplete:

> There seemed so much renunciant consequence involved,
> When independent questioning self should yield, indubitant
>   and absolved.

(ll. 57-64)

This is a problem that also spoils many of the other poems, most noticeably 'Rogation' (1959), which is further damaged by excessive alliteration:

> Indwelt redemption, doubted and denied,
> Concord no sanctity could comprehend,
> Mercy immeasurable and multiplied,
>
> World watcher, armed and influent to befriend.
> Hope and humility, resistless Rood,
> Beyond our bodements bring beatitude.

That same year, Sassoon wrote 'Arbor Vitae', in which he uses a tree as a metaphor for "grace in me defined". The poem is a success, not only because the metaphor works well, but also because the poet has managed to present it in a simple and graceful tone and rhythm:

> This tree all winter through
> Found no green work to do –
>   No life
> Therein ran rife.
>
> But with an awoken year
> What surge of sap is here –
>   What flood
> In branch and bud.
>
> So grace in me can hide –
> Be darkened and denied –
>   Then once again
> Vesture my every vein.

Unfortunately most of the other later poems miss this lightness of touch; they are short, compact and top-heavy, expressing the poet's unconditional surrender:

> Because I have believed, I bid my mind be still.
> Therein is now conceived Thy hid yet sovereign Will.
> Because I set all thought aside in seeking Thee,
> Thy proven purpose wrought abideth blest in me.
>
> ('Proven Purpose', ll. 1-4)

In 1960 the Stanbrook Abbey Press published *The Path to Peace* in an expensive, limited edition. In this anthology of thirty poems, Sassoon's pilgrimage is traced from his early 'Before Dawn' (1909) to 'A Prayer at Pentecost' (1960). Its title juxtaposes Sassoon's personal pilgrimage with *The Road to Ruin*, his 1933 volume in which he had warned the world of a new world war.[19] To celebrate the poet's eightieth birthday in September 1966, the Arts Council funded the publication of *An Octave*, which consisted of eight of his later poems, introduced by Charles Causley.[20] In spite of repeated requests by his publisher, none of these post-conversion poems were ever included in later editions of his *Collected Poems*, "Seems somehow wrong", he wrote after Faber's last request in 1964 (232). This may seem a surprising statement for a poet who always regarded his poetry as his "true biography". Perhaps it was because – like John Bunyan *Pilgrim's Progress* which ends when Christian and Hopeful enter the Celestial City and the Golden Gates shut behind them – he too felt that the long and arduous pilgrimage which his poems had chronicled had come to an end when he was received into the Catholic Church.

EPILOGUE

A STRANGER ON EARTH

I

During the last ten years of his life, following his conversion, Sassoon was no longer interested in his posthumous literary reputation, though he felt that it would be by the *Sherston Trilogy* that he would be remembered: "the war poems (the significant and successful ones) will end up as mere appendices to the matured humanity of the *Memoirs*" (*LC*, 14). In June 1965 he received the Honorary Degree of D. Litt. at the University of Oxford. Academic recognition now meant little to the 78-year-old, and he only accepted because he knew it would give pleasure to his friends. The Latin citation (for which David Cecil had been one of the advisors) called Sassoon an eminent artist whose prose works "*Commentarii Venatoris Vulpium* et *Tribuni Peditum*" had portrayed "the good qualities of the horse and the senseless barbarities of the war". Sassoon's only objection to the speech was that no reference was made to his spiritual journey: "I suppose 'the world' was being on the safe side, as usual".[1] This reference to the world outside as an almost alien presence is typical of Sassoon's state of mind.

Ever since the 1930s, contemporary literature had passed him by largely unnoticed; though he continued to read Georgian poets such as de la Mare, Hodgson, Blunden, Masefield and Andrew Young, he paid little or no attention to later developments like the Auden generation, the poets of the 1940s and the Movement poets. The one poet that did excite him was Dylan Thomas, probably because he felt Thomas' poetic talent was un-intellectual and akin to his own:

D.T.'s poetic cosmos is a good instance of splendid irrationality, a defiance indeed of 'rational thinking'. Many of them are written in a private language of his own from which I

252

fail to interpret the meaning. Rhapsodies, controlled by a tight technique of verse-craft. They make my own poverty of language painfully apparent. But I believe that D.T. would have agreed with my suggestion that the poetic impulse is a visitant from elsewhere. He too must have had moments when he wondered what his symbolic effusions amounted to – though in his case, the word-magic is indisputable.[2]

But his admiration was for the poems only, for he thoroughly disapproved of Thomas's life-style – just as in his youth his mother had condemned Swinburne's eccentric behaviour as one unbefitting a poet.

The battle between the Modernists and the Neo-Georgians had been decided in the late 1920s, when J.C. Squire's *London Mercury* went into decline and the Neo-Georgians as a movement disappeared. From then on, literary criticism generally either ignored or condemned Georgian poetry (without distinguishing between the original Georgians and the Neo-Georgians), though it has rightly been pointed out that "much of the disapproving commentary on the Georgians is attributable to critics who were really advocating another kind of poetry".[3] In his 1961 address 'To Criticize the Critic', T.S. Eliot acknowledged that in his early attacks on the Georgians he was "implicitly defending the sort of poetry" he wrote himself.

The reaction against Modernism which was noticeable in the 1950s was not unrelated to the Second World War. When G.S. Fraser observed in 1955 that

English culture, in the last few years – in reaction, maybe, to shifts of world power – has become much more self-protectively insular. The bright young men no longer read Kierkegaard, Kafka, Sartre, and what have you, but rediscover Bagehot, George Gissing, 'Mark Rutherford', or Arnold Bennett[4]

he was in fact drawing attention to a kind of cultural withdrawal, not dissimilar to that of the Georgian poets after the Great War. The reaction in the 1950s was probably *not* due to shifts in world power as Fraser suggested (political consequences would not have concerned everybody directly), but to those after-effects of a world war that were immediately felt by all the people: a nation that was licking its social and economic wounds was not interested in the outside world. That was what had happened after the Great War, when the Georgian movement had displayed similar insular tendencies (in a literal sense reflected in the many titles referring to England and the British Isles).

Like the Georgians before them, the Movement poets of the 1950s worked in a social and cultural post-world war climate, and it is interesting to see that their reaction against Modernism is marked by a reappraisal of the Georgian poets and their concerns. For one thing they returned to the very Georgian question of the poet and his readership. Though most of the Movement poets were university-educated and quite content to write for a similarly intellectual audience, they thought the poet could not simply ignore the reader altogether:

> The Movement believed indifference or hostility to the reader to be responsible for what they saw as the obscurity of Modernist poetry. Awareness of the reader, they believed, helped the poet to 'restrain his oddities' and was a prerequisite for a relationship of equality and trust: as [D.J.] Enright puts it "the poet should do the work, his fair share of it, and not leave it to the researching reader to seek clues on other ground." The Modernists destroyed this relationship by failing to concern themselves with the reader's likely reception of the poem, and his possible difficulties with its meaning.[5]

The most outspoken critic of Modernism among the Movement poets was Philip Larkin. In his insistence on the enjoyment that literature should give to as wide an audience as possible, he takes a view that is identical with that of the Georgians in general and Sassoon in particular; he too argued against an intellectualizing of poetry, condemning the shift from a general readership to an academic audience:

> It is not sufficient to say that poetry has lost its audience, and so no longer need consider it: lots of people still read and even buy poetry. More accurately, poetry has lost its old audience, and gained a new one. This has been caused by the consequences of a cunning merger between poet, literary critic,

and academic critic (three classes now notoriously indistinguishable): it is hardly an exaggeration to say that the poet has gained the happy position wherein he can praise his own poetry in the press and explain it in the classroom [...]
In short, the modern poetic audience, when it is not taking in its own washing, is a *student* audience, pure and simple. At first sight this may not seem a bad thing [...] But at bottom poetry, like all art, is inextricably bound up with giving pleasure, and if a poet loses his pleasure-seeking audience he has lost the only audience worth having, for which the dutiful mob that signs on every September is no substitute.[6]

Larkin went further than any other Movement poet in linking his condemnation of Modernism to a revaluation of the Georgians, and his views on poetry were to a large extent identical with theirs. In his essay 'Fiction and the Reading Public', David Lodge writes that novelists

recognize (in a way which I suspect is not true of poets) that their fortune in the market – the readiness of strangers to risk or expend money on their creative work – is a significant criterion of achievement.[7]

But the idea that poets are less market-oriented is a post-Georgian concept: the Georgian poets *did* believe that good poetry could be enjoyed by a wide audience; their ideal was the popularization of good poetry (an ideal Edward Marsh realized with his *Georgian Poetry* anthologies) and they did regard popular success as a measure of the poet's achievement. Larkin's poetic career reflects this Georgian ideal in that it combined critical acclaim with popular success, but though he never made a secret of his preference for the Georgian poets (particularly as editor of the *Oxford Book of Twentieth-Century Verse* in 1973, in which he included many Georgians, as well as Neo-Georgians like Squire, Shanks and Turner), his own successes never led to a Georgian revival.

II

Of the Georgian writers who were included in one or more of the first three *Georgian Poetry* anthologies (i.e. Abercrombie, Drinkwater, W.H. Davies, James Stephens, John Masefield, W.W. Gibson, James Elroy Flecker, de la Mare, Bottomley, and Sassoon) Walter de la Mare and Sassoon have been the most successful: most of their works are still in print and continue to sell.

The comparison between de la Mare and Sassoon is useful, in that it illustrates one of Sassoon's essential limitations. Both writers regarded themselves as poets, though both did write prose as well; counted among the Georgian poets, both men were in fact extreme individualists, who never thought of themselves as belonging to any movement; in their outlook both were extremely English, showing little or no interest in foreign cultures; in their writing they were drawn to their childhood, which they associated with innocent happiness, and, especially in de la Mare's case, with an as yet unrestrained imagination; and both were essentially religious men, very much interested in the metaphysical. When, in December 1961, Sassoon was asked to unveil the memorial tablet to de la Mare in St Paul's Cathedral, he remembered him in his address as

> interested in the most ordinary things, though his mind dwelt so much on things intangible and visionary. And in all relationships the homeliest of men.
>
> I have known no one who could so stimulate and heighten one's perceptiveness. Absorbing and interpreting all that came his way, he could communicate his questing consciousness to others, sending them away with re-christened eyes.[8]

Sassoon's pilgrimage was a quest induced by a desire to find inner peace and to re-establish a disturbed harmony, *not* by a boundless curiosity and an eagerness to know and understand the world around him. All those who have recorded their personal memories of Walter de la Mare keep coming back to his desire to learn and to know;[9] Sassoon, on the other hand, never developed a questioning attitude: his rejection of the upper-middle-class values his mother had taught him was caused by the horrors of a world war, but it was an impulsive reaction rather than a balanced evaluation; as a result he veered to the other extreme of left-wing Socialism, not realising until later that this was a position that suited him even less. His interests in the world around him were limited at the best of times, and once he embarked on his spiritual pilgrimage he grew so preoccupied with his own condition that he withdrew into a solipsistic state of mind, creating a cocooned existence that was not unlike the safe and protective world in which his mother had brought him up. It was as if the 'Heytesbury Hermit' (as he was known in the neighbourhood) had learnt the hard way the wisdom of what Blaise Pascal had said in one of his *Pensées*: "All the misfortunes of men derive from one single thing, which is their inability to be at ease in a room in their own home".[10]

III

It is a paradoxical fact that the man whom friends and acquaintances remembered as both reticent and modest, was in his writings so self-obsessed that almost his entire *oeuvre* is devoted to his own self. Sassoon's authorship is unique for its extreme limitations, and as a writer he lacked a complete dedication to his art: he is absorbed in himself as a person rather than a writer absorbed in himself as a subject for his art. For his reputation as a poet it is to be regretted that he was never able to unlearn the artificial word-music that had appealed to him as a child: as his speech was affected by a slight stammer, so his poetry is affected by this tendency to write word-music. By following Pater's dictum on all art aspiring to the condition of music, he neglected some of his strongest points as a writer: his sincerity, his natural simplicity and his impressive descriptive qualities.

On the closing pages of *Siegfried's Journey*, the then 59-year-old Sassoon gave a personal view on life:

Once in a lifetime, perhaps, a man may be the instrument through which something constructive emerges, whether he be the genius giving birth to an original idea or the anonymous mortal who makes use of an opportunity which will never recur. It is for the anonymous ones that I have my special feeling. I like to think of them remembering the one time when they were involved in something unusual or important – when, probably without knowing it at the time, they, as it were, wrote their single masterpiece, never to perform anything comparable again. Then they were fully alive, living above themselves, and discovering powers they hadn't been aware of. For a moment they stood in the transfiguring light of dramatic experience. And nothing ever happened to them afterwards. They were submerged by human uneventfulness. (*SJ*, 221)

On the whole this seems a pretty fair description of his own life. One of the ironies of it was that his "constructive moment" was brought about by one of the most destructive events the world had ever known. His literary executor, Sir Rupert Hart-Davis, writes that in later life Sassoon "was annoyed at always being referred to simply as a war poet",[11] but it was in the war that Sassoon stood as a soldier-poet in "the transfiguring light of dramatic experience", and it was the war that established him as a poet. Sassoon himself had always shared his mother's conviction that he was destined to be a poet: his war-poetry gave him his breakthrough, bringing him to the attention of a wider reading public.

But when reading the early pieces he preserved in his *Collected Poems* one cannot help thinking that if it had not been for the war, Sassoon would probably have remained a very minor Georgian poet, forever writing about sunrises and fauns, without ever achieving the artistry of a W.H. Davies or Walter de la Mare. The young Sassoon was on the whole a trivial poet, who lacked both passion and originality, and had simply nothing to say. And so it is fair to say that Sassoon's literary career was made by the Great War: not only did it provide him with a subject, but it also made him write with passion and conviction. Also, it was the war that was directly responsible for the mental crisis that occupied Sassoon for the rest of his life. The crisis itself is both the source of inspiration for, as well as the main theme of his later poetry and it also made him investigate his past, which is the subject of the autobiographical prose works.

But if the war made the writer, it also well-nigh destroyed the man. The rude severance of the links with his past life left him completely unsettled, and in almost forty years after the war Sassoon remained spiritually adrift, until his conversion to the Roman Catholic faith gave him the peace of mind he had been craving for. The mental wounds that the war caused took a long time to heal, though this may have been at least partly due to the fact that Sassoon was singularly ill-equipped to build up a fruitful existence after the war. Apart from the short time he acted as literary editor of the *Daily Herald* in 1919, Sassoon never held a job in his life, and his leisurely existence, safeguarded by his father's annuity and his aunt's inheritance, left him too much alone with his own memories and never gave him the healthy distractions that a working life might have brought.

His limited education was also an important factor in his slow recovery after the war: his thinking would have been greatly facilitated by a more ordered and trained mind. His mother's decisions to keep him at home until he was twelve and to take him home whenever he was in poor health were factors that certainly contributed to his sloppy education. His defensive and suspicious attitude towards Modernism and intellectuals was due to the realization – after his first encounters with intellectuals in London and at Garsington – that his limited education excluded him from a career as an intellectual man of letters. It seems to have left him with an enormous chip on his shoulder and to have led him to the rather simplistic view that the contemporary world was dominated and all but destroyed by scientists and intellectuals.

His mother's influence weighed heavily on him throughout his life. He was undoubtedly the victim of an over-protective upbringing, for seen from a distance, his post-war journey seems a regressive process in which he tries to re-create the safe world of his childhood. Ezra Pound described poets as the "antennae of the race", but Sassoon's later poetry clearly shows a man whose spirit was not on speaking terms with the *Zeitgeist*; his world was the late-Victorian/Edwardian world of his mother. His pilgrimage took him in an opposite direction from the society he lived in, for starting out in the 1920s as a traditional poet in an experimental age and relatively uneducated in a literary world that was ever more dominated by intellectuals, he returned to the life-style of an Edwardian country-gentleman in an ever more urban, socialist and classless society, and ended up a devout Catholic in what he saw as a godless and secular world.

Sassoon was a natural loner, but it seems likely that these reclusive tendencies were aggravated by his homosexuality. Reading his books one realizes that he never describes himself in a relationship as an equal partner, since in nearly all his friendships he is either an apprentice (Denis Milden/Norman Loder, Rivers, Hardy, Gosse, Ross,

Beerbohm, Head, Hodgson, E.M. Forster), or a fatherly figure, giving advice and (financial) assistance (David Thomas, Owen, Blunden, Gabriel Atkin, Stephen Tennant).[12] It cannot be a coincidence that Sassoon is in the apprentice role in most of his literary friendships and the elder partner in homosexual relationships.

Sassoon obviously never came to terms with his homosexuality. Though in the early 1920s he toyed with the idea of making it the subject of his first novel, it never became a theme in his work. That he even considered such a controversial project as a homosexual novel is not all that surprising when one considers Sassoon's state of mind in the early 1920s. At the time, he still regarded himself as a writer whose reputation was based on his rebellious war poetry. This assessment was largely correct, but his conclusion, that he was therefore a literary rebel who needed to tackle controversial subjects was completely erroneous. Sassoon was not a rebel: his natural inclination was to suppress rather than to expose. In the event he published six autobiographical prose works in which the sexuality of the main characters is never discussed. The note he added in the 1930s to his 1921 diary about homosexuality being a bore because "the intelligentsia [had] capured it"[13] is a very thin excuse which may have deluded himself, but which will convince nobody else.

Sassoon's attitude towards his sexual problems is best illustrated in his relationship with T. E. Lawrence. They had first met in November 1918, after Lawrence had asked Edward Marsh to introduce him to the author of *Counter-Attack*. Though after this first meeting Sassoon referred to Lawrence as "a little Oxford archeologist" (*D1*, 280), their friendship quickly matured. Both men were complex personalities and never felt comfortable with their own sexuality; Lawrence's repressive instincts were in this respect even stronger than Sassoon's. When in 1962 Sassoon was asked to contribute to a television programme about T. E. Lawrence, he refused ("I will not be TVd!"), but he also added that he felt Lawrence ought to be judged "by what he was to others – not by his tortured inward self".[14] The friendship between Lawrence and Sassoon must have been based on the recognition of the other's "tortured inward self" that was not to be approached.

This respect for the hidden depths of the inward self also characterizes Sassoon as an autobiographer. On his quest for autognosis he never went so far as to confront himself with those facets of his personality he preferred to suppress. It accounts for a basic dishonesty in the auto-biographies in which he never even alludes to, let alone investigates, his sexuality. Perhaps his marriage in 1933 can be seen as an escape from his homosexuality. When it broke up, his response was to withdraw from the world altogether. Did the Heytesbury Hermit seek solitude or was he escaping from all intimate human relationships that might bring out latent feelings and emotions he could not cope with? Robert Graves once accused Sassoon of never being quite open with his friends and of sacrificing friendship to loyalty. The distinction is telling: friendship suggests interaction, intimacy, openness and development. In comparison loyalty is one-sided, stable, and not only does it not require intimacy, but once it has been established it does not require any contact at all.

The importance of Sassoon's homosexuality for his writing lies in the fact that it was one of the skeletons in his cupboard he was trying to escape from in his nostalgic prose works. But its importance should not be exaggerated: it was never the main driving force behind his writing. In his war poetry it had been his sense of responsibility for his men, his anger and indignation that had made him speak out. In his prose works it is his desire to escape, not only from his homosexuality, but also, and more importantly, from his war memories and from a world he felt increasingly alienated from.

IV

The war seems also to have been responsible for one of the oddest characteristics of Sassoon's writing. There is one striking difference between his early verse and war poetry on the one hand, and prose works and later poetry on the other: the post-war Sassoon is a writer who cannot write fiction.

In his early poems he regularly described imaginary scenes and settings, and in his war poetry – particularly in the descriptive pieces – he created (though usually without much success) a *persona* of what he considered to be the 'common' soldier. But already in his satirical verse it was noticeable how Sassoon could not keep the 'I' out of the poems (and in his case the 'I' is always himself, never a fictional *persona*), and this autobiographical element comes to dominate his later poetry, which is the record of his personal pilgrimage.

Similarly, in his prose works, George Sherston could admittedly be regarded as a fictional character in *Memoirs of a Fox-Hunting Man* (though even there he is, as Sassoon himself said, a simplified version of the author), but by *Memoirs of an Infantry Officer* and *Sherston's Progress* the characters of Sherston and his creator have become indistinguishable. Sassoon's later prose works are all non-fiction: three autobiographies and his Meredith biography, and even in this last work the instances of 'authorial intrusion' are numerous. Sassoon himself put it all down to an uneventful life and a lack of experience:

> I have often wondered, how much I might have done had more material for writing about come my way, for I needed the stimulus of experience. But I have seldom *sought* experience, and most of it has been imposed on me by circumstance. And the quietist in me was usually uppermost in me. (*LC*, 16)

But on reflection this does not seem a convincing explanation, since plenty of material for writing had come Sassoon's way: in the 1920s he met everybody worth meeting in London, he sat at dinner tables with the rich and famous, dined at his club with writers, painters amd musicians, stayed for weeks at a time at Ottoline Morrell's Garsington, and travelled abroad – to France, Holland, Germany, Austria, and Italy – on various occasions. His diaries over the period 1915-1925, published posthumously, testify to a hectic social life, and give many fascinating glimpses of some of the leading members of the English social and cultural world. In comparison, Walter de la Mare's life was decidedly uneventful, and he was never short of material to write about.

It might be argued that it was the gentlemanly·code that made Sassoon decide against using this material for his books, that he felt he could not gossip nor use personal knowledge about people he had met and events he had witnessed or heard about in the London clubs and restaurants or at Garsington. This must undoubtedly have been the case in the autobiographies, and *Siegfried's Journey* in particular, but it will not do as an explanation for not writing fiction. Sassoon need not have presented his characters and stories under as thin a veil – immediately recognizable for friends and acquaintances alike – as Aldous Huxley did in *Crome Yellow*. If he had had the imaginative powers to make up a story he could have created composite characters, used different settings, or employed any of various other ways of disguising his sources.

V

"First found beliefs remain", Sassoon wrote in 'World Without End' (in *Emblems of Experience*, 1951), and he could be extremely dogmatic in adhering to these beliefs without ever questioning or investigating them. Though a great self-analyser in many other fields, Sassoon is never at his best when discussing his own authorship. He never wavered in his conviction that his mother was right when she believed that he was destined to be a poet, never questioned the outdated concept of what she thought being a poet entailed.

And so, after the war, he remained in his tastes a late Victorian-Edwardian writer, baffled by *The Waste Land* and David Jones' *The Anathemata* ("quite beyond me"),[15] happy to see his friend Edmund Blunden appointed Professor of Poetry at Oxford instead of Robert Lowell ("a poet I have never perused"), and, though only in his private correspondence, outspoken in his condemnation of Modernist developments in the arts ("all arts have gone the same way – dry bones and caricature and discontent and distortion and ungracious ingenuity").[16] After the war he reverted to an almost Victorian position in which he expected poetry to be "morally uplifting". When T.S. Eliot was awarded the Order of Merit in 1948, Sassoon wrote to Max Beerbohm that he regarded this announcement "with dissatisfaction", adding that he wondered what future generations would get out of his work: "What *has* he said that will ring on for their ears?" (*LMB*, ·101). For Sassoon, *The Waste Land* was not only virtually incomprehensible, but also purely pessimistic in its portrayal of a civilization which was beyond hope. But though the mature Sassoon expected poetry to carry an uplifting message, and though he distanced himself from his war protest, he never condemned his own war poetry for its horrific realism. He came to see the religious theme of his later poetry as a natural development from the prophet role he had adopted as a war poet.

In 1936 the editors of *The Collected Works of Isaac Rosenberg* asked him to contribute the introduction (initially they had asked W.B. Yeats, but he had refused, not believing in war poetry as a genre). Sassoon readily accepted: "The only thing that matters is that Rosenberg should be given his due as one of the best of the young poets who perished in the war".[17] Sassoon felt especially strongly for Rosenberg's poetry because he believed they had something in common: in his 'Foreword' he wrote that he recognized in Rosenberg "a fruitful fusion between English and Hebrew culture. Behind all his poetry there is a racial quality – biblical and prophetic".[18] An element of identification is immediately recognizable: what Sassoon found in Rosenberg is what he had also found in himself: a prophetic and religious urge, and he believed these to derive from the same source: their Jewishness. That is why, towards the end of his life, he wrote to Felicitas Corrigan that he sometimes surmised "that my eastern ancestry is stronger in me than the Thornycrofts. The daemon in me is Jewish".[19]

Sassoon's pilgrimage was a slow and burdensome one, but in the end he managed to create a harmony between all the contradictory elements in his past. His conversion to the Roman Catholic faith was important to him in that it gave a theological foundation to his belief in a spiritual kinship that transgressed the bounds of time and place. What had begun to take shape in *Rhymed Ruminations* – a belief that there was no essential difference between distance in time and distance in space – was then underpinned by the Catholic teaching of the Communion of Saints: it accounted for the almost physical reality that the spiritual presences of friends he had lost in the war, poets he felt akin to, and anonymous representatives of a decent humanity in past generations had always had for him.

It is this silent, spiritual struggle, recorded in his writings, that cannot fail to move and impress the serious student of Sassoon's work. It evokes an interest and sympathy for Sassoon as an individual, in spite of a poetic expression that is at times far from flawless. His reputation as a poet will probably have to rest on his war poetry: its historical importance is beyond question, but its simplicity of style has often led critics to underestimate the literary qualities that the best descriptive poems and most effective satires undoubtedly have. But his greatest achievements are to be found among his prose works, not only *Memoirs of an Infantry Officer*, which as a war memoir is of both historical and literary import-ance, but in *Memoirs of a Fox-Hunting Man* and *The Old Century*, the prose works dealing with Sassoon's youth and childhood years, in which he showed that, if really inspired by his subject, he was a writer who was capable of more than he is generally given credit for. *Memoirs of a Fox-Hunting Man* in particular merits a serious reading, not only for its meticulous and vivid style, but also for its clever composition and unexpected depths of writing which reveal Sassoon as a skilled craftsman and serious artist.

Siegfried Sassoon is a novelist *manqué* in that a lack of imaginative power – possibly a result of the mental wounds that the war inflicted – meant that he was a masterful prose writer who never succeeded in exerting his artistic talents in the writing of fictional works. With the exception of his war poetry – which is in this respect his least characteristic work – his writings are as isolated and insular as was Sassoon the man: they have no place in the canon of English literature, they are not representative of the literary period they were written in, but they will continue to draw readers for the sheer pleasure that they give and the poignant and touching story that they tell. As such they are a fitting monument to their creator, a humane and intensely private man, whose life and career were shaped by the Great War, and who must often have wondered if it had all been worth it.

Asked about her husband's career a few years after his death, T.S. Eliot's wife Valerie said that "He felt that he had paid too high a price to be a poet, that he had suffered too much".[20] Looking back on his almost forty years' pilgrimage, Siegfried Sassoon might well have said the same thing, since he had fulfilled his childhood ambition of becoming a poet, but in the process the romantic ideas he had had about being a poet had turned out to be so many illusions that were painfully unlearned. His desire for death was strong in the last years of his life. In March 1966 he wrote to Felicitas Corrigan:

O dear, I say to myself, if only things would stop happening! Not that much does happen to my seclusion. I just go on being told that I am a war poet, when all I want is to be told that I am only a pilgrim and a stranger on earth, utterly dependent on the idea of God's providence to my spiritual being.

But the game goes on, so I must put on my pads and make my way to the wicket. The wicket – O please, dear St Peter, don't delay too long in opening it to me![21]

Sassoon's language echoes *The Pilgrim's Progress*. When Christian and Faithful are questioned by the men at Vanity-Fair they tell them "that they were pilgrims and strangers in the world, and that they were going to their own country, which was the heavenly Jerusalem".[22] The enharmonic change on 'wicket' introduces one last time a recurring symbol in Sassoon's work. The man who used G. F. Watts's picture of Death coming to the door of the House of Love as the symbol of the Great War ending his happy youth at Weirleigh, who started his spiritual pilgrimage as "a suppliant at the door" at Henry Vaughan's grave, now asked for the wicket gate of Heaven to be opened unto him.

Siegfried Sassoon died at Heytesbury House on 1 September 1967, a week before his eighty-first birthday. In a sonnet, written on his death, Michael Thorpe remembers him as:

> A lean, anonymous horse-riding man,
> Jogging along the Wiltshire downland;
> That was the truest picture, of one
> Who rode away from the crowd[23]

It was by the time he had moved into Heytesbury House and published *Vigils*, in 1935, that Sassoon had begun to turn his back on the crowd, on the world, and even on life itself. He had always liked to quote Walter Savage Landor's well-known quatrain:

> I strove with none, for none was worth my strife:
> Nature I loved, and next to Nature, Art:
> I warmed both hands before the fire of life;
> It sinks; and I am ready to depart.

By the time of his death Siegfried Sassoon had been ready to depart for over thirty years.

NOTES

PREFACE

1. William Empson, *Arguefying* (London, 1988), p. 125.

PROLOGUE: FAMILY TIES

1. Dame Felicitas Corrigan, *Siegfried Sassoon: Poet's Pilgrimage* (London, 1973), p. 17.
2. See Keith Middlemass, *Edward VII* (London, 1975), p. 44.
3. See Stanley Jackson, *The Sassoons: Portrait of a Dynasty* (London, 1968), pp. 84-88.
4. Jackson (1968), p. 75.
5. In 1871 her sister Laura became the second wife of Lawrence Alma-Tadema (1836-1912), the Dutch-born painter who in the 1880s and 90s achieved popular successes with his imaginary scenes from classical Greece, Rome and ancient Egypt.
6. Jackson (1968), p. 76.
7. In *The Old Century* there is mention of a cook and two maids, with a nurse – later replaced by a German governess – to look after the boys. The male element consisted of the head-gardener, two under-gardeners and Richardson the groom.
8. Philip Hoare, *Serious Pleasures: the Life of Stephen Tennant* (London, 1990), p. 88.
9. His book collecting may have reminded him of his grandfather Sassoon David Sassoon, who had spent his leisure hours building up a library of rare Hebrew manuscripts. Cf. Jackson (1968), p. 38.
10. Cf. Sassoon's own account of this venture in *The Old Century*, pp. 279-82.
11. Corrigan (1973), pp. 55-6.
12. Rupert Brooke's last girlfriend, the actress Cathleen Nesbitt (1888-1982) records in her memoirs, *A Little Love* (London, 1977), that she met Brooke later that same day and that he was full of indignation about Sassoon's remark. That she should recall such a trivial incident over sixty years later (and at the time Sassoon was still a complete unknown) is hard to believe, especially since, according to Sassoon's version, Brooke did not really make an issue out of it.

CHAPTER 1: YOUNG NIMROD

1. Holbrook Jackson (1913), *The Eighteen-Nineties* (Harmondsworth, 1939),
    p. 53. It is extremely doubtful whether Swinburne can simply be regarded
    as one of the Pre-Raphaelites. He did count many of them among his
    friends (his 1866 *Poems and Ballads* were dedicated to Burne Jones and he
    greatly admired Rossetti), but unlike his Pre-Raphaelite friends he was
    well-read in French literature: he was considerably influenced by the
    French aesthetes, an influence that dated back to his first reading of
    Baudelaire's *Les Fleurs du Mal* in the expurgated edition of 1861. Cf.
    William Gaunt, *The Aesthetic Adventure* (London, 1945), p. 35.
2. Michael Thorpe, *Siegfried Sassoon: a Critical Study* (London, 1966), p. 5.
3. Corrigan (1973), p. 15.
4. Robert Graves, *In Broken Images: Selected Letters 1914-1946*, ed. by Paul
    O'Prey (London, 1982), pp. 73, 74.
5. *In Broken Images*, p. 28.
6. Cf. 'The Merciful Widow', 'If Wordsworth Had Written "The Everlasting
    Mercy"' and 'If Mr. Masefield Had Written "Casabianca"', all reprinted in
    J.C.Squire, *Collected Parodies* (London, 1921).
7. Harold Williams, *Modern English Writers: Being a Study of Imaginary
    Literature* (London, 1918), p. 97.
8. D.H. Lawrence's *Love Poems and Others* (Duckworth, 1913), published
    the same year as Sassoon's 'Daffodil Murderer', contains such poems as
    'The Collier's Wife' and 'Violets', which show that he had a better ear for
    local dialect.
9. Four poems from *The Old Huntsman* were deleted from the *Collected
    Poems*: 'Special Constable', 'Liquor-Control', 'Policeman' and 'Gibbet'
    (which had been first published in the privately printed *Melodies*, 1912).
10. Virginia Woolf in a review of *The Old Huntsman* in the T.L.S. (31 May
    1917). Wilfred Owen in a letter to his father, 26 August 1917 (Wilfred
    Owen, *Collected Letters*, ed. by Harold Owen and John Bell (London,
    1967), Letter no. 543, p. 456). Sassoon himself referred to the poem as "a
    mere verse exercise", cf. Corrigan (1973), p. 203.
11. First published in *The Listeners and Other Poems* (1912).
12. Quoted from Elaine Showalter, *Sexual Anarchy* (New York, 1990), p. 174.
13. Letter to Edward Carpenter, 27 July 1911. Quoted in Tsuzuki, *Edward
    Carpenter* (Cambridge, 1980), pp. 147-48.

CHAPTER 2: AN OFFICER AND TEMPORARY REBEL

1. See Tony Ashworth, *Trench Warfare 1914-1918* (London, 1980), p. 21.
2. Ivor Gurney, *War Letters*, ed. by R.K.R. Thornton (London, 1984), p. 29.
    Cf. also p. 130, where he refers to four sonnets that were intended as a
    1917 answer to Brooke's sonnets.

3.   'War Diary', 12 June 1917. In: Herbert Read, *The Contrary Experience* (New York, 1973), p. 89.

4.   Robert Graves (1929), *Goodbye to All That* (Harmondsworth, 1982), p. 146. Graves' autobiography, though always readable, is not always reliable. For one thing 'To Victory' was written in January 1916, and Sassoon was first in the trenches in November 1915 (though admittedly before March 1916 only with working parties).

5.   See *Ottoline at Garsington: Memoirs of Lady Ottoline Morrell 1915-1918*, ed. by Robert Gathorne-Hardy (London, 1974), pp. 90-1.

6.   Organizational tables of the British Army are given in Haythornthwaite, *A Photohistory of World War One* (London, 1993). For Sassoon's experiences, cf. his contribution to J.C. Dunn's, *The War the Infantry Knew 1914-1919* (London, 1989), p. 306.

7.   *Raymond Asquith: Life and Letters*, John Joliffe, ed. (London, 1987), p. 206.

8.   Charles Carrington, *Soldier from the Wars Returning* (London, 1965), pp. 159-60.

9.   Henri Barbusse: *Le Feu* (1916). An English translation by W. Fitzwater Wray appeared in 1917 under the title *Under Fire*. Page reference is to the Everyman edition (London, 1965), p. 44.

10.   Cf. Sassoon's footnote to 'In the Pink' in *The War Poems*, ed. by Sir Rupert Hart-Davis (London, 1983), p. 22, where he adds that the poem was refused by *the Westminster* "as they thought it might prejudice recruiting!!".

11.   This first draft is included in the *Diaries 1915-1918*, pp. 49-50. That he omitted the final stanza when he revised 'A Working Party' for publication in *The Old Huntsman* was probably due to the fact that he considered it too sentimental, going on as it does about "widows grieving down the streets in black / And faded mothers dreaming of bright sons".

12.   Jon Silkin, *Out of Battle: the Poetry of the Great War* (Oxford, 1978), p. 132.

13.   Corrigan (1973), p. 21.

14.   *War Poems*, p. 47. The somewhat apologetic tone of these lines is probably due to the fact that they were written after Sassoon's conversion to Roman Catholicism.

15.   Herbert Read, *Collected Poems* (London, 1966), pp. 37-40. First published in *Naked Warriors* (1919), the volume singled out by T.S. Eliot in the July 1919 issue of the *Egoist* as containing "the best war poetry that I can remember having seen".

16.   Permission had been granted, but it was soon discovered that Graves' nerves had suffered so badly that on 7 June he was sent to Osborne Palace on the Isle of Wight (once Queen Victoria's summer retreat where Sassoon's grandmother Mary Thornycroft had gone to paint portraits of the Royal Family and now another convalescent home for officers).

17.   *Ottoline at Garsington*, p.181.

18. *The Collected Letters of Katherine Mansfield 1903-1917* (Oxford, 1984), p. 310.

19. In *Diaries 1915-1918*, pp. 173-74.

20. Sassoon gives his own account of this action in the final chapter of *Memoirs of an Infantry Officer*. For a discussion of this account, cf. pp. 134-35.

21. Cf. Paul Levy, *G.E. Moore and the Cambridge Apostles* (Oxford, 1981), p. 289. Lytton Strachey based his defence on these grounds when he appeared for a tribunal in March 1916; cf. Michael Holroyd, *Lytton Strachey: a Biography* (New York: Holt, 1980), p. 626.

22. Cf. Bennett's second judicious letter, reprinted in Sassoon's *Diaries 1915-1918*, pp. 180-81. Bennett agreed with Robert Ross that Sassoon must have been " a little deranged", cf. his letter to Ross in Bennett, *Letters Vol. III* (London, 1970), pp. 36-7.

23. Robert Hanmer's letter in *D1*, 178; for Graves' response, cf. *In Broken Images* (London, 1982), p. 77.

24. *The War the Infantry Knew 1914-1918*, p. 372.

25. Five days earlier, on 4 June 1916, Wilfred Owen had joined the 5th (reserve) Battalion of the Manchester Regiment at Milford Camp, Surrey, as a newly commissioned 2nd Lieutenant.

26. Cf. Frank Swinnerton, *The Georgian Literary Scene* (London, 1946), p. 244.

27. Denis Winter, *Death's Men*, pp. 59-60.

28. Wilfred Owen, *Collected Letters* (London, 1967), p. 484.

29. Ibid., p. 485.

30. The first time Owen's mother heard about his meeting with Sassoon was in a letter dated 22 August (the same date as the Leslie Gunston letter), but in this letter Owen only mentions the second meeting, without referring to the first one. In his *Wilfred Owen: the Last Year* (London, 1992), p. 39, Dominic Hibberd places this first meeting "on about 16 August", though he does not explain why he mentions this particular date. Sassoon's own suggestion that it was "One morning at the beginning of August" (*SJ*, 58), would seem to be incorrect, in spite of its vagueness.

31. Hibberd (1992), p. 10.

32. For the first letter, cf. *Collected Letters*, p. 486; Sassoon's remarks about Gunston's poetry were omitted from the *Collected Letters*, but quoted in Hibberd (1992), p. 42.

33. *Collected Letters*, pp. 487, 547.

34. Ibid., p. 496.

35. Cf. Sassoon's pencilled in changes to 'Anthem for Doomed Youth', in *The Collected Poems of Wilfred Owen*, ed. by C. Day Lewis (London, 1984), pp. 185-88.

36. Sassoon also described this scene in a letter to E.M. Forster, though he there left out the sexual feelings it aroused (cf. Forster, *Selected Letters: vol. I* (London, 1985), p. 290, note 2).

37. Martin Taylor, ed., *Lads: Love Poetry of the Trenches* (London, 1989), p. 18.
38. Ibid., p. 17.
39. Paul Fussell, *The Great War and Modern Memory* (London, 1975), p. 272.
40. Cf. Taylor, *Lads: Love Poetry of the Trenches*, p. 17.
41. *The Diaries of Lady Cynthia Asquith 1915-1918* (London, 1987), p. 366.
42. Carrington, *Soldier from the Wars Returning*, p. 220.
43. John Oxenham, *All's Well!* (London, 1916), p. 7.
44. This is, of course, in many ways an unfair comparison: Oxenham's poems were published 18 months before Sassoon's *The Old Huntsman*. Unfortunately Oxenham's sales figures are scarce as the Methuen files were lost in the Blitz. Yet Oxenham's massive output is in itself a measure of his popular appeal: *All's Well* (1915), *The King's High Way* (1916), *The Vision Splendid* (1917), *The Fiery Cross* (1917), *Hearts Courageous* (1918), and the sequel to *All's Well: All's Clear* (1919).
45. V. de Sola Pinto: *Crisis in English Poetry* (London, 1963), p. 164. Pinto (1895-1969), later Professor of English at the University of Nottingham and co-editor of D.H. Lawrence's *Complete Poems*, was Sassoon's second-in-command during the latter's last months in France in the spring and summer of 1918.
46. Jon Silkin, in his Introduction to *The Penguin Book of First World War Poetry* (Harmondsworth, 1979), p. 28.
47. That same day Sassoon was shot in the head by one of his own men, when returning from a patrol in no man's land. He was eventually invalided home.
48. John Middleton Murry, 'Mr. Sassoon's War Verses', reprinted in *The Evolution of an Intellectual* (London, 1927), p. 75.
49. pp. 77-8.
50. Perhaps Murry was particularly critical of Sassoon because he had not forgiven him for giving up his war protest and returning to the front.
51. Gilbert Frankau, 'The Other Side', in *The Judgement of Valhalla* (London, 1918), p. 50. Frankau (1884-1952) served with the Royal Field Artillery and was invalided home with delayed shell-shock in February 1918. After the war he became a prolific and successful novelist. He used his war experiences in *Peter Jackson, Cigar Merchant* (London, 1920).
52. 'The Poet of the War', in Murry (1927), p. 86.
53. Silkin (1979), p. 47.
54. Silkin (1978), p. 158.
55. Ibid.
56. E.M. Remarque uses a similar juxtaposition in the title and the penultimate paragraph of *Im Westen Nichts Neues* (1929), where he describes the death of the hero: "Er fiel im Oktober 1918, an einem Tage, der so ruhig und still war an der ganzen Front, dass der Heeresbericht sich nur auf den Satz beschränkte, im Westen sei nichts Neues zu melden" ("He fell in October 1918, on a day that was so quiet and still on the whole front, that the army

report confined itself to the single sentence: 'All quiet on the Western Front'").

57. *The Diaries of Cynthia Asquith 1915-1918*, p. 381. Bernard Freyberg, later 1st Baron Freyberg (1889-1963) and Governor-General of New Zealand, was one of the best-known war heroes. For his heroic exploits at Gallipoli, see. ibid, p. 503. For a discussion between Cynthia Asquith and him on Sassoon's war protest, see. pp. 380-81.

58. Sir Rupert Hart-Davis in his introduction to *The War Poems*, p. 11.

59. Charles Kay Ogden (1889-1957) had founded the *Cambridge Magazine* in 1912 and remained its editor until 1922. In the 1920s he developed 'Basic English' together with I.A. Richards.

60. Thorpe (1966), p. 34. Sassoon himself was also quite pleased with this poem, cf. *Siegfried's Journey*, p. 71.

61. Cf. Katherine Mansfield, *Collected Letters – Vol. 2* (Oxford, 1987), pp. 256-61; Virginia Woolf, *Letters – Vol. 2* (London, 1976), pp. 262, 270 & *Diaries – Vol. 1* (Harmondsworth, 1979), p. 174; Sassoon, *Diaries 1923-1925*, p. 59.

62. Douglas Goldring, 'The War and the Poets' in: *Reputations: Essays in Criticism* (London, 1920), p. 109.

CHAPTER 3: GEORGIAN POET

1. Bertrand Russell, *Autobiography 1914-1944* (London, 1971), p. 89.

2. In a letter to Edward Marsh, quoted in Hassall, *Edward Marsh: Patron of the Arts* (London, 1959), p. 467.

3. Quoted in: Robert H. Ross, *The Georgian Revolt: Rise and Fall of a Poetic Ideal 1910-1922* (London, 1967), p. 227.

4. H.D., *Bid Me To Live* (London, 1984), p.7.

5. An early influence on the Modernists, and an example of their European outlook, was 'Futurism' and its vociferous advocate Filippo Marinetti. The first Futurist manifesto was published in February 1909, followed by a 'New Futurist Manifesto' in May 1913 (which appeared in an English translation in *Poetry and Drama*). Before the war, T.E. Hulme published his articles in *The New Age* and held private and public lectures in London between 1911 and 1914. Imagist propaganda was published in *The New Freewoman* by Rebecca West (1913), the 'Preface' to *Some Imagist Poets* (1915) by Richard Aldington and in *The Egoist* by F.S. Flint. The Vorticist programme was published in Wyndham Lewis's *Blast* (2 issues, June 1914 and July 1915).

6. E.J. Hobsbawm, *The Age of Empire 1875-1914* (New York, 1987), p. 226.

7. Quoted in Gillett, *The Victorian Painter's World* (Gloucester, 1990), p. 48.

8. Their popularity was reflected in public honours: Frederick Leighton (1830-96) was the first painter to receive a peerage and was elected President of the Royal Academy; Edwin Landseer, Luke Fildes, Alma-

Tadema and Edward Poynter (1836-1919) were all knighted. Poynter was also appointed Director of the National Gallery and succeeded Leighton and Millais as President of the Royal Academy.

9.   Cf. William Gaunt, *The Pre-Raphaelite Tragedy* (London, 1975), pp. 150, 142.

10.   From *The Savoy*, October 1896. Reprinted in *Victorians on Literature and Art*, ed. by Robert L. Peters (New York, 1961), p. 322.

11.   'The Grey Rock' (1913), ll. 53-8.

12.   He is remembered for his vigorous attack on Edmund Gosse in October 1886. Pointing out the numerous inaccuracies in Gosse's *From Shakespeare to Pope* earned him no more than the Poet Laureate's famous rebuff; speaking up for his friend, Tennyson referred to Collins as the "louse upon the locks of literature". Cf. Anthony Kearney, *The Louse on the Locks of Literature* (Edinburgh, 1986), pp. 52-69 and Thwaite (1985), pp. 276-97.

13.   John Churton Collins, *Ephemera Critica* (Westminster, 1901), pp. 14-15.

14.   Ibid., p. 25.

15.   C.K. Stead, *The New Poetic*, (London, 1964), p. 49.

16.   Quoted in Joy Grant, *Harold Monro and the Poetry Bookshop* (Berkely, 1967), p. 42.

17.   Lascelles Abercrombie, *The Theory of Poetry* (London, 1924), pp. 49-50.

18.   Ross (1967), p. 48.

19.   Arthur Waugh, 'The New Poetic', reprinted in *Georgian Poetry 1911-1922: the Critical Heritage*, Timothy Rogers, ed. (London, 1977), p. 144.

20.   William Watson, 'The Adjective', in *The Poems of Sir William Watson 1878-1935* (London, 1936), p. 175.

21.   Russell (1971), p. 52.

22.   Ronald Blythe, *The Age of Illusion: England in the Twenties and the Thirties* (Harmondsworth, 1964), p. 25.

23.   Cf. my 'Georgian Poetry's False Dawn', in *Neophilologus* Vol. LXXV, No. 3, July 1991, pp. 456-69.

24.   John Drinkwater, *Discovery* (London, 1932), p. 92.

25.   Cf. Rogers (1977), p. 153.

26.   In his influential *New Bearings in English Poetry* (Harmondsworth, 1979; first published 1932) F.R. Leavis refers to John Drinkwater as the man who "may perhaps claim to be the representative Georgian poet [...]" (p. 51). Leavis had little time for the Georgians and discussed them without making the distinction Georgian / Neo-Georgian. The first three *Georgian Poetry* anthologies make clear that awarding Drinkwater the status of 'Representative Georgian Poet' is not justified.

27.   Quoted in Hassall (1959), p. 464.

28.   Edward Marsh, *A Number of People* (London, 1939), p. 323.

29.   Donald Davie, *Ezra Pound* (Chicago, 1982), pp. 17-18.

30.   John Drinkwater, 'Art and Nationality', in: *Essays by Divers Hands, vol. XVI*, ed. by Dr. G.P. Gooch, F.R.S.L. (London, 1937), pp. 137-155. Drinkwater had died seven months earlier, on 25 March 1937.

31.   pp. 145, 150.
32.   Ezra Pound, 'How to Read', first published in the *New York Herald*, 1928. Reprinted in *Literary Essays,* T.S. Eliot, ed. (London, 1985), p. 34.
33.   J. Middleton Murry, 'Present Condition of English Poetry', in: *Aspects of Literature* (London, 1920), p. 145.
34.   Edward Shanks, *My England* (London, 1938), pp. 62, 64. Shanks admits that "like all true efforts this produced a number of falsities", and then, without naming poet or title, quotes for an example – the Neo-Georgian's revenge – a few lines from John Drinkwater's 'Cotswold Love' (pp. 64-65).
35.   By a morbid irony of fate, two of the young composers who were killed in the war served with Rupert Brooke in the Hood Battalion and were present at his graveside when he was buried at Skyros. W. Denis Browne was killed at Gallipoli six weeks later; the Australian-born Frederick Kelly completed his *Elegy, 'In Memoriam Rupert Brooke'* for string orchestra in June 1915, but was killed at the Somme in November 1916. Arguably the severest loss for British music was the death of George Butterworth, killed in action at the Somme in August 1916. He composed the orchestral Rhapsody *A Shropshire Lad*, and, like Ivor Gurney, set some of A.E. Housman's poems to music.
36.   During the war years Holst composed *The Planets*, Delius his *A Song before Sunrise*, while Parry, requested by the Poet Laureate Robert Bridges to write a patriotic song, obliged with his beautiful setting of Blake's 'Jerusalem'.
37.   Lewis Foreman (ed.), *From Parry to Britten: British Music in Letters 1900-1945* (London, 1987), p. 86. The editor notes that "Bliss's attitude was permanently coloured by the view he took then, a very positive influence in his activity after the War as a champion of the new and in the development of a highly personal style which took little if anything from Germanic models".
38.   When George Sherston visits the Caledonian Hotel in Edinburgh in 1917, he notices that the hotel musicians are playing "Mendelssohn's (German) Spring Song" (*SP*, 39).
39.   'Victorians', in *Poems 1930-1940* (London, 1940), pp. 252-53.
40.   E.M. Forster: *Selected Letters – vol. I* (1985), p. 294.
41.   Quoted in Patrick Howarth, *Squire: Most Generous of Men* (London, 1963), pp. 134-35.
42.   Cf. Maurice Hewlett's definition of poetry: "It is perhaps the Expression of Emotion in terms of Beauty", quoted in *The Later Life and Letters of Sir Henry Newbolt* (London, 1942), p. 164.
43.   Abercrombie (1924), p. 16.
44.   Ibid., pp. 49, 64.
45.   The text of the lecture was published by the University as a pamphlet in May 1939. Page references in the text are to this pamphlet.

CHAPTER 4: SATIRICAL INTENT

1.   He supplemented his income by occasionally selling some of the signed
     first edition copies that had been given to him by their authors, though he
     was not best pleased when somebody else followed the same procedure
     with one of his own books. When Sassoon learned that a copy of his 1912
     play *Hyacinth* (privately printed in an edition of thirty-five copies) turned
     up on a book-stall, he immediately bought it, "Don't know whose copy it
     was. Rather annoying" (*D2*, 289).

2.   The name suggests that Lewis thought Sassoon was related to the 'filthy'
     rich Sassoons he and Ezra Pound so much disliked. Though a distant rela-
     tion, Sassoon neither knew nor ever met Sir Victor Sassoon (1881-1961).

3.   Thorpe (1966), p. 40.

4.   Cf. Rupert Hart-Davis's note on Rivers in *Diaries 1920-1922*, p. 47 n.2.

5.   Ronald W. Clark, *Freud: the Man and the Cause*, (London, 1980), p. 386.

6.   Frequent guests were C.K. Scott Moncrieff (1889-1930), who after the war
     translated Proust's *Remembrance of Things Past* (1922-31); William More
     Adey (1858-1942), who published the first English translation of Ibsen's
     Brand (1891), together with Ross ran the Carfax picture gallery (1900-08)
     and was joint-editor the *Burlington Magazine* (1911-19); Philip
     Bainbrigge (1891-1918), skilled author of porno-graphic ballads (he
     exchanged scholarly but highly obscene verses and parodies with Scott
     Moncrieff), killed in action in the Battle of Epehy, September 1918. Other
     regular guests included Osbert Sitwell, Ross's elder brother Alec, and his
     nephew Sir Squire Sprigg (editor of the *Lancet*).

7.   Cf. Thwaite (1984), pp. 360-61 and *Selected Letters of Henry James to
     Edmund Gosse 1882-1915*, ed. by R.S. Moore (Baton Rouge, 1988), pp.
     296-97.

8.   In *Siegfried's Journey* Robert Ross is regularly mentioned, but Sassoon
     never once refers to the Douglas/Crosland trials. Osbert Sitwell is also
     reticent on the subject, cf. *Noble Essences* (London, 1950), p. 150.

9.   E.M. Forster, *Selected Letters – vol. I* (1985), p. 303.

10. Cf. Douglas Goldring, *The Nineteen Twenties: a General Survey and Some
     Personal Memories* (London, 1945), p. 163.

11. *Diaries 1923-1925*, p. 98. Frank Schuster (1840-1928), the son of a
     wealthy Jewish Frankfurt banker, was an elderly homosexual, wealthy mu-
     sic-lover and party host. His sister Adela had been one of Oscar Wilde's
     loyal friends and benefactors. Sassoon was a frequent guest at his London
     house in Old Queen Street (where Fritz Kreisler once tried out the Elgar
     Violin Concerto accompanied by the composer) and Bray-on-Thames, and
     a regular member of the entourage that accompanied Schuster on his fre-
     quent visits abroad. In 1924 Sassoon, the then reluctant socialite, recorded
     a highly critical description of Schuster in his diary (*D3*, 109-11). On
     rereading his diaries in 1938 he added a footnote saying that this was "not
     a very good summing up of Schuster" and made amends by writing a more
     sympathetic version (reprinted in *D2*, 293-4).

12.   *The Poems of Lascelles Abercrombie*, (London, 1930), p. vii.
13.   Reprinted in: Edgell Rickword, *Essays & Opinions 1921-31*, ed. by Alan Young (Cheadle Hulme, 1974), pp. 193, 258.
14.   Sassoon first came across the verb 'Columbussed' in Aylmer Strong's *A Human Voice* (1917). The author had presented him with a copy in September 1917, when Sassoon was at Craiglockhart. This is the "volume of portentously over-elaborated verse" that Wilfred Owen and Sassoon had such fun with on their last evening together (cf. *SJ*, 64-5). My thanks to Dominic Hibberd for this information.
15.   One of the worst examples in Sassoon's work occurs in the sestet of 'At the Grave of Henry Vaughan' (*The Heart's Journey*, XXIII), where a line that runs on into the next one and then stops (too) abruptly is further marred by a piece of bracketed authorial wisdom that only disturbs the poem's intimate mood: "Here faith and mercy, wisdom and humility / (Whose influence shall prevail for evermore) / Shine.".

CHAPTER 5: THROUGH THE WICKET GATE

1.   A reference to Tennyson's popular tear-jerker 'Enoch Arden' (1864).
2.   F. B. Millett, J. M. Manley & E. Rickert, *Contemporary British Literature*, (London, 1935), p. 275.
3.   In almost all reference works, the year of birth of W.J. Turner is given as 1889. This has been a most successful deception on the part of Turner, who was actually born in 1884. This fact was first pointed out by the Swiss scholar H. W. Häusermann in an article published in *English Studies* (Amsterdam, 1962), though no one seems to have taken much notice of it. That he was right is borne out by *Diaries 1920-1922*, p. 197, where Sassoon writes that in July 1922 he happened to look in Turner's passport "and found that he is two years older than me". It is to be feared that this piece of evidence will do little to correct this widespread error. The footnote on Turner in this same volume (p. 16) reads: "Australian poet and music critc (1889-1946)".
4.   "I did not find my real poetic voice until 1924, with the H. Vaughan sonnet" (*LC*, 13).
5.   Sassoon included two poems from *Picture Show*, one love poem (V) and the Robert Ross elegy (XVII).
6.   Geoffrey Keynes (1887-1982) was John Maynard Keynes' younger brother. In his youth he was a close friend of Rupert Brooke; he later became a successful surgeon, book collector and bibliographer.
7.   Geoffrey Keynes, *The Gates of Memory* (Oxford, 1983), p. 233.
8.   Bernard Bergonzi, *Heroes' Twilight* (London, 1965), p. 108.
9.   T. S. Eliot, 'The Music of Poetry', in *Selected Prose*, Frank Kermode, ed., (London, 1975), p. 111.
10.   For the Georgians on this subject cf. Lascelles Abercrombie's 'Poetry and Contemporary Speech' (1914) and 'Colloquial Language in Literature'

(1931); for the opposite view cf. Ezra Pound on Wordsworth, whom he constantly accuses of preferring the 'ordinary' word to 'le mot juste'. For an amusing account of an Abercrombie/Pound confrontation on the subject, cf. Noel Stock, *The Life of Ezra Pound* (San Fransisco, 1982), p. 159.

11.   Peter Ackroyd, *T.S. Eliot: a Life* (New York, 1984), p. 230.

12.   Thorpe (1966), p. 209.

13.   Henry Vaughan, 'Child-hood', ll. 31-6. All quotations from Vaughan's work are taken from *The Complete Poems*, ed. by Alan Rudrum (Harmondsworth, 1983).

14.   First published in 1934 in a private edition containing 22 poems, the first trade edition that was published in an edition of 2000 copies in November 1935 contained 35 poems.

15.   From Tennant's journal. Quoted in Philip Hoare, *Serious Pleasures: the Life of Stephan Tennant* (London, 1990), p. 251.

16.   Hoare, *Serious Pleasures*, p. 91.

17.   Quoted in Hoare, *Serious Pleasures*, p. 180.

18.   George Sassoon in a letter to the author, 23 March 1996.

19.   Geoffrey Keynes, *The Gates of Memory*, p. 234.

20.   *Selected Letters of T.E. Lawrence*, David Garnett, ed. (London, 1941), p. 357.

21.   Dennis Wheatley, *Officer and Temporary Gentleman 1914-1919* (London, 1978), p. 118. Wheatley (1897-1977) was a prolific author of novels of the occult.

22.   Quoted in Michael Thorpe's Introduction to *The Old Century*, p. 16.

23.   Lawrence in a letter to Sassoon, 17 December 1934. See *Selected Letters of T.E. Lawrence*, David Garnett, ed. (London, 1941), p. 363.

24.   Stephen Leacock's (1869-1944) humorous works include *Literary Lapses* (1910), *Nonsense Novels* (1911), *Arcadian Adventures with the Idle Rich* (1914) and *Frenzied Fiction* (1918).

25.   Quoted in Corrigan (1973), p. 40.

26.   Edmund Blunden (1896-1974) had in fact been 'discovered' by Sassoon when the latter was editor of *the Daily Herald* (cf. Blunden's *Poems 1914-1930*, pp. v-vi and *Siegfried's Journey*, p. 146). Blunden co-edited an edition of John Clare's verse in 1920, and a volume of Clare's autobiographical writings in 1931.

27.   Whistler (1905-44), a young artist famous as a mural decorator and bookillustrator, and friend of Cecil Beaton and Osbert Sitwell. Sassoon had met him through Stephen Tennant and had felt attracted to him. Hoare (1990), pp. 140-42 recounts how initially there was an element of rivalry between Sassoon and Whistler: both were striving for Tennant's affection.

28.   Cf. James King, *The Last Modern: a Life of Herbert Read* (London, 1990), pp. 282-83.

29.   Cf. Corrigan (1973), p. 246.

30.   Ibid., p. 96.

31.   Ibid., p. 166.

CHAPTER 6: MEMOIRS OF A FOX-HUNTING MAN

1. When he reread this passage in his diaries in 1939, Sassoon added the following note: "Homosexuality has become a bore; the intelligentsia have captured it. S.S." (*D2*, 53, n.1).

2. Forster, *Selected Letters – Vol. I* (1985), p. 316. Forster destroyed these stories in 1922.

3. A possible reason for the failure of Sassoon's pure fiction-writing might be his inability to create a convincing persona. The characters he created, both in his poetry and his prose, were either one-dimensional and 'flat' or a (more or less fictionalized) self-portrait.

4. Forster (1985), p. 290, note 2.

5. Quoted in Thorpe (1966), p.70.

6. J.B. Priestley: *The Edwardians* (London, 1970), p.57.

7. Cf. Edward Thomas, *The Heart of England* (Oxford, 1982), pp. 157-58; Helen Thomas, *As It Was and World Without End* (London, 1978), p 135; John Masefield, *Grace before Ploughing* (London, 1966), pp. 39-40.

8. All page references in the text are to the first edition, ninth impression, published by Faber & Faber in February 1930.

9. Robert Graves: *In Broken Images: Selected Letters 1914-1946* ed. by Paul O'Prey (London, 1982), p. 208. *Memoirs of an Infantry Officer* had then not yet been published, but by March 1930 the manuscript had been completed.

10. David Daiches, *The Present Age - from 1920* (London, 1958), p. 202.

11. Paul Fussell, *The Great War & Modern Memory* (London, 1977), p. 96.

12. Ibid., p. 90.

13. Sassoon was an avid reader of Wordsworth and the chapter division of *Memoirs of a Fox-Hunting Man* is not unlike that of *The Prelude* (whose subject, 'Growth of a Poet's Mind', is of course the underlying subject of Sassoon's autobiographies *The Old Century* and *The Weald of Youth*). The ironic relevance of *The Prelude*, Book IX, 'Residence in France', will not have escaped him.

14. Sir Geoffrey Keynes: *The Gates of Memory* (Oxford, 1983), p.233.

15. Edward Marsh, *A Number of People* (London, 1939), p. 236.

16. Ibid.

17. Cf. Sassoon in a letter to Felicitas Corrigan, 5 August 1960: "But we live in an unhomely age and I have always been rather Cranford minded – appropiately, for Knutsford, the original of Cranford, was a market town of my Thornycroft forbears". Corrigan (1973), p. 168.

18. R.S. Surtees (1805-64) was the son of a country squire and worked as a sporting journalist until he succeeded to his father's position in 1838. He is the Dickens of the hunting novel and author of such classics as *Jorrock's Jaunts and Jollities* (1838), *Mr. Sponge's Sporting Tour* (1852) and *Facey Romford's Hounds* (1865).

19.   V.S.Pritchett: *The Living Novel & Later Appreciations* (New York, 1964), p. 91.

20.   Cf. *Sherston's Progress*, pp. 64-5 and *The Weald of Youth*, pp. 32-5.

21.   Walter Pater, *Marius the Epicurean* (1885), Ian Small, ed. (Oxford, 1986), Ch. VIII, p. 76.

22.   Ibid., Ch. XXIII, p. 215.

23.   The barbed wire threat for the huntsman was real enough, though. Cf. *The Weald of Youth*, pp. 156-57, where he describes the trouble the Master of the Atherstone had in persuading farmers not to use barbed wire.

24.   Catherine Gordon, *British Paintings of the 19th Century* (London, 1981), p.72.

25.   Text from manuscript. The poem is reprinted in *Diaries 1915-1918*, p. 263 and Rupert Hart-Davis' edition of the *War Poems*, p. 122.

26.   George apparently forgot that his Surtees hero John Jorrocks was also a self-made man: in chapter two of *Jorrock's Jaunts and Jollities* he is described as "a substantial grocer in St. Botolph's Lane, with an elegant residence in Great Coram Street, Russell Square".

27.   George Orwell's story of the London poor going hop-picking in Kent was not published until seven years later, in *A Clergyman's Daughter* (1935).

28.   Cf. Sassoon's war poem 'Memorial Tablet', ll.13-4: "Once I came home on leave: and then went west... / What greater glory could a man desire?".

29.   Cf. *Diaries 1915-1918*, pp. 122, 123, 126, 127.

30.   George Moore, *The Brook Kerith* (London, 1952), p. 372.

31.   *The Brook Kerith*, p. 304.

32.   David Jones was also struck by the solemn ritual of 'stand-to', cf. *In Parenthesis* (London, 1982; first published 1937), Part 4, note 3, p. 202. R.H. Mottram refers to the men emerging from the dug-outs in biblical terms, only he compares it with the Judgment Day resurrection: "At dusk, directly the light is too dim to see movement from one trench to another, there's a most extraordinary scene. Do you remember the old Doré picture of the Resurrection? [...] Men that have lain hidden in or just behind the lines suddenly appear out of their holes" (from: *Sixty-Four, Ninety-Four* (1925), the second volume of *The Spanish Farm Trilogy* (London, 1927), pp. 280-81.

CHAPTER 7: MEMOIRS OF AN INFANTRY OFFICER

1.   Cf. *Memoirs of an Infantry Officer*, pp. 74-8 & *Diaries 1915-1918*, pp. 82-4. Sassoon made only some minor changes, the most interesting of which is that whenever the diaries mention "Huns" this is replaced in the book by "Germans".

2.   Brian Finney, *The Inner I: British Literary Autobiography of the Twentieth Century* (London, 1985), p. 172.

3.   All page references in the text are to the first edition, published by Faber & Faber in September 1930.

4. Edmund Blunden, *Undertones of War* (Harmondsworth, 1982), p. 242.
5. When Graves published his *Lawrence and the Arabs* in 1927, he wrote to Edmund Gosse asking him if he would not like to review the book. Sassoon considered this a reprehensible form of log-rolling. Shortly after the death of Thomas Hardy in January 1928, Graves wrote to Sassoon asking him if he might be interested in writing a short and lively biography. Sassoon wrote back saying that he regarded this proposal part of the "vulgar uproar" surrounding Hardy's death. In his reply Graves made abundantly clear that he did not believe in literary 'elders and betters': "I treat everyone as an equal unless they prove themselves inferior".
6. Cf. *In Broken Images*, pp. 196-209 & 220-33.
7. Cf. pp. 150-51 in the Penguin edition.
8. Though Graves also served in the Second Battalion RWF, Dr Dunn did not ask him to contribute to his book. Dunn had been sent an advance copy of *Goodbye to All That* and had written to Graves in November 1929 to draw his attention to several inaccuracies. He was angered when Graves quoted parts of his confidential letter in an article in the *Daily Mail*. Graves' offer to supply Dunn with material for his book was not taken up. Cf. Keith Simpson's 'Introduction' to *The War the Infantry Knew* (London, 1989), pp. xxx-xxxii.
9. Cf. *Memoirs of a Fox-Hunting Man*, p. 11.
10. *Alice In Wonderland*, Chapter IV.
11. Cf. Sassoon's poem 'On Passing the New Menin Gate', in *The Heart's Journey*. The names of 54,889 soldiers with no known grave are engraved on this gate.
12. At the beginning of the war there had been a 'White Feather Crusade', when young women presented white feathers to young men in civilian clothes, thus subtly persuading them to go and 'do their bit'. Cf. Arthur Marwick, *The Deluge: British Society and the First World War* (London, 1973) p. 50.
13. Sassoon's account differs in details from that of Robert Graves in *Goodbye to All That* (Penguin edition, pp. 213-17). Graves accepted Sassoon's objections though no corrections were made. Cf. *In Broken Images*, pp. 199, 202.
14. Craig Raine, 'Siegfried Sassoon' (1973), in: *Haydn & the Valve Trumpet* (London, 1990), pp. 165, 167.
15. Though Raine gives some pertinent examples, he apparently takes *Memoirs of a Fox-Hunting Man* to be a volume of straight autobiography, completely disregarding its finer points. Also, one cannot help feeling that his critical judgment has been impaired by his dislike of the world of the fox-hunter, and his sympathy for the infantry officer's stand against the war.
16. *The Great War and Modern Memory*, p. 104.
17. Cf. Jon Silkin, *Out of Battle*, p. 132: "although he was in contact before and during the war with Edward Marsh and the Georgians, nothing in the

Memoirs indicates either contact with, or interest in, the Imagists". Silkin here clearly confuses biographical knowledge about Sassoon's career and the limitations of the Sherston persona: George Sherston is not a writer and there is nothing in the *Memoirs* that links him with the contemporary literary world: it is true that the Imagists are never mentioned, but there is nothing in the *Memoirs* that suggests contact with, or interest in, Marsh and the Georgians either.

18.   George Parfitt, *Fiction of the First World War*, (London, 1988), p. 142.
19.   Cf. *Goodbye to All That*, pp. 215-16.
20.   *In Broken Images*, p. 199.

CHAPTER 8: SHERSTON'S PROGRESS

1.   All page references in this chapter are to the first edition, published by Faber & Faber in September 1936.
2.   The role of the peaceful hunting-world Sassoon described in *Memoirs of a Fox-Hunting Man* is in this respect comparable to that of the simple and pleasant metre and rhyme schemes in Sassoon's bitterest war poems.
3.   W.H.R. Rivers, *Instinct and the Unconscious* (Cambridge, 1920), p. 2.
4.   W.H.R. Rivers, *Conflict and Dream* (London, 1923), p. 171.
5.   "I have just been to Cambridge to stay with W.H.R. Rivers, ethnologist and psycho-analyst. This fellow is one of *the* most interesting" (Letter to Hugh Walpole, 12 December 1919; *Letters of Arnold Bennett: Vol. III* (London, 1970), p. 116).
6.   The reference is to Frances Cornford's 'Rupert Brooke': "A young Apollo, golden-haired / Stands dreaming on the verge of strife / Magnificently unprepared / For the long littleness of life".
7.   The religious metaphor is not that far-fetched: at one stage Sherston refers to Rivers as "my father-confessor" (59).
8.   Thorpe (1966), p.103.
9.   In this respect it is interesting to note that *The Old Century*, the first volume of his straight autobiographies, was published in September 1938, exactly 2 years after *Sherston's Progress*.
10.   Edmund Blunden describes a similar incident in *Undertones of War* (Harmondsworth, 1982), p. 59.
11.   Sassoon was not the first to do so; in 1930 Henry Williamson had published his satirical war novel *The Patriot's Progress*.
12.   Cf. John Bunyan, *The Pilgrim's Progress* (Harmondsworth, 1965), p. 104. D. Felicitas Corrigan attributes this line wrongly to Valiant-for-Truth (cf. Corrigan (1973), p. 32 / *Pilgrim's Progress* (1965), p. 348).

CHAPTER 9: THE PAST REVISITED

1. All page references in this section are to the Faber & Faber paperback edition (with an introduction by Michael Thorpe), London, 1968.

2. Brian Finney, *The Inner I: British Autobiography of the Twentieth Century* (London, 1985), p. 180.

3. Though we are told about some of his mother's friends (like Nellie Gosse and Helen 'Wirgie' Wirgman), Sassoon remains silent on the subjects of friends of his own age.

4. All in all, some fifty novelists, poets, painters and musicians are mentioned by name.

5. It was later reprinted in Pater's *Miscellaneous Studies* (London, 1895), pp. 172-196. Page references in the text are to the 1907 Macmillan edition.

6. In September 1924 Sassoon had also visited Edingthorpe. The notes in his diary are extensive, and it is obvious that he used them in writing this episode (cf. *D3*, 201-202).

7. T.S. Eliot, *East Coker*, ll. 18-22. It is not inconceivable that *The Old Century* was a minor source of inspiration for Eliot. The book was published by Faber and Faber (where Eliot had been an editor since 1925) in September 1938. The exact date of the composition of Eliot's poem cannot be established, but "The first reference to *East Coker* is in a letter from John Hayward [...] dated February 1940"; cf. Helen Gardner, *The Composition of 'Four Quartets'* (London, 1978), p. 16.

8. Walter Pater, *Imaginary Portraits* (London, 1890), pp. 27-8.

9. Gerald Monsman, *Walter Pater's Art of Autobiography* (New Haven, 1980), p. 37.

10. And of course there is the religious concern, not present in 'The Child in the House', but a dominant theme in Pater's *Marius*.

11. Gwen Raverat (1885-1957), grand-daughter of Charles Darwin. She worked as a wood-engraver and illustrator and had been one of the Neo-Pagans, the circle of friends that gathered around Rupert Brooke when he was at Cambridge 1906-1909.

12. Richard Church, *The Golden Sovereign* (London, 1957), p. 92. His autobiographical trilogy consists of *Over the Bridge* (1955), *The Golden Sovereign* (1957) and *The Voyage Home* (1964).

13. All page references in this section are to the Faber & Faber paperback edition (London, 1986).

14. Thorpe (1966), p.139.

15. Ibid., p.145.

16. His real name was Jozua Marius Willem van der Poorten Schwartz (1858-1915). He had adopted his pseudonym in 1891 "because it was an alias with a Dutch look that English readers might possibly be able to pronounce".

17. Corrigan (1973), p. 66.

18. All page references in this section are to the first edition, published by Faber & Faber in December 1945.

19. Thorpe (1966), p. 160.

20. That the publishers continue to re-issue the book without an index is therefore most regrettable.

21. Thorpe (1966), p.169.

22. Four years later, when he needed money, Sassoon "carried up to town three first editions of Drinkwater, which I sold to Sotheran's for £10!" (*D3*, 54).

23. Sassoon was not the only one to experience Drinkwater's self-promotion: "I had a nice lunch with John & his wife. Except that I had to undergo the ordinary ordeal – 'What had I read of his & how did I like it?'. *The Letters of Rupert Brooke*, ed. by Sir Geoffrey Keynes (London, 1968), p.605.

24. And it was at his request that Sassoon contributed to the magazine, cf. *In Broken Images*, pp. 102-103. Sassoon later claimed that his quarrel with Graves was mainly due to "his subjection to Laura Riding [the Modernist poet], I was driven away by her intense egotism and eccentricity" (*LC*, 21). His correspondence with Graves in the early 1930s tells a different story.

25. Other members included Bertrand Russell, Lytton Strachey and Clive Bell.

26. Among these COs were, at one time or another, Clive Bell, Aldous Huxley, Gerald Shove (a young Cambridge economist, married to the Georgian poet Fredegond Shove), David Garnett, and the painter Duncan Grant.

27. *Ottoline at Garsington: Memoirs of Lady Ottoline Morrell 1915-1918*, ed. by Robert Gathorne-Hardy (London, 1974), p. 122.

28. A recent biography claims that she was also the model for Lawrence's Lady Chatterley. Cf. Miranda Seymour, *Ottoline Morrell: Life on the Grand Scale* (London, 1992).

29. Vita Sackville-West, *The Edwardians* (London, 1930), p. 32.

CHAPTER 10: GOD'S TREASURE

1. All page references in this section are to the Arrow Books edition (London, 1959).

2. Keynes, *The Gates of Memory*, pp. 237-39. T.E. Lawrence had already doubted the wisdom of Sassoon's marriage. After meeting Hester shortly before the marriage in December 1933 he wrote to Lady Astor: "she was honestly in love with him, and in terror of her life of proving inadequate. I tried to cheer her up, without being foolishly optimistic. I liked the foolhardy creature. Fancy taking on S.S." (*T.E. Lawrence: Selected Letters*, Malcolm Brown, ed. (New York, 1992), p. 479).

3. Ackerley recorded their life together in *My Dog Tulip: Life with an Alsatian* (1956).

4. Diary-entry 13 July 1949. Quoted in Peter Parker, *Ackerley* (New York, 1989), pp. 302-303.

5. 'The Pulley', l. 14.

6. A six-page extract from this manuscript is published in *Diaries 1920-1922*, pp. 15-22.

7. George Sassoon in a letter to the author, 26 January 1994.

8. The main source of information for this last phase in Sassoon's career is Dame Felicitas Corrigan's *Siegfried Sassoon: Poet's Pilgrimage* (London, 1973). Though this is an extremely valuable book, it is somewhat hampered by the fact that its author is a true disciple of the author of *Meredith*, with the result that as a biographer she is even more sympathetic in her approach, and even less critical in her judgments. Still, this does not seriously affect the book, since it consists mainly of Sassoon's poems, letters and diary-entries. All further page references in this chapter are to this book.

9. Sassoon knew *The Dynasts* well, quoting several passages in his 1916 diary (cf. *Diaries 1915-1918*, p. 81).

10. 'To My Mother' was an older poem, first published separately on 24 September 1928. That Sassoon decided to include it in *Common Chords* was probably because it was his first volume to appear since his mother's death in 1947.

11. Sassoon was never particularly interested in philosophy, but it is interesting to see that his life's philosophy as it here emerges – that there is no harm in finding consolation in memories which in your heart of hearts you know to be distorted and untrue – is reminiscent of the survival mechanism that the German philosopher Hans Vaihinger had formulated in his *Die Philosophie des Als-Ob* (1911). Vaihinger (1852-1933) said that thinking was essentially another means in the struggle for survival. If man can develop 'fictions' which he knows not to be true in the ordinary sense, but which *do* serve him to whatever purpose, this makes them useful in life, and therefore *true* (truth, according to Vaihinger, being all that is useful in the struggle for survival). There is no evidence to suggest that Sassoon had ever read or read about Vaihinger, but it is not at all unlikely that he had. Vaihinger's philosophy was first presented to a wider audience in Havelock Ellis' best-selling *The Dance of Life* (1923). In a footnote to the Vaihinger chapter, Ellis explains that a few years earlier, he had published an article on Vaihinger in *the Nation & Atheneum*, a periodical to which Sassoon occasionally contributed (Cf. *The Dance of Life* (London, 1928), p. 79 note 1). An English translation of Vaihinger's book, entitled *The Philosophy of 'As If'* appeared in 1924. But even if Sassoon was not familiar with Vaihinger's writings, the fact remains that many of his poems as well as *The Old Century* are perfect illustrations of Vaihinger's survival theories.

12. It was Grey (1862-1933) who at the outbreak of the Great War on 3 August 1914 said that "The lamps are going out all over Europe; we shall not see them lit in our lifetime", supposedly to his friend Edward Tennant, 1st Baron Glenconner (1859-1920), an elder brother of Margot Asquith. In 1922, two years after Lord Glenconner's death, Edward Grey married his

widow Pamela (1871-1928). Sassoon had visited Grey at Fallodon Hall in
the late 1920s, during his affair with Stephen Tennant. Cf. Hoare (1990)
and Simon Blow, *Broken Blood: The Rise and Fall of the Tennant Family*
(London, 1987).

13. This is the quality in Sassoon's poetry that must have appealed to Philip
Larkin, who named Sassoon among his twelve 'exemplars'. A desire to
submerge his individuality in the cyclical movement of Nature is also the
underlying theme in Larkin's own later poetry. See my 'The Return to the
Native' in *In Black and Gold: Contiguous Traditions in Post-War British
and Irish Poetry*, C.C. Barfoot, ed. (Amsterdam, 1994), pp. 95-117.

14. Though Sassoon presents this explanation as one that satisfies him
completely, this was not the last time he wondered about his soul's
survival in heaven. In *The Tasking* he still asks "How do you handle my
dispersal – / Nameless, unlanguaged, and deminded? / Shall psyche thrive,
no more purblinded? / Answer me that, O Universal" ('The Dispersal', ll.
9-12).

15. The influence of Henry Vaughan is also present in the use of the definite
article-noun form in many of the poems' titles.

16. The lower-cased "he" in the last line quoted seems intentional, since it
occurs both in the *Collected Poems* and the Corrigan printing. The
previous line, however, refers to God as "He" and "His"; which makes it
likely that the lower-case "he" is an uncorrected typing error.

17. Henry Head (1861-1940), an eminent neurologist, knighted in 1927. He
had been a friend and associate of W.H.R. Rivers, who introduced him to
Sassoon. He and Geoffrey Keynes had saved Virginia Woolf after her
suicide attempt in October 1913. During the war he treated the war poet
Robert Nichols. Head became a close friend of Walter de la Mare. Sir
Rupert Hart-Davis calls him "After W.H.R. Rivers the chief father-figure
in S.S.'s life" (*D3*, 34 note 5).

18. These opening lines are in mood and setting remarkably similar to those of
Philip Larkin's 'Church Going'. Though Larkin named Sassoon as one of
his favourite poets, 'Church Going' was actually written a few years *before*
'Lenten Illuminations'.

19. In *The Pilgrim's Progress*, Evangelist refers to Christian's pilgrimage as
"the way of peace" (Penguin ed., 1965, p. 53).

20. The eight poems were: 'Rogation' (1959), 'Arbor Vitae' (1959),
'Unfoldment' (1960), 'A Prayer at Pentecost' (1960), 'Awaitement' (1960),
'Proven Purpose' (1964), 'A Prayer in Old Age' (1964) and 'Sight
Sufficient' (1957). *An Octave* was published in a limited edition of 150
copies.

EPILOGUE: A STRANGER ON EARTH

1. Corrigan (1973), p. 102.
2. Diary entry, 13 December 1953, in Corrigan (1973), pp. 150-51.

3. Myron Simon, *The Georgian Poetic* (Berkely, 1975), p. vii.

4. G.S. Fraser, 'The New Poets', in *New World Writing* (1955). Quoted in Eric Homberger, *The Art of the Real: Poetry in England & America since 1939* (London, 1978), p. 87.

5. Blake Morrison, *The Movement: English Poetry and Fiction of the 1950s* (Oxford, 1980), pp. 133-34.

6. Philip Larkin, 'The Pleasure Principle', in *Listen* 2 (Summer-Autumn 1957). Quoted in Blake Morrison (1980), p. 127.

7. David Lodge, 'Turning Unhappiness into Money: Fiction and the Market', in *Working with Structuralism* (London, 1986), p. 163.

8. Corrigan (1973), pp. 216-17.

9. One of the best examples is Russell Brain's *Tea with Walter de la Mare* (London, 1957), in which Brain (a neurologist) recalls conversations he had with de la Mare in the 1950s. He shows how even late in life de la Mare was still keen to talk and think about just anything, and how he kept wondering about the mysteries of life (though anybody who has two neurologist friends whose names are Henry Head and Russell Brain has at least something to wonder about).

10. Pascal, *Pensées* ii, 139 (ed. L. Brunschvicg, 5th edn., 1909).

11. Sir Rupert Hart-Davis in his introduction to the *War Poems*, p. 11.

12. The only possible exceptions might have been his friendships with Stephen Colwood [Gordon Harbord] in *Memoirs of a Fox-Hunting Man* and Allgood [Marcus Goodall] in *Memoirs of an Infantry Officer*, friends from before the war – but they were both killed in the trenches.

13. See Chapter 6, note 1.

14. Corrigan (1973), p. 230.

15. Sassoon considered Jones' *In Parenthesis* (1937) "an important war record", though he qualified this by adding that it did not "reach" him like Edmund Blunden's *Undertones of War* (Cf. Corrigan, 232). Jones had in fact served as a private in Sassoon's own Regiment, the Royal Welch Fusiliers.

16. Cf. Corrigan (1973), pp. 232, 241 and 112 respectively.

17. Quoted in Joseph Cohen, *Journey to the Trenches: The Life of Isaac Rosenberg 1890-1918* (London, 1992), p. 181.

18. *The Collected Works of Isaac Rosenberg*, Ian Parsons, ed. (London, 1979), p. ix.

19. Corrigan (1973), p. 17.

20. Peter Ackroyd, *T.S. Eliot: a Life* (New York, 1984), p. 334.

21. Corrigan (1973), p. 242.

22. *The Pilgrim's Progress* (Penguin edition, 1965), p. 127.

23. Michael Thorpe: 'For S.S. (Died September 1st, 1967)', ll. 3-6. In: *By the Niger and Other Poems* (London, 1969), p. 81.

INDEX

Writings are entered under the names of the authors concerned.

Entries in **bold** type contain biographical information.

In references to Notes the page number is immediately followed by an 'n' and the number of the note.